The Talmud of Relationships, Volume 1

"Finally, an opening to the Talmud for all to enter! A master teacher, Amy Scheinerman addresses topics that are key to our most important relationships and self-understanding. She deftly walks us through the logic of the passage, asking thought provoking questions along the way, and allowing us to draw our own conclusions."

—RABBI LOUIS RIESER, teacher, scholar-in-residence, and author of *The Hillel Narratives*

"Amy Scheinerman gently and adroitly guides us through some of the most fascinating and provocative passages of talmudic literature. . . . *The Talmud of Relationships* amply demonstrates that talmudic/rabbinic literature retains its power to speak to the spiritual issues we face individually and communally, even more than a millennium and a half later."

—GAIL LABOVITZ, associate professor of rabbinic literature, Ziegler School of Rabbinic Studies

"Amy Scheinerman does it again. She takes the most obscure Talmudic texts and makes them come alive, right before your eyes. And the best part: the 'aha' moment is not short-lived. Amy's insights will stick to your bones and add value and meaning to your life."

—RABBI STACY OFFNER, Temple Beth Tikvah, Madison, Connecticut

"A treasure trove of insight, information, and meaning which invites us into the world of the rabbis and the Talmudic tradition. Be prepared to experience the Talmud come alive as we learn to navigate engrossing texts, and also reflect upon our own relationships: who we are and who we aspire to be."

—RABBI NORMAN COHEN, professor of Midrash at HUC-JIR and author of *The Way into Torah*

The Jewish Publication Society expresses its gratitude for the generosity of the sponsors of this book.

Dr. Jeffrey S. and Susan J. Aronowitz in honor of our son, Jordan Adam, the light of our lives.

University of Nebraska Press
Lincoln

The Talmud of Relationships, Volume 1 *God, Self, and Family*

RABBI AMY SCHEINERMAN

The Jewish Publication Society
Philadelphia

© 2018 by Amy Scheinerman

All rights reserved. Published by the University of Nebraska Press as a Jewish Publication Society book. Manufactured in the United States of America.

Library of Congress Cataloging-in-Publication Data
Names: Scheinerman, Amy, author.
Title: The Talmud of relationships / Rabbi Amy Scheinerman.
Description: Philadelphia: Jewish Publication Society; Lincoln: University of Nebraska Press, [2018] | Includes bibliographical references.
Identifiers: LCCN 2017056782
ISBN 9780827612648 (pbk.: alk. paper)
ISBN 9780827614383 (epub)
ISBN 9780827614390 (mobi)
ISBN 9780827614406 (pdf)
Subjects: LCSH: Talmud—Criticism, interpretation, etc. | Jewish way of life. | Jewish ethics. | Interpersonal relations—Religious aspects—Judaism.
Classification: LCC BM504.2 .S3314 2018 | DDC 296.1/206—dc23 LC record available at https://lccn.loc.gov/2017056782

Set in Merope by E. Cuddy.
Designed by L. Auten.

To my husband, Prof. Edward Scheinerman, with gratitude for four decades of love, companionship, conversation, and laughter. I have loved sharing our lives, and I look forward to growing old with you.

CONTENTS

Acknowledgments xi
Introduction: Why Talmud? xiii

Part 1. The Core: Relationships with God and Self

1. Finding Our Place: Babylonian Talmud,
   Tractate Menachot 29b 3
2. Controlling Our Anger: Babylonian Talmud,
   Tractate Berakhot 7a. 17
3. Understanding Our Suffering: Babylonian
   Talmud, Tractate Berakhot 5a–b 41
4. Approaching Prayer: Mishnah Berakhot
   4:2 and the Accompanying Gemara from
   the Babylonian and Jerusalem Talmuds. 71

Part 2. First Sphere: Family Relationships

5. Honoring Our Parents: Jerusalem Talmud,
   Tractate Pe'ah 1a, 5b–6b. 97
6. Affirming Our Sexuality: Babylonian
   Talmud, Tractate Nedarim 20a–b .123
7. Balancing Family and Study: Babylonian
   Talmud, Tractate Ketubot 61b, 62b–63a 145

Appendix: Theodicy, the Problem of God's Justice. 169
Glossary 179
Notes 189
Bibliography. 209

ACKNOWLEDGMENTS

While it is always a pleasure to acknowledge one's blessings, the opportunity to thank the people who helped bring my first books to fruition is an exceptional delight.

My thanks to Rabbi Barry Schwartz, director of the Jewish Publication Society, who invited me to write this book. Barry's timing could not have been more perfect, since this was just the project I had been contemplating and hoping would be possible. I am grateful for his encouragement and support.

My thanks to Joy Weinberg, the JPS managing editor, for her superb editing. Joy's meticulous and sensitive attention to detail, nuance, and tone are matched by her wisdom, warmth, and patience.

My thanks to the University of Nebraska Press (UNP), JPS's partner in publishing *The Talmud of Relationships*, for their vital role in this exciting project, Elizabeth Zaleski of UNP, and Michele Alperin for her excellent questions and masterful editing.

My thanks to the wonderful colleagues and communities who have invited me in to serve as their weekend scholar-in-residence, affording me the opportunity to share what I love and to learn with them.

My thanks to my husband, Edward Scheinerman, for his steadfast and unwavering support and encouragement throughout the process of writing and revising, as well as for schlepping home piles of books from the Johns Hopkins University library.

Finally, a special thanks to my dear friend, colleague, and *chevruta* partner, Rabbi Louis Rieser, who opened Talmud to me in an entirely new way, and whose friendship has been an extraordinary gift.

INTRODUCTION   *Why Talmud?*

The Hasidic master Rebbe Nachman of Bratzlav told this parable: Once a Jewish man who lived in Austria dreamed that a valuable treasure lay buried under a bridge in Vienna. Determined to find it, he packed a bag and journeyed two days and two nights until he reached the bridge. Then he stood there wondering what to do, since searching during daylight would provoke suspicious questions.

A soldier came by and asked him, "What are you looking for?"

The man told the soldier about his dream.

The soldier replied, "I feel sorry for you, you crazy dreamer! Believing in dreams is nonsense. I, too, dreamed once of a valuable treasure that lay buried in a cellar." And then, to the man's amazement, the soldier not only located that treasure in the town where this Jewish man lived, but also mentioned his name.

The soldier continued, "I have no idea where this town is or who this man is, but I would be crazy to try to find him."

The man nodded politely, turned around, and headed home. Upon his arrival he went straight down to his cellar and began digging. In time he unearthed a chest containing a great treasure. The man declared, "The treasure has always lain buried in my house, but I had to leave my home and travel far away in order to discover it was under my feet all along."[1]

It is time to unearth the treasure that lies buried in our cellars. That treasure is Talmud.

For modern, liberal Jews, Tanakh (Hebrew Scripture), and particularly the Written Torah (the Five Books of Moses), has become their central religious text. But in reality the core text of Judaism has, for a very long time, been the Talmud. While Torah continues to play a central role in the inspiration, identity, and history of the Jewish people, we are Rabbinic Jews, not biblical Jews. The Rabbis of the Talmud in the second through sixth centuries CE filtered, interpreted, and enlarged Written Torah to create our Judaism—a set of ethical and ritual traditions based on three pillars: Talmud Torah (study), worship, and *gemilut chasadim* (deeds of loving-kindness).[2]

Why Do We Need Talmud?

If Jews had a Torah, why was there a need for the Talmud? One insight is Talmud's sobriquet for Talmud itself: "Oral Torah." When the Romans destroyed the Second Temple in 70 CE, the nation of Israel was traumatized and the Land of Israel decimated. Without the sacrificial cult presided over by the *kohanim* (priests), it was unclear how the Israelites could continue to serve God. Bereft of the Temple, how could they maintain their covenant with God?

Stepping into this void, over the course of many centuries, the Rabbis shaped what we know as Judaism. The Jewish traditions of sacred texts, religious practices, ethical values, customs, and ideals—all interwoven with a cultural emphasis on learning and teaching, questioning and debating, family and community—have withstood the vicissitudes of history and traveled with Jews through time and space ever since. Rabbinic tradition and methodology proved flexible enough to adapt to the contingencies of life, sturdy enough to support the Jewish people during dark times, and idealistic enough to provide challenge and inspiration throughout.

At the core of Judaism stands a set of sacred texts—Mishnah, Tosefta, two Talmuds (one from Babylonia, one from the Land of Israel), many compilations of midrash, a wide assortment of commentaries, numerous legal codes, and works of philosophy and mysticism—that transmit tradition from generation to generation. Talmud, the edited transcript of a four-centuries-long study session that began nearly two thousand years ago, is primary among these sacred texts.

In every age Talmud is studied, debated, and internalized by a new generation of learners. Talmud invites each learner into the conversations and debates of the ancient study houses, providing a way to explore the big questions and deepest concerns of living and arrive at one's own answer.

Why I Wrote This Book

As a teenager I longed for deep ideas, intense conversation, and religious meaning. Deep ideas could be found in the literature I read in school, but it lacked religious meaning and rarely led to intense conversation.

In high school I belonged to my synagogue's youth group. The wonderful friendships I formed enlarged my life. One spring, at a weekend retreat, a rabbinical student I had never met (and whose name I regret I cannot recall) came to teach us. It was several weeks before Passover, and he brought a short text, perhaps a paragraph or two in length, pertaining to the upcoming festival.

I was mesmerized. This brief text was unlike anything I had ever read. It opened up important and meaningful conversation on many issues, each deeper and more profound than the last. After an hour of discussion and peeling away the layers, we were still going strong.

I asked the rabbinical student where the text came from.

"From the Talmud," he replied.

I had never heard of the Talmud, despite having attended religious school weekly since first grade. Feeling that I had discovered something amazingly wonderful, I asked, "Is there more of this?"

He laughed gently and said, "Yes. There are twenty volumes."

In college I came to realize that in order to study Talmud I would need to learn both Aramaic and Hebrew. I knew neither, but that memory of just a paragraph of Talmud still pulled at me.

In rabbinical school I acquired some of the tools to learn Talmud. Yet I did not have another experience like the one on that spring afternoon in high school.

For many years I struggled with Talmud, trying to wrest from it the profound sense of meaning and connection I had first experienced. It took a long time. Along the way, books and articles helped propel me and inspire me to keep learning.

Perhaps it has something to do with middle age (or perhaps I finally grew up?), but eventually things began to click into place. I think it has to do with a very special friend, Rabbi Louis Rieser. We met at a rabbinic study retreat nearly a decade ago. I was already a fan of his thinking and writing, having read several of his articles about Hillel (that would subsequently be published in *The Hillel Narratives*). We became *chevruta* (study partners) for the week, and enjoyed our learning and conversations so much that we decided to continue after the formal week of learning ended.

Learning with a partner is a time-honored way to study Talmud, but not one I had experienced in rabbinical school, which in those days followed the Western academic model ("Keep your eyes on your own paper").

Each week we would log on to Skype and begin by sharing our lives. Then we would open the Talmud and settle into learning, unpeeling layers of meaning and layering them with our personal and professional experiences as rabbis. We did not always study Talmud—the Torah commentaries of classical Hasidic masters occupied some of our time—but we always returned to Talmud, and it felt like coming home.

When we learned together, the terse sentences sprouted longer chains of meanings—implications for the way people live together and relate to one another, for the way communities function and people treat one another, and for the relationships that define and determine our lives. Some days we would look at a text and think, "It's flat, not much here," but then a single question would inspire three ideas and six more questions . . . and soon the "dull" or "inscrutable" text was a complex, magnificent three-dimensional palace of insights.

Over the years I have had the privilege of teaching Talmud locally, as well as in congregations around the country. Often I have experienced the joy of hearing other people say, "This stuff is wonderful and so meaningful!" and "I want to learn more of this!" As a teacher who knows this feeling from the inside out, it doesn't get better than that.

The purpose of this book is to share my learning and the wonder of Talmud with you. No particular background is required; my goal is to open Talmud to anyone who is interested. I hope that's you.

Why Was Talmud Written?

We can view the genesis of the Talmud through three lenses.

First, the turmoil of the first century, including the decimation of the priestly leadership in the wake of the Jerusalem Temple's destruction, created a void and gave rise to a community of scholars who ultimately authored the Talmud. Shaye Cohen, scholar of Hebrew literature and philosophy, expresses this view:

> In 70 CE, the temple was destroyed, the high priesthood and the Sanhedrin ceased to exist, and the priests lost not only their jobs but also the institutional base of their power. The Jewish community of the land of Israel no longer had a recognized social elite or "establishment," and the Jews of the Diaspora no longer had a center that bound them together. This was a vacuum the rabbis tried to fill. Ultimately they succeeded, but victory was gained only after a struggle. The rabbis were opposed by various segments among the wealthy and the priesthood and by the bulk of the masses in both Israel and the Diaspora. The local aristocracies, especially in the cities, were not going to subject themselves voluntarily to the hegemony of the new power group; the priests still thought of themselves as the leaders of the people; and the masses were indifferent to many aspects of rabbinic piety. The rabbis triumphed over their opponents among the aristocracy and the priesthood by absorbing them into their midst, or at least coming to

terms with them. The rabbis triumphed over the indifference of the masses by gradually gaining control of the schools and synagogues. The exact date of the triumph is hard to determine, but it was not earlier than the seventh century CE.[3]

Second, the Rabbis' rise was a function of their persistent political struggles. Stuart A. Cohen, scholar of Jewish political theory and practice, advances this view:

[The eventual hegemony of rabbinic Judaism in the life of the Jewish people] was not inevitable. Neither was there anything haphazard about the process whereby it occurred. In the political arena, as in others, the rabbis had to struggle for the realization of their ambitions—often from positions of intrinsic constitutional inferiority. If the enormity of their achievement is to be properly assessed, appropriate note must be taken of the persistence with which they pursued an essentially political campaign. Their avowed purpose was to confound the contrary aspirations of rival contestants, some sacerdotal, others civil, for whatever communal authority native Jewish agencies could still claim to command.[4]

Third, the Talmud is the realization of an innovative, experimental intellectual and religious project. Barry Holtz, scholar of Jewish education, offers this wonderful lens:

Consider for a moment the following thought experiment. Let us think of the Babylonian Talmud not as we usually do—not as a vast compendium of laws, legends, debates, and interpretations, but as a massive, multivolume, postmodern, experimental volume. Wilder than *Moby Dick*, beyond the imagination of James Joyce, more internally self-referential than anything dreamed up by David Foster Wallace. Hundreds of pages of dialogue, of discussions that start but never end; organized, it seems on the surface, by free association, and filled with hyperlinked cross-references across the wide expanse of its domain. It has no beginning and no conclusion. It just is. It is as if the Talmud expects that you have read it all before you've read a single page.[5]

Torah contains a wealth of ethical injunctions meant to shape how we live in community with one another—for example, business laws, civil and criminal laws, social justice laws—but many of these laws are geared for an ancient agricultural or shepherding society. The Sages (I use the term synonymously with Rabbis) sought to extend these values and priorities into their contemporary, increasingly urbanized and complex environment. They generated oral teachings, passed down from master to disciple, that included interpretation of Torah's laws for their more modern settings, as well as Rabbinic legislation, wisdom, and memories of how ritual had been conducted in the Second Temple.

Toward the end of the second century R. Yehudah ha-Nasi (Judah the Prince), living in *Eretz Yisrael* (the Land of Israel), feared that these oral traditions and teachings would be lost, and directed that they be committed to writing. The result of this herculean effort is the Mishnah (meaning "study" or "review"), a terse and compact catalog of practices and legal rulings complete with debate, minority opinions, and an occasional brief story or sermon.

Jews in the academies of *Eretz Yisrael* and Babylonia (where Jews had lived since the destruction of the First Temple and exile of 586 BCE) studied the Mishnah in depth, exploring its implications, debating the logic of its rulings, telling their own stories, providing anecdotal illustrations of principles articulated, and more. Over the next few centuries the Sages of both *Eretz Yisrael* and Babylonia produced a Gemara (meaning "learn") containing the Rabbis' questions, analyses, discussions, and debates. Actually they produced two Gemaras: one composed in Babylonia (the Babylonian Talmud, or Bavli) and the other in the Land of Israel (the Jerusalem Talmud, or Yerushalmi).

The Jerusalem Talmud, composed primarily in the academies of Tiberias and Caesarea and completed around 400 CE, is the shorter of the two Talmuds; it clocks in at seven volumes. (While the Bavli contains Gemara discussions for sixty-three tractates of the Mishnah, the Yerushalmi has Gemara for only thirty-seven tractates.) When people say "the Talmud," they are referring to the twenty-volume-long Babylonian Talmud, composed and redacted primarily in the academies of Sura and Pumbedita and completed around 600 CE, which has long enjoyed precedence. Thus far, the Bavli enjoys far more influence and attention than the Yerushalmi.

The Five Books of Moses have come to be called *Torah she-bi-khtav* (the Written Torah) and the Talmud *Torah she b'al peh* (Oral Torah) because the Rabbis made the audacious and brilliant claim that the People of Israel received the Talmud at Mount Sinai at the same time that Moses received the Torah. Unlike Torah, however, which was immediately written down, the Talmud was transmitted orally from generation to generation for fourteen hundred years until, at the end of the second century CE, R. Yehudah ha-Nasi arranged that the Mishnah be written down.

This is a remarkable claim, given that Talmud is packed with the names and teachings of the Rabbis, who lived between the second and sixth centuries (long after Sinai!). Historically, extraordinary Sages had combined the laws and values of the Written Torah, the needs of their contemporary communities, and their keen rational skills of logic and argumentation to produce a masterpiece of religious literature with enduring spiritual value. The Rabbis' larger claim was their way of asserting divine authority for their project, which was to live in covenant with God in a world without the Temple.

The first chapter and verse of Pirkei Avot (Ethics of the Ancestors)—arguably serving as the introduction to Talmud—begins with a beautiful image of *shalshelet ha-kabbalah* (the chain of tradition). Here is how Talmud explains its origin, which it locates in the same experience of revelation that gave the People of Israel the Torah:

Moses received the Torah from Sinai and transmitted it to Joshua, and Joshua [transmitted it] to the elders, and the elders [transmitted it] to the prophets, and the prophets transmitted it to the members of the Great Assembly. They said three things, "Be deliberate in judgment, raise up many students, and make a fence around the Torah." (Pirkei Avot 1:1)

According to tradition, the Great Assembly was a synod of 120 Sages, scribes, and prophets who governed Israel from the end of the biblical period of prophets and who were active from the eighth through the fifth centuries before the Common Era, through the early Rabbinic period of the first two centuries CE. Today, many scholars question whether the Great Assembly ever existed; the Rabbis may have imagined such an institution to form a bridge from the biblical prophets to the beginning of the Rabbinic period—and hence an unbroken chain for transmission of the tradition.

Whether or not the Great Assembly is historical or legendary, the opening of Pirkei Avot demonstrates that the Rabbis are deeply invested in their claim that they are the rightful heirs of the Torah tradition, the latest link in an unbroken chain of divine revelation that goes back to Mount Sinai. Moses, Joshua, the elders, the prophets, the members of the Great Assembly, and the Rabbis are all links in this chain, as is every generation after them. When Pirkei Avot 1:1 speaks of the Torah, it intends to include the Oral Torah (the Talmud) as well.

Reconciling the claim that both Written Torah and Oral Torah were given at Mount Sinai with history is less confounding when we realize that Pirkei Avot is not making a historical claim at all. Rather, it is the Rabbis' way of declaring that Oral Torah has the same *authority* as Written Torah; it is the Sages' literary assertion that their enterprise commands the same respect and religious authority as the Five Books of Moses.

The Rabbis support their claim that Talmud has "Sinai status" in a most ingenious way; they tell a time travel story. Moses, the Giver of

Torah, goes "back to the future." He doesn't find Dr. Emmett Brown or his parents, but he does find R. Akiva—Akiva b. Yosef, a *tanna* of the latter first century and early second century. Swept some fourteen centuries into the future, Moses finds himself sitting in the back row of R. Akiva's classroom. As remarkable as it is that the Rabbis imagined time travel so long ago, perhaps even more significant is that they paired R. Akiva with Moses, whom the Rabbis called *Moshe Rabbenu* (Moses, our rabbi) and who is revered as the Giver of Torah. It is no coincidence that legend holds that R. Akiva lived 120 years—like Moses.

Legend also holds that Akiva b. Yosef rose from obscurity—an unlettered shepherd who caught the eye of the daughter of his wealthy employer—and became the preeminent Sage of his generation. Quoted extensively in Mishnah, R. Akiva is attributed with systematizing halakhah (Jewish law) by developing hermeneutics (methods of biblical interpretation) to interpret the Bible in the realms of both halakhah and midrash. So great is his contribution to the development of Rabbinic Judaism, it is not unreasonable to dub R. Akiva the second Moses (as our story in chapter 1 of this volume subtly does).

With Talmud, the Sages reshaped Torah to thrive after the Second Temple's destruction. Consider the festivals observed to this day. The Written Torah (Five Books of Moses) instructs us to observe three yearly pilgrimage festivals that have deep roots in agricultural and shepherding cultures: Sukkot, Passover, and Shavuot.[6] When the Temple stood in Jerusalem, those who were able traveled to Jerusalem to celebrate these festivals. They brought sacrifices for the *kohanim* (priests) to offer on the altar in the Temple or purchased sacrifices once they arrived in Jerusalem. Each festival called for different sacrifices and celebratory rituals.

Today nearly two millennia have passed since Jews worshiped in this manner, but thanks to the Rabbis these festivals remain a vibrant and lively facet of Jewish life. Reshaping the festivals for life in exile, the

Rabbis identified them with the national myth that explains when, how, and why the People of Israel came into existence. Each yearly cycle of celebration tells the story of Israel.[7]

So, too, with other aspects of Jewish life. Without an altar on which to offer sacrifices to God, the Rabbis developed an order of daily prayers for worship and composed specific prayers to be used for all occasions. They put liturgical "flesh on the bones" of life-cycle passages mentioned in Torah, such as marriage and death, creating a rich tradition that taps into the sacred stories of the Jewish people. Hence in Talmud we find many traditions of the Passover seder, the order of prayers in the siddur (prayer book), the marriage ceremony under a chuppah (wedding canopy) with a ring and ketubah (marriage contract) — and, beyond these rituals, extensive discussions of Jewish values and ethics that inform our lives.

Taken together, the teachings, customs, practices, and laws the Rabbis developed and recorded in the Talmud provided the Jewish people with the traditions they needed not only to survive, but also to thrive.

Geography of the Talmud

Mishnah is the substrata, or foundation, of the Talmud. Specifically it is a collection of tannaitic oral teachings and descriptions of Second Temple practices from the first two centuries of the Common Era. Rabbi Yehudah ha-Nasi commissioned its writing in *Eretz Yisrael* at the end of the second century CE, lest the oral teachings be forgotten. Some modern scholars have speculated that the Mishnah was originally a set of lecture notes (which helps explain the tight and terse style of Mishnah) that came, in time, to be viewed as a sacred religious text.

On top of this foundation — and what now constitutes the bulk of the Babylonian Talmud — is Gemara. Nominally an elucidation of Mishnah, Gemara is in reality a lengthy and complex compilation of edited transcripts reflecting four centuries of conversations and debates launched and inspired by the Mishnah, along with additional notes, stories, and material. Gemara was probably written down in its present form (following a process of editing and redacting) toward the end of the sixth century CE.

The first printed edition of the Talmud—Daniel Bomberg's in Italy between 1520 and 1523—established the general formatting used to this day. A section of Mishnah is followed by the Gemara that discusses it. The commentary of the great French commentator Rashi (Rabbi Shlomo Yitzhaki) is printed on the inner margin near the binding. The commentary of the Tosafists (medieval rabbis from France and Germany, by and large Rashi's students, sons-in-law, and grandsons) is printed in the outer margin. Additional commentaries are often published at the end of each volume.

The Vilna edition of 1835 standardized the content and numbering of each folio or page (*daf*), beginning with *bet* (page 2). Initially the cover was considered the first page, but sometime afterward another explanation arose: there is no page 1 because there is no beginning or end to Talmud study—not only is it a lifelong pursuit, but discussions continue from generation to generation. Accordingly, the first page of each tractate is 2a. The recto (front side) is called *alef* (a) and the verso (reverse side) *bet* (b). Hence "BT Berakhot 25b" means Babylonian Talmud, Tractate Berakhot, page 25, verso side. The folios of the Jerusalem Talmud, abbreviated JT, are often named a, b, c, and d, but some publishers are renaming the folios using only a and b to conform to the standardized system employed for the Babylonian Talmud.

Finally, when a mishnah alone is cited, this is customarily done by chapter and the number of the mishnah within that chapter. Hence, M Berakhot 4:2 means Mishnah, Tractate Berakhot, chapter 4, second mishnah, and will be identified that way in a printed edition of the Mishnah. In the Talmud, however, M Berakhot 4:2 will be found on *daf* 28b. Hence I often cite both references for clarity—M Berakhot 4:2; 28b—to enable the reader to locate the text quickly in either publication.

The Texts in Talmud

Within Talmud we encounter a wide variety of discussions ranging from complex legal analysis, to folklore, to theological reflection and speculation. Discussions and decisions pertaining to civil law, criminal law, business ethics, and religious rites and observances are interspersed with discussions and legal dictates concerning family relationships, ethical conundrums, relations with non-Jews, and advice to scholars and community leaders. Even more: you can occasionally find a recipe, medicinal advice, magical incantations, strategies for avoiding evil spirits and dybbuks—and a dash of locker-room humor.

Talmud evinces a deep and thorough understanding of people. The Rabbis recognized the best and the worst in us—the realities of human proclivities, passions, aspirations, and potential—and from there charted a course for Jewish living. They discussed and enshrined the values that are the hallmark of Torah: love of God, family, and community; social justice, compassion, and human dignity; tzedakah (righteousness),[8] *gemilut chasadim* (deeds of loving-kindness),[9] and *derekh eretz* (decency);[10] Torah study and learning.

They also dove into the pool of theology and offered a broader array of views of God than Torah. They abstained from dictating dogma or creed, but did make generous use of metaphor, often imagining God's psyche and emotional states in starkly human terms. Particularly in the *aggadah* (stories), the Rabbis attribute to God a wide range of intense emotions, including passion, compassion, anger, and jealousy. On several occasions they depict God as dangerously irrational and potentially out of control. The Rabbis' struggle to understand the world in which they find themselves crosses paths with their struggle to understand God and divine will. Human fallibility and divine temperament sit side by side in the study house, often overlapping, and open for examination and discussion.

Embedded too in Talmud are many stories (*aggadah*, from the Hebrew root for "tell" or "recount"). Cloaked in deceptively simple exteriors, these multifaceted tales discuss and illustrate highly sophisticated and potent religious ideas. Sometimes the stories illustrate a point, other times undermine the point, and always deepen the conversation taking place. By studying and discussing them and peeling away the layers, we discover ourselves in the stories: our relationships, our challenges and dilemmas, our dreams and aspirations, our frustrations and sorrows, our ideals and successes. Talmud is filled with treasures to be savored.

Talmud is even more than this. It teaches us, by its example, that disagreement and debate are healthy and good because they generate more ideas and deeper thinking. Thus, we are free to differ over just about every issue imaginable. At the same time, *how* we engage with one another in conversation, debate, and analysis is enormously important. The Rabbis understood that disagreement can lead to a healthy generation of new ideas or it can become malicious and cruel, and thereby rupture a relationship. They taught the concept of *machloket l'shem shamayim* (a controversy for the sake of heaven) as a criterion to ensure that one remains within a healthy boundary. The motivation for the disagreement is key: if one's purpose is to trounce, demean, and demoralize one's opponent, the approach is morally wrong. Debates that deteriorate into rancor and hostility do not result in Torah learning; their only lasting effect is to damage the people involved—and, ultimately, the broader community. Pirkei Avot encapsulates this important teaching:

> A controversy for heaven's sake will have lasting value, but a controversy that is not for heaven's sake will not endure. What is an example of a controversy that is for heaven's sake? The debates of Hillel and Shammai. What is an example of a controversy that is not for heaven's sake? The rebellion of Korach and his followers.[11]

This text impugns Korach, who fomented a rebellion against Moses and Aaron in the wilderness (Numbers 16). Korach presented his claims as a valid disagreement—thus, as if he were serving heaven—when in reality his true motivation was to gain power and control over the community. In contrast Pirkei Avot holds up as exemplars Hillel and Shammai, the leaders of the two predominant schools of thought in the Jewish community in the late first century BCE and early first century CE when Oral Torah was first developing.[12] The Talmud records more than three hundred matters in which Hillel and Shammai voiced differences of opinion. Because their goal was to foster Torah learning and serve God, and they thereby conducted their disputations honestly and civilly, their disagreements are deemed appropriate. Talmud teaches:

> For three years there was a dispute between Bet Shammai and Bet Hillel, the former asserting, "The halakhah ['legal ruling'] is in agreement with our views" and the latter contending, "The halakhah is in agreement with our views." Then a *bat kol* ['heavenly voice'] issued forth, announcing, "Both these and these are the words of the living God, but the halakhah is in agreement with the rulings of Bet Hillel."
>
> If both are "the words of the living God" what was it that entitled Bet Hillel to have the halakhah fixed in agreement with their rulings? Because they were kind and humble, they studied their own rulings and those of Bet Shammai, and were even so [humble] as to mention the opinions of Bet Shammai before their own.[13]

Talmud sets the bar wonderfully high for civil conversation and debate—teaching us to ask questions, think deeply, argue passionately, reason intelligently, seek responsible answers, remain civil—and keep our sights on heaven.

It's All about Relationships

How would you identify yourself? By your profession, religion, age, ethnicity, sexual orientation, accomplishments, possessions, background, appearance, personality, or life goals? Or perhaps by your religious beliefs and political commitments? Would you describe yourself as an athlete, a Ravens fan, a woodworker? Imagine that all these categories—all the attributes and descriptors we assign to ourselves and others assign to us—are the weft or crosswise threads of the tapestry of our lives. They change as we weave through time, lending our tapestry an easily identifiable color and texture, as well as a recognizable look: "Oh, that tapestry is Sarah!" or "Anyone can see that tapestry is Abraham!" While we might recognize another by their weft threads, that is usually not enough for us to recognize ourselves.

Warp threads, by contrast, are the lengthwise threads strung tightly to the loom, holding the weaving together. They are the relationships of our lives, the people we love and who love us, those whom we take care of and those who nurture us: parents, children, partners, other relatives, friends and neighbors, teachers, colleagues—and God, however we may conceive God.

Unlike weft threads, warp threads enable us to discover who we are. In the end it is through our relationships with others that we come to know our own selves. Ralph Waldo Emerson wrote, "Other men are lenses through which we read our own minds."[14]

The talmudic stories chosen for this book all speak to our life relationships: with ourselves, with God, with our families, within the Jewish community, and beyond. I selected them because they are marvelous stories in and of themselves and because they offer us a lens through which to examine pressing concerns in our lives and issues of great importance in our world.

My hope is that as each of us works to improve our relationships through the lens of Talmud, the tapestry of our lives will grow ever more beautiful.

Using This Book

Talmud is a difficult text to read. Therefore, the traditional way to learn is with a guide (teacher) and a study partner (*chevruta*), the very same way the Talmud came into being in the study houses of Babylonia and

Eretz Yisrael. To this day, people study Talmud with a *chevruta* partner and in small groups.

This book is intended to be your *chevruta* partner (but by all means find yourself a study partner with whom to share it) or to be used as a classroom, family, or informal study text. Each chapter begins with an overview, "Why Study This Passage?," intended to orient the reader toward the theme of the story and provide the literary and historical background needed to understand and appreciate the passage. Subsequently, "A Broad View to Begin" places the passage into the larger picture of Rabbinic discussion about a moral or theological principle of concern. Next comes "Exploring the Nooks and Crannies of Our Passage" in which the passage is presented in English translation, together with detailed explanation and analysis. From there, "Continuing the Conversation" offers provocative questions arising from the passage and related texts to ponder on one's own or discuss with others. Finally, the concluding section, "Summing Things Up," places the chapter's larger relationship discussion into perspective. Some readers may wish to begin by reading this summary.

Translations and Abbreviations

Translation can be tricky business. A brochure translated from Mandarin into English, dubbed the worst-ever translation, illustrates this: "Getting There: Our representative will make you wait at the airport. The bus to the hotel runs along the lake shore. Soon you will feel pleasure in passing water. You will know that you are getting near the hotel, because you will go round the bend. The manager will await you in the entrance hall. He always tries to have intercourse with all new guests."[15]

Another example: The first week my husband and I lived in Israel as students, before we knew Hebrew, we received a hand-scrawled note from his relatives in Netanya. They had called the university switchboard and the Israeli student on duty took their message and helpfully translated it to English for us. Here's what we received: "We order you to come on

Shabbat, but you must not come." Bewildered, we decided that if they had gotten in touch that meant they wanted us to visit, so we hopped a bus and showed up Friday afternoon. Some months later, we learned that the verb *l'haz'min* means both "invite" and "order," and that *atem lo mukhrachim* means "you don't have to." Our invitation would have been better translated, "We invite you to come, but you don't have to if you don't want to."

An Italian proverb has it that *traduttore tradittore*—"the translator is a traitor." While translations never fully substitute for the original text, I hope that my translations will elucidate rather than skew or obscure the Talmud's meaning. I have tried to achieve a balance between the cadence of Talmud and the needs of an English reader.

Talmud is written primarily in a terse Aramaic, sprinkled with Hebrew and punctuated with biblical verses, sayings, and proverbs. A conversation or story will often favor pronouns over names (e.g., "he said to him"). I have added names in square brackets (e.g., "[R. Yehoshua] said to [Rabban Shimon b. Gamliel]") for clarity, as well as additional explanatory verbiage (also in square brackets) to assist the reader.

Talmud does not supply citations for biblical verses; the Rabbis presume we have the entire Tanakh (Hebrew Scripture) memorized and accessible on a ROM chip in our brains. If only! Thus, they often cite only a section of a verse, and occasionally not even the most germane part of it. Moreover, the surrounding verses are sometimes equally important. It is generally a good idea to look up verses used as prooftexts to check their context and read the verses before and after them. Just in case you haven't had that ROM chip installed yet (mine is still on order), I often provide the full biblical verse plus citation, including the part of the verse not quoted by the Talmud in square brackets, to help the reader appreciate why this particular verse is used as a prooftext.

When quoting the Tanakh (Hebrew Scripture), I have generally used the New Jewish Publication Society translation[16] or the gender-sensitive adaption of the JPS Torah translation[17] except where I determined that my own translation would better convey the original Hebrew as the Sages understood it, and thereby help the reader better understand the Talmud's use of, and interpretation of, Scripture. In addition, I use my own translations in a few instances to reduce needlessly gendered language in the Prophets and Writings.

Here are three abbreviations you will see frequently in connection with talmudic citations:

M: Mishnah
BT: Babylonian Talmud (Bavli)
JT: Jerusalem Talmud (Yerushalmi)

Two additional abbreviations relate to people: The first is "R.," which connotes "Rabbi." As a title, "Rabbi" derives from *rav*, meaning "master" or "teacher." Rabbi, meaning "my teacher," came to be used by *tanna'im* (the Sages whose opinions are recorded in the Mishnah) and *amora'im* (the Sages of the Gemara) in the Land of Israel. *Rav* is the honorific title the *amora'im* in Babylonia generally used from the third century onward. The second is "b.," an abbreviation for "ben" (son) that, when used in a name, connotes "son of." Hence R. Yitzchak b. Avraham means "Rabbi Yitzchak, the son of Avraham." There is also a glossary in the back of this book; please reference it as needed.

Welcome to Talmud!

Welcome to the Talmud, a magnificent and crucially important work of Jewish sacred literature, the treasure that has been beneath our feet all along. I hope this book will whet the appetite of those of you tasting Talmud for the first time, as well as prove equally challenging, enriching, and delicious to those of you who have studied Talmud, making all of us hungry for more.

The Talmud of Relationships, Volume 1

PART 1 **THE CORE**

Relationships with God and Self

1 Finding Our Place
Babylonian Talmud, Tractate Menachot 29b

> Ben Bag-Bag taught: Turn it over and over—everything is in it. Scrutinize it and grow old and gray with it, but do not turn away from it, for there is no better portion than it.
> —Pirkei Avot 5:24

Why Study This Passage?

There is Torah (the Five Books of Moses) and there is *torah*, interpretations and applications of the sacred text. The Masoretic text of the Torah has been set since the tenth century CE, but the quest to explore its meaning, promulgate interpretations, and apply them to our lives began long before the tenth century and continues to this day.[1] Judaism rests on the textual pillar of Torah, and Jewish tradition has grown and thrived thanks to the pursuit of *torah* in each generation. In the first through sixth centuries of the Common Era, that pursuit by the *tanna'im* and *amora'im* gave birth to Mishnah and Gemara—Talmud. Our passage reveals R. Akiva's sagacious legacy in establishing interpretive traditions that have facilitated our continuing quest for *torah*, and the central role that interpretation plays in Jewish life and tradition. If Moses gave us the Written Torah, R. Akiva is the architect of the Oral Torah.

In some ways R. Akiva, who lived in the first and second centuries, is among the most enigmatic of the Sages. Whereas Moses grows up in the opulence of a pharaoh's palace, numerous talmudic accounts attribute to Akiva humble beginnings and portray a life that began in extreme poverty. In one version of his life story, R. Akiva is an unlettered shepherd who learns the alphabet only at the age of forty, yet becomes the foremost Sage of his time. In romantic accounts found in Talmud and midrash, it is his employer's daughter, Rachel, who recognizes Akiva's potential and insists that he study with the Sages to reach his potential. In one account (*Avot de-Rabbi Natan*), Rachel lives in destitute poverty for more than twenty years while Akiva pursues learning, rises to become a great Sage, and returns home with twenty-four thousand disciples in tow. That R. Akiva's success and importance are described in various Rabbinic stories in such glorious, hyperbolic language is a testament to his significance far more than it is an accurate historical record.

R. Akiva's colleagues see him as a peacemaker in the mold of Aaron; the stories about his ability to handle delicate and dangerous situations sensitively are legion. For example, Talmud reports that after a tempestuous argument in the *bet midrash* (study house), R. Eliezer b. Hyrcanus refused to abide by the majority decision and the Rabbis voted to excommunicate him, but feared he would use his magical powers to seek revenge.

> The Sages said, "Who shall go and inform [R. Eliezer that he has been excommunicated]?"
>
> R. Akiva said, "I will go lest someone inform him inappropriately and thus destroy the entire world."
>
> What did R. Akiva do? He donned black garments and wrapped himself in black and went and sat at a distance of four cubits from R. Eliezer.
>
> R. Eliezer said, "Akiva, what happened today?"
>
> R. Akiva replied, "Master, it appears to me that your companions are avoiding you."

Thereupon, R. Eliezer also rent his garments, took off his shoes, got down off his chair, and sat on the ground, all the while tears streaming from his eyes.[2]

Even more importantly, R. Akiva's contributions as the systematizer of halakhah set the nascent Rabbinic movement on a solid intellectual and procedural footing. Prior to R. Akiva, Jewish legal tradition consisted of a collection of accumulated oral laws and customs arising from logic and interpretation of Torah by a small handful of Sages. R. Akiva developed sophisticated methods for the organization and formulation of Jewish law through logic and scriptural interpretation. Akiva's hermeneutics and halakhic exegesis (methods of deriving new halakhah by interpretation of biblical texts) would come to form the foundation of Rabbinic Judaism.

R. Akiva taught that nothing in the Written Torah (Five Books of Moses) is without significance; every word and even every letter is replete with meaning. Every jot and tittle of Torah can be interpreted to extract sweet meaning, both in the present and in the future when the need arises.

Consider how R. Akiva found meaning within the first seven words — the very first verse — of Torah: *When God began to create heaven and earth* (Genesis 1:1). In the Hebrew the words for "heaven" and "earth" are each preceded by the Hebrew particle *et*, which has no translatable meaning except for marking the subsequent word as a direct object. In a midrash R. Ishmael challenges R. Akiva to explain how *et* could have significance in this verse.

> R. Akiva replied, "If it stated, *When God began to create heaven and earth*, we might have maintained that heaven and earth are also divine powers [i.e., 'gods']." [R. Akiva] then cited to [R. Ishmael]: *For this is not a trifling [or: 'empty'] thing from you* (Deuteronomy 32:47) and if you find it [the *et*] trifling (or: empty of meaning), that is your fault because you were unable to interpret it [correctly]. No, "*et* the heavens" is [written] to

include the sun and moon, the stars and planets; and "*et* the earth" is [written] to include trees, grass, and the Garden of Eden.[3]

For R. Akiva even the tiny particle *et* that cannot be translated conveys a world of meaning, telling us of the fullness of God's creative power.

In R. Akiva's hands Torah became a gold mine for continually unearthing new treasures. We might call these new treasures *torah*: *torah* (written with a lowercase "t") here meaning ongoing revelation that arises from studying Torah.

This is why the enterprise of halakhah has proved itself expandable, flexible, and applicable throughout the past nineteen centuries in the far-flung places Jews have lived. Torah, for R. Akiva, is not merely a book; it is a *process* of reading, interpreting, and discerning God's will in response to whatever question, situation, or dilemma confronts us.

R. Akiva's brilliant innovations suggest that we should speak not only of Torah, the text that has been handed down to us, but also of *torah*, the process of interpreting the Written Torah to find new direction, meaning, wisdom, and truth for our lives. The newly revealed *torah* then becomes folded into the ever-growing, ever-expanding Torah tradition.

R. Akiva is also credited with establishing the hermeneutical methods that gave rise to PaRDeS — an acronym formulated in the Middle Ages for *P'shat*, *Remez*, *D'rash*, and *Sod*, four progressive levels of Torah interpretation that Jews have acknowledged ever since:

P'shat — contextual meaning
Remez — symbolic or allegorical meaning
D'rash — homiletical meaning
Sod — esoteric or mystical meaning

Midrash *Pesikta de-Rav Kahana*, reflecting on R. Akiva's groundbreaking approach to Torah and halakhah, tells us that he "discovered things that were unknown even to Moses."[4] The talmudic story you will read in this chapter illustrates and enlarges on the midrash's claim.

The talmudic context of this story reveals much about the Sages' intent in telling the tale. The story is found in the order Kodashim (Holy things) amid a discussion of a mishnah stipulating that merely a part of a ritual object found to be defective can invalidate the whole. For example, if one letter of a Torah scroll is *pasul* (unfit) because the ink has been rubbed off, then the entire scroll is deemed *pasul* and cannot be used for a public reading until it is repaired. Leading up to our story in the Gemara, God explains details of the Torah not explicit in the Torah text itself. How could it be that there is more to Torah than meets the eye? If we do not plumb the full depth of Torah's meaning, is our understanding *pasul* because it is in some sense incomplete, like the Torah scroll on which a letter has been rubbed away? The Rabbis' very enterprise is to enlarge and expand on the meaning of Torah, applying it to ever-new realms of life.

Certainly, Moses could not have known or foreseen this. What would Moses think if he knew what became of his Torah in the hands of the Rabbis?

Exploring the Nooks and Crannies of Our Passage

The scene is set in heaven. Moses has not only climbed to the peak of Mount Sinai, but has ascended to heaven, where he sees God putting the finishing touches on the Torah.

> Yehudah said in the name of Rav: When Moses ascended to the heavens, he saw God sitting and tying crowns to the letters [of the Torah]. Moses asked, "What is staying Your hand?"
>
> God replied, "There is a man who will be in the future, after many generations, named Akiva b. Yosef, who will find in every jot and tittle mounds of *halakhot* ['laws'].

God, apparently in no hurry to give the Torah to Moses, is tying *tagin* (crowns) on the letters. *Tagin* are small strokes or flourishes, the only decoration permitted on a *sefer Torah*.

Moses is impatient. Why is God delaying revelation? God replies that these decorative tittles, too, are an integral part of Torah because they will enable future generations to extend the teachings of Torah beyond *p'shat*. Mitzvot are to be found not only in the words, but also in the *tagin*, if properly understood and interpreted. A man named Akiva son of Yosef, in particular, will derive a whole world of laws from these seemingly superfluous decorations. Not surprisingly, Moses wants to know who this remarkable man is.

> Moses said, "Master of the Universe, show him to me!"
> God said, "Turn around."
> Moses turned around and [found himself] in the eighth row of students in R. Akiva's academy, but he had no idea what they were saying. His strength deflated.

The verb "turn around" appears numerous times in the story. On each occasion the unexpected arises. Moses turns around and is instantaneously transported from Mount Sinai into the future. He finds himself sitting in R. Akiva's classroom.

Why are we told that Moses's time travel lands him, specifically, in the eighth row of R. Akiva's academy? The traditional classroom hierarchy in the time of the Sages placed the better students in the front row. Weaker students sat behind them. Moses is in the last row. The story confirms this placement: Moses doesn't understand anything he hears.

How could Moses, the great Lawgiver, be unable to follow R. Akiva's lesson? Perhaps the story seeks to convey Moses's poor self-image and sense of inadequacy as he listens to R. Akiva teach laws about which he knows nothing (after all, he has not yet received the Written Torah, let alone the Oral Torah). The eighth row of R. Akiva's classroom connotes Moses's humility and inexperience with Rabbinic hermeneutics and the Rabbis' reverence for him as *Moshe Rabbenu*, the quintessential teacher, Rabbi, and prophet.

However, the number eight has yet another connotation: completion. The world was created in seven days. The eighth day was the first complete day following Creation. Hence *brit milah* (covenant of circumcision) takes place on the eighth day: it completes the body.

> The class asked R. Akiva about a certain matter, "Whence do we know this?"
> He replied, "It is a law transmitted to Moses at Sinai."
> Moses's mind was put at ease.
> He turned to God [and asked], "If you have someone like this, why are you giving the Torah through me?"
> God said, "Silence! This is what arose in My mind!"

We have come to the heart and soul of the story. We don't know what R. Akiva is teaching his students. Is it something new R. Akiva discovered? Is it his personal interpretation or opinion? What matters most is its source. R. Akiva's teaching is *already encoded in the text*; it was, in some sense, already there at Sinai waiting for a Sage to discover and teach it.

R. Akiva's response, that his teaching is contained in Torah, does not mean that the precise words or idea can be found in its pages, but that it is legitimately, authoritatively derived from Torah. This is an example of the laws that God intended for R. Akiva to uncover; this is a halakhah "encoded in the crowns." This is what the enterprise of doing *torah* is about.

Moses's innate humility kicks in here. He asks why God doesn't give Torah through R. Akiva instead, given that R. Akiva can deliver not only the Written Torah but also an interpretation of the jots and tittles, the Oral Torah. God's response is unexpectedly harsh. "Silence! This is what arose in My mind!" is tantamount to "Don't you dare to question Me!" Moses will hear these words a second time.

Moses continued, "Master of the Universe! You showed me his Teaching, now show me his reward."

God said, "Turn around."

He turned around and saw that R. Akiva's flesh was being weighed out in the marketplace.

Moses confronted God, "This is Torah and this is its reward?!"

God said, "Silence! This is what arose in My mind!"

Moses assumes that a teacher as marvelous as R. Akiva will be rewarded for revealing and teaching more *torah*. This is an ironic presumption, given that Moses, who leads Israel out of Egypt and through the wilderness for forty years, is not permitted to set foot in the Land of Israel. He is not rewarded either. To say that R. Akiva was not rewarded, however, is an understatement. Our story alludes to a talmudic tradition that R. Akiva was brutally martyred by the Romans for publicly violating Emperor Hadrian's edict against studying and practicing Torah.[5]

Moses, shocked by what he sees, challenges God's justice. And again God cuts off conversation with "Silence! This is what arose in My mind!" Is God being imperious and unfeeling? Or is this an expression of *hashgachah* (divine providence), a Jobian claim that we are incapable of comprehending God's cosmic plan?

An alternative way to understand God's surprising retort is that the universe *is* "the mind of God." Everything that happens, all that befalls us, occurs not because God is a cosmic micromanager or divine puppeteer whose will and agency determine all events, but rather because God inheres in all Creation. In this view, "Silence!" is the Rabbis' admonition: "Don't ask that question. It is a dangerous theological path to follow, leading to despair and hopelessness. Don't think that Torah brings a tangible reward like winning the lottery; it doesn't work that way." Torah, we are reminded, is not a talisman that protects us from evil and suffering. It is a source of wisdom and insight to cope with all that life dishes out.

As Written Torah describes its own introduction into the world of the Israelites in Exodus 19 and 20, Talmud describes the seeds God sows within Written Torah in the form of *tagin* to facilitate the emergence of Oral Torah in future generations. Written Torah looks into the mirror and sees Oral Torah reflected back; Moses looks in the mirror and sees the teachings of R. Akiva reflected back. The process of *torah*, whereby we seek and find wisdom and meaning in our sacred texts, involves both looking into the text and into ourselves. The Rabbis believe that by its very nature Torah offers an unending font of interpretive possibilities and new meanings in each generation, symbolized by the *tagin*. While R. Akiva is a singular case of an extraordinary individual who made unique contributions to the Rabbinic enterprise, every generation is capable of finding new meaning in the text in response to the questions they pose and the challenges they face.

Continuing the Conversation

1. What Does This Say about the Nature of Revelation?
What do we mean when we use the term "Revelation"? It is often said that "God *revealed* the Torah to Moses at Mount Sinai" and that "Torah is God's revelation." But what does that mean, particularly in light of Talmud's understanding of its own genesis? Our story suggests two possibilities.

The first possibility is that God encodes laws in the *tagin* attached to the letters of Torah so that future generations will discover them when the need arises. This suggests that God's revelation happened once and is complete. Everything we need is already contained in Torah. After Sinai our efforts are directed at unlocking, discovering, and decoding meaning that is already implicit in the text.

Alternatively God builds flexibility into Torah, providing *tagin* that future generations can employ to find the meaning, wisdom, and laws they need for their lives. In this way revelation is progressive and ongoing, ever flowing from our open-minded encounter with Torah.

Which perspective best mirrors your view?

2. But We're Not Moses or Akiva!

Does anyone today consider their insights into Torah to be on par with Moses or R. Akiva? The Rabbis invite us to dive deeply into Torah, swim around, and create more *torah*. Does that mean that our views and insights are God's will?

Rabbi Naftali Tzvi Yehudah Berlin (1816–93, also known as the Netziv), born into a family of esteemed Jewish scholars, served as dean of the famed Etz Chayyim Yeshiva in Volozhin, which reached its zenith during his forty-year stewardship. In his innovative Torah commentary *Ha'amek Davar* (Delve into the matter), the Netziv argues that there is an organic relationship between the Written Torah (of Moses) and the Oral Torah (of R. Akiva) by drawing an interesting analogy between Torah interpretation and scientific research:

> Scientific scholars cannot claim in their hearts that they have understood all the secrets of nature.... In fact, they cannot be sure that their own research is true since they have no clear test. A later individual or generation can, through research, contradict the previous scientific construction. So, too, researchers into the nature of Torah cannot claim to have considered all the changes and all that requires thought. There is no certainty that what they have explained is the true intention of the Torah. So, all we can do is do our best with what we have.[6]

The Netziv is counseling humility, which in itself is valuable, but also far more. What is he saying about the nature of Torah interpretation and halakhah?

3. Renewing Ourselves through Interpretation

Does it ever seem strange, or perhaps amazing, to you that the entire Jewish community reads the same book, the Five Books of Moses, over and over again, year after year, generation after generation, all on the same weekly schedule? Of course we do not just read; we interpret, finding new life and meaning in ancient words.

Rabbi Shlomo Ephraim Luntschitz (1550–1619, Poland), in his popular commentary to the Torah *Kli Yakar* (Precious vessel), interprets the *mincha chadashah* (new meal offering) of Leviticus 23:15-16 in a novel manner. He writes: "The Torah must be new for each person every day as the day that it was received from Mount Sinai. For the words of Torah shall be new to you, and not like old matters that the heart detests. For, in truth, you are commanded to derive novelty each and every day."

The only way for Torah to be new is for us to seek new interpretations. Rabbi Luntschitz goes beyond invitation; he considers it to be a sacred obligation to interpret Torah in a way that resonates for your soul and for your life.

Do you agree? Why, or why not?

4. The Question of Original Meaning

Gerald Bruns, scholar of English language and hermeneutics, is less concerned with any objective truth that the Bible might be understood to articulate, than the manner in which every reader brings his or her own self to the text in the process of study and interpretation. He puts it this way: "What is at stake with respect to the Scripture is not what lies behind the text in the form of an original meaning, but what lies in front of it where the interpreter stands. The Bible always addresses itself to the time of interpretation: one cannot understand it except by appropriating it anew."[7] Bruns is saying that engaging with Torah is not about going through the text; it's about letting the text go through us.

How do you think the Rabbis who originally told the story of Moses in

R. Akiva's academy would respond to Bruns? Do you agree with Bruns? Have you succeeded in letting the text go through you?

5. Another Way to View Torah

We usually think of "Torah" as a noun, the proper name of a set of Five Books that tradition says God revealed to Moses on Mount Sinai. (In English, the term Pentateuch, from the Greek for "five scrolls," is often used.) The Hebrew root, *yud-resh-heh*, means to "teach" or "guide" (not law!). Perhaps we might think of Torah as a verb: "doing *torah*" would mean studying and searching for meaning and wisdom in both the Written Torah and the Oral Torah.

What is gained by thinking of Torah as a verb rather than as a noun? "Let's go do *torah*!"

Summing Things Up

In the hands of the Sages Torah became far more than a holy book or a collection of holy books. Torah became the ongoing process of interpreting and exploring our holy books.

The Sages expanded our idea of Torah beyond Written Torah to also encompass Talmud (Oral Torah)—and, beyond that, future interpretations of both as successive generations search for meaning, direction, and wisdom for living their lives in covenant with God. For the Sages, everything we need is in Torah (both Written and Oral) because the Jewish approach of study and interpretation is flexible and expandable: Torah provides a launching pad into all the important questions we ask and conversations we need to hold. Ultimately, it is the vehicle to finding the answers we need.

We also have R Akiva to thank for establishing interpretive traditions that have facilitated our continuing quest for *torah*. After all, as Pirkei Avot 1:1 tells us, "Moses received the Torah from Sinai and transmitted it to Joshua, and Joshua [transmitted it] to the elders, and the elders [transmitted it] to the prophets, and the prophets transmitted it to the members of the Great Assembly." Understood here is that the members of the Great Assembly transmitted it to the Sages and, thanks to Talmud, the Sages transmitted it to us. R. Akiva and his colleagues gave us the tools to carry on the tradition of interpretation in our lives—and so, the tradition of robust insight and revelation continues, growing ever richer with each generation.

2 Controlling Our Anger
Babylonian Talmud, Tractate Berakhot 7a

R. Shimon b. Elazar said in the name of Chilfa bar Agra in R. Yochanan b. Nuri's name: One who rends his garments out of anger, or breaks his vessels out of anger, or he who scatters his money out of anger should be regarded in your eyes as one who engages in idolatry, because such are the wiles of the evil inclination: today it says, "Do this," tomorrow it says, "Do that," until it bids him, "Go and serve idols," and he goes and serves them.

—BT Shabbat 105b

Why Study This Passage?
What is it like to be in the presence of someone who erupts like a volcano in anger, spewing the hot lava of accusations and fury?

I do not have in mind the righteous anger provoked by injustice and the sight of human suffering, which can sometimes pave the way to instituting greater justice and mitigating suffering. Rather, I am thinking of the banal emotion we all experience, some of us occasionally, and others of us with alarming frequency.

In general, anger is a self-centered, instinctual, and universal emotional response to feeling criticized, disrespected, degraded, humiliated, cheated, or ignored. Such anger is dangerous, both to the one who expresses it and to those on whom its lava is disgorged.

For the fuming person, anger can be dangerous regardless of whether it is expressed or suppressed—leading to high blood pressure, headaches, and heart problems. A *Journal of the American College of Cardiology* meta-analysis of more than two dozen studies revealed that anger and hostility are associated with chronic heart disease (CHD) events in both healthy people and those already afflicted with CHD.[1] An article in the *Journal of Medicine and Life* expressed it this way:

> Anger can have a direct impact upon cardiovascular diseases through the HPA [hypothalamic-pituitary-adrenal] axis and the sympathetic nervous system, their activation leading to an excessive liberation of corticosteroids and catecholamine. The liberation of such stress hormones can produce an avalanche of events, including hemodynamic and metabolic modifications, vascular problems, and disorders of the cardiac rhythm.[2]

Suppressing or internalizing anger is also dangerous, sometimes leading to anxiety and depression.[3] Numerous studies demonstrate evidence of the connection between "anger-in" (suppressed anger, or anger turned inward) and both depression and anger. Research psychologists note: "Strong associations have been reported between depression and anger-in . . . [as well as] evidence for associations between anxiety and anger-in."[4]

The stress of anger eats away at the one who experiences the anger. As the Buddha taught: "You will not be punished *for* your anger; you will be punished *by* your anger. . . . Holding on to anger is like grasping a hot coal with the intent to throw it at someone else; you are the one who gets burned." Mark Twain put it this way: "Anger is an acid that can do more harm to the vessel in which it is stored than to anything on which it is poured."

Moreover, anger is dangerous to those on the receiving end. Too often it leads to violent behavior.

Following a number of highly publicized horrific mass shootings in this country,[5] it became fashionable to blame mental illness for violent crime, since those who committed these attacks were often discovered to have been seriously ill. But the vast majority of people who suffer mental illness do not engage in violent behavior, and most murderers are not mentally ill. The common factor is not mental illness; it is anger.

Clinical psychologist Laura L. Hayes recounts the case of a "sweet, diminutive, elderly patient" who suffered from schizophrenia and was committed to a psychiatric hospital because she had stabbed another customer at a supermarket. At her commitment hearing, she responded to a query concerning whether she had heard voices: Yes, the voices in her head had told her *not* to hurt the man she was about to stab, but he had infuriated her by getting into the express checkout lane ahead of her with more than ten items. Hayes concludes: "Violence is not a product of mental illness; violence is a product of anger. When we cannot modulate anger, it will control our behavior."[6]

In April 2015 violent riots broke out in Baltimore in the wake of Freddie Gray's death, which had resulted from fatal injuries sustained while in police custody. Anger was unquestionably hanging thick in the air. More than one media commentator attributed the violence to pent-up anger. One protester, watching a CVS store that had been set on fire, observed to a National Public Radio reporter: "I see no shame in being violent to be heard because if you can't do it peacefully then what other option do you have?"[7] Mahatma Gandhi might have replied, "I object to violence because when it appears to do good, the good is only temporary; the evil it does is permanent."

Keenly aware of the interplay between anger and violence, the Rabbis find a surprisingly creative way to help us view—and control—our tempers with a measure of objectivity. Rather than discussing human anger, they talk about God's anger. God's anger thus allows us to reflect on our own. And if God's anger is unjustified and controllable, ours is too—all the more so.

Torah describes God's frequent bouts of rage and their destructive results. When God's anger erupts into the world, human lives are at grave risk. God's fury over human corruption in Noah's generation causes the Flood that consumes humanity. When Korach and his minions rebel against Moses, God causes the earth to open and swallow them.

Torah views God's anger from the human perspective, concentrating on how the people experience divine wrath. But the Rabbis imagine God's anger from within the Divine, asking: How does God experience anger? How does God feel about God's own anger? What does God do about it?

By exploring divine anger from the inside, the Rabbis afford us an empathetic excursion through our own anger and create a safe place for us to consider difficult questions: What makes us angry? Is our anger justified or overblown? What effect does our anger have on others? How can we gain mastery over it?

It may seem absurd to contemplate divine anger as a means of discussing human anger. Aren't the two wholly different? For the Rabbis, the answer is a resounding No. They recognize that anger, divine or human, surges from both self-protection and self-promotion. In their telling, God's emotions are as intense as ours, and often bear similar effects. God's love is empowering, just as our love of others can empower them. God's anger is destructive; so is ours. In the same way, God's efforts at self-control teach us self-moderation, and God's ability to set anger aside sets a standard for each of us to follow.

A Broad View to Begin

What is it like to be God? This is not a question we usually ask, but it preoccupied the Rabbis. To understand what it means to be fully human, and to be godlike, the Sages first asked: What is it like to be God? Since people are created *b'tzelem Elohim* ("in the image of God" or "on the model of God"), we (the Sages) need to understand what it means to be God in order to understand what it means to be godlike, and we need to understand what it means to be godlike in order to understand what it means to be fully human.

In our own time, to answer questions about how God thinks, we can begin by considering how we human beings conceive and talk about God. Let's consider three (of many possible) models.

First, we might imagine God to be a Being with authority over humanity and power over the world. Concerning this Being, we might ask: Does God have a body? A mind? Does God see, hear, and emote as we do? Does God respond to our behavior, both good and bad? Does God intervene in history and shape the course of events?

Second, we might conceive God as an abstraction: a physically intangible idea, principle, or force that motivates. Examples of abstract "God-ideas" include goodness, holiness, and the power that enables personal salvation. Here we might ask: Can we interact with an idea, principle, or value? How does an idea, principle, or value motivate human behavior? Can it require specific human behaviors?

Third, we might think about God as a projection of our thoughts and feelings, such as our fears and aspirations. If this is the case, is God the consolidation of the best or the worst within us, or perhaps a combination of both? If God derives from our imaginations and feelings, is the very idea of God constructive or destructive?

However we conceive God—as a Being, in abstract terms, or as a psychological projection—speaking about God in other than human terms is all but impossible for us. Because we human beings experience the world as embodied creatures, we are limited in our ability to imagine existence and interact with the world in any other way.

Here we are tapping into a larger discussion in the world of philosophy and religion: how are we to understand religious claims concerning God (regardless of the tradition they derive from), given that all manners of claim and belief are expressed in human language that derives from human experience? Roger M. White, philosopher of language and religion, explains:

> [The] use of "human" language in talking about God is inevitable. If we are to use language at all to talk about anything whatsoever, we have no alternative but to use language in a way that is intelligible to us as human beings. Every way of talking that could be grasped by a human being must be such that it could be learnt by a human being, and explained to a human being: we simply cannot step outside the human condition and use language in a way that transcends the limits of our comprehension. . . . The language we use to talk of God must therefore be a language that relates to our experience.[8]

Our ancestors spoke about God in anthropomorphic terms, as if God has a body. For example,

> [Adam and Eve] heard the sound of the God Adonai moving about in the garden at the breezy time of day; and the man and his wife hid from the God Adonai among the trees of the garden. The God Adonai called out to the man and said to him, "Where are you?" (Genesis 3:8–9)

God moves about and makes noise; hence God has a physical presence. God talks to Adam; hence God has a mouth or some other organ to produce sound. Why is it that God cannot see Adam? One interpretation: for the author of this story God is not everywhere, but rather located in time and space, much like people.

Our ancestors also spoke about God in anthropopathic terms—they ascribed to God a rich and varied, but distinctly human, array of emotions. For example, when God realizes that the Israelites have built an idol, a golden calf, to worship in the wilderness, *Adonai spoke to Moses, "Hurry down, for your people, whom you brought out of the land of Egypt, have acted basely."... Adonai further said to Moses, "I see that this is a stiff-necked people. Now, let Me be, that My anger may blaze forth against them and that I may destroy them, and make of you a great nation"* (Exodus 32:7,9–10).

Here we find God exhibiting emotions we readily identify as human: anger, jealousy, resentment. God has an id.

Then something remarkable happens:

But Moses implored his God Adonai, saying, "Let not Your anger, Adonai, blaze forth against Your people, whom You delivered from the land of Egypt with great power and with a mighty hand. Let not the Egyptians say, 'It was with evil intent that [Adonai] delivered them, only to kill them off in the mountains and annihilate them from the face of the earth.' Turn from Your blazing anger, and renounce the plan to punish Your people. Remember Your servants, Abraham, Isaac, and Israel, how You swore to them by Your Self and said to them: I will make your offspring as numerous as the stars of heaven, and I will give to your offspring this whole land of which I spoke, to possess forever." And Adonai renounced the punishment planned for God's people. (Exodus 32:11–14)

Moses's address to God sounds much as it would if he were speaking to a powerful human being, and not the Divine Creator and Sovereign of the universe. He appeals to God's reputation in the world, something God cares about deeply; apparently God has an ego. He recalls God's promise to the Patriarchs to make their progeny a great nation; God has a superego as well.

In the end God relents and renounces the intended punishment.

Throughout this episode and many others in the Bible God is described as emotionally volatile, often with a hairpin trigger, swinging between deep love for Israel and fury at her behavior.

At the same time, another strand of thought found anthropomorphic descriptions of God discomfiting—primitive, unsophisticated, and insufficiently intellectual on the one hand, and inadequately spiritual on the other.

In the Septuagint, the earliest Greek translation of the Tanakh (written in the third and second centuries BCE in Alexandria, Egypt), the attempt to avoid describing God in human terms is evident. The Septuagint is especially adept at expunging references to God's body and emotions. The "image of God" is rendered "glory of God." The "mouth of God" becomes the "voice of God" (though that doesn't entirely solve the problem, does it?). The Septuagint suppresses Hebrew Scripture's full-bodied description of God's emotions, as well.

Yet, with human emotions—especially anger—excised, so too are repentance and pity. The Septuagint's God appears to resemble the character often played by John Wayne, a lone cowboy on the prairie who does not experience emotion like the rest of us. Some Jews perceive this God as a sterile version of the emotionally dynamic divine being we meet in the Torah. Without a rich emotional life, this God no longer appears to serve as a divine model of repentance and mercy. Some people believe this model of God lacks depth because it lacks pathos. For others, this is a preferable model, inspiring control, stability, and reason above emotional volatility.

Early Rabbinic literature from the first and second centuries CE took a somewhat different approach. Throughout Hebrew Scripture, the Rabbis tended to suppress descriptions of God that suggest God is a cosmic superhuman who intervenes in the events of our world, especially in our individual lives. Often, they substituted Elijah or a *bat kol* (heavenly voice) for God's role in a story, distancing God from the realm of action in everyday life. In addition, they often introduced descriptions of humanlike behavior attributed to God with the term *ki'vi'yakhol* (as though it were possible) to signal the reader that their words are not to be interpreted at face value—for, after all, God is not like a human—but rather to be understood as figures of speech employed because we humans lack the capacity to speak of God in any other terms.

From the third century CE onward, however, the Sages of Babylonia were reveling in the image of an embodied God. Many of their stories are filled with beautiful, poetic, and literary descriptions that draw us into a world of deep meaning that transcends literalism.

It is not entirely clear what inspired the shift from a tannaitic style of speaking about God that was largely devoid of anthropomorphic and anthropopathic characteristics to the robust, full-bodied style of the *amora'im* (Rabbinic authorities from 200 through 600 CE) in Babylonia. I suspect that the events of 70 CE — in which the Romans destroyed the Temple, decimated the country, and deflated Jewish hopes for regaining sovereignty over the Land of Israel—took a deep toll in the ensuing decades. To the people, God, who throughout the Hebrew Scripture had promised to protect Israel from her enemies and had repeatedly assured them that the Land of Israel would be their patrimony and possession forever, felt increasingly distant, even out of touch. God did not save them from Roman conquest nor protect them from Roman oppression. Perhaps the experience of God's "distance" is mirrored in the general avoidance of anthromorphism and anthropopathism in tannaitic writing of the first two centuries. With time, however, the need to feel emotionally close to God may have precipitated a return to anthropomorphic and anthropopathic language. Or perhaps, once the sting of 70 CE was no longer as acute, the Rabbis recognized that only from the depth of human embodied reality could they speak to spiritual experience.

The context for our passage is a discussion about prayer. The Rabbis established prayer as a mitzvah, a Jewish religious obligation that replaces the sacrifices originally made in the *Mishkan* (wilderness Tabernacle) and later in the *Bet Mikdash* (Temple[s] in Jerusalem). When the Jerusalem Temples stood, sacrifice was the primary mode of worshiping God. After the Second Temple was destroyed in 70 CE, sacrifice was replaced by prayer as the essential link between Israel and God.

If we pray, it is natural for the Rabbis to imagine that God prays as well.

For us, this may seem strange and counterintuitive. But for the Rabbis, we pray *because* God prays: we follow God's model.

If we accept the premise that God prays, what questions follow?

Exploring the Nooks and Crannies of Our Passage

R. Yochanan bar Nafcha lived at the end of the second century and well into the third century CE. Born in Tzippori (Sepphoris), a major center of study in *Eretz Yisrael*, and orphaned at a young age, he was adopted by Rabbi Yehudah ha-Nasi, the patriarch and compiler of the Mishnah, who is called simply "Rabbi" throughout Mishnah and Talmud. Early in his life Rabbi began teaching Yochanan Torah. Although Rabbi died when Yochanan was fifteen years old, the boy continued to study Torah. Eventually he moved to Tiberias, where he began his own school. Like his mentor, he became a Sage of great repute.

Our passage begins with a teaching that R. Yochanan learned from R. Yose ben Chalafta, a student of R. Akiva who lived in the second century CE and started his own school for Torah study. R. Yochanan, in the name of R. Yose, makes the extraordinary claim that God prays daily. He exploits a feature of Hebrew grammatical construction to justify this remarkable assertion.

> Yochanan says in the name of R. Yose: How do we know that the Holy One, blessed be God, prays? Because it says: *I will bring them to My sacred mountain and let them rejoice in My house of prayer [literally: "the house of My prayer"]* (Isaiah 56:7). It does not say "their prayer" but rather "My prayer"; hence the Holy One Blessed be God prays.

The prophet Isaiah, speaking of the end of days, described the Temple as *bet tefillati*, *bet* meaning "house" and *tefillah*, "prayer." In context, *bet tefillati* means "My house of prayer"—but could also be parsed "the house of My prayer." R. Yose exploits this grammatical curiosity to assert that "My prayer" proves that God prays. What is more, R. Yose (as

R. Yochanan explains to us) points out that Isaiah did not say "their prayer," which would refer to prayers God gives people to say, but rather "My prayer," further proof that God prays.

If we accept the premise that God prays, what questions arise in your mind? If you're pondering any of these three questions—What prayer does God pray?, When does God pray?, Why does God pray?—Talmud answers all three.

R. Zutra b. Toviyah is a student of Rav, the Sage who founded an academy of Jewish study in Sura in third-century Babylonia. He offers a response to the first question in the name of his distinguished teacher:

> What does God pray? R. Zutra b. Toviyah said in the name of Rav, "May it be My will that My mercy may suppress My anger, and that My mercy may prevail over My [other] attributes, so that I may deal with My children through the attribute of mercy and, on their behalf, stop short of the limit of strict justice."

The Rabbis consider the poles of God's interaction with humanity to be defined by judgment (*din*) and mercy (*rachamim*), themes that continue to loom large in the High Holy Day liturgy. Rosh Hashanah is also known as *Yom ha-Din* (Day of Judgment). The belief endures that when God is angry with us, God sits in judgment and metes out punishment. And so throughout the day we pray for God's mercy. Our prayers acknowledge that God is weighing our deeds from the previous year—both good and bad—in order to decide whether we merit another year of life. If we do, we are written into the Book of Life (*Sefer Chayyim*) for the coming year. And even if we don't—if our good deeds do not outweigh our bad deeds—God might nonetheless choose mercy and award us life in the coming year.

We might think God's decisions concerning judgment and mercy are considered, rational, and reasonable, but the Rabbis suggest otherwise. Apparently God has what we would call an anger-management problem.

God too would prefer to be dispensing mercy rather than judgment, but struggles to suppress divine anger in favor of divine mercy. This is why God prays daily for restraint and self-control.

Talmud next introduces a *baraita* (mishnaic-era teaching) about a High Priest named Yishmael b. Elisha. (Talmud frequently refers to R. Yishmael b. Elisha, his grandson, who lived in the latter half of the first century and beginning of the second century. Occasionally there is a confusion between grandfather and grandson, as seems to be the case here. Since the Yishmael mentioned in our passage has a tête-à-tête with God in the Holy of Holies, this must be the grandfather.)

> It was taught: R. Yishmael b. Elisha says, "I once entered into the innermost part [of the Sanctuary—the Holy of Holies] to offer incense and saw Akatriel-Yah,[9] the Lord of Hosts, seated on a high and exalted throne. God said to me, 'Yishmael, My son, bless Me!' I replied, 'May it be Your will that Your mercy may suppress Your anger, and Your mercy may prevail over Your other attributes, so that You may deal with Your children according to the attribute of mercy and may, on their behalf, stop short of the limit of strict justice!' And God gave me a nod of the head." From this we learn: the blessing of an ordinary person must not be considered lightly in your eyes.

Among the Mayo Clinic's "10 tips to tame your temper" are "#4: Take a timeout," and "#10: Know when to seek help." God follows both tips.

Where can God go for help? To the one place where God meets human beings face-to-face for one-on-one conversation: the Holy of Holies in the Temple.

God summons Yishmael b. Elisha, the High Priest, to enter the Holy of Holies. Astonishingly, God then asks Yishmael for a blessing, and is rewarded with a wonderful blessing: precisely what God prays for daily.

This account suggests two possibilities. First, the prayer Rav told us God utters daily was learned from Yishmael; God visiting Yishmael in the Holy of Holies is the backstory to God's prayer. If this is the case, then God, to whom *we* pray, learned to pray from a human being. Such is the power of prayer, but also the power of a blessing.

The second possibility is that Yishmael sagely and intuitively discerns God's deepest need and desire, and accordingly provides a prayer that reinforces God's effort to achieve self-control over divine anger. Yishmael responds with patience and love—and above all, mercy!—not with judgment or anger. This is indeed a blessing, and Yishmael is a model of self-restraint for God.

In either case, these blessings are powerful.

Furthermore, the Rabbis observe, "The blessing of an ordinary person must not be considered lightly in your eyes." What do they mean by this?

One explanation might be that if God on High can seek and receive the blessing of a human being, we as individual human beings should not view with disdain the blessing of someone we consider "ordinary" or "beneath us." Rather, we ought to accept other people's blessings graciously and gratefully.

But there is another way to understand the Rabbis' comment. After all, Yishmael b. Elisha is not an ordinary person; he is the High Priest. Perhaps the Rabbis are suggesting that we should not think of *ourselves* as "ordinary people" whose blessings are of little value to others. Rather, we should see ourselves as the High Priest Yishmael b. Elisha in relation to God! Our blessings can bestow comfort, strength, and support—sometimes even more than we might imagine.

Note that upon receiving Elisha's blessing, God nods in assent, an expression of approval and appreciation. The Rabbis draw a beautiful lesson from this: Every blessing is precious when it is heartfelt. The status of the one who bestows it is immaterial; the sincerity, depth of caring, and content of the blessing are what matter.

The Gemara now returns to the subject of anger, and asks a practical question of human relations.

> Yochanan further said in the name of R. Yose: How do you know that we must not try to placate a person when he is angry? For it is written: *My face will go and I will give you rest* (Exodus 33:14).[10] The Holy One, blessed be God, said to Moses: Wait until My countenance of wrath will have passed by, and then I shall give you rest.

This is excellent practical advice. It can be dangerous to attempt to placate someone who is enraged; often it only adds fuel to the fire.

R. Yose uses as his prooftext Exodus 33:14, where God either assures Moses, "I will go in the lead and will lighten your burden,"[11] or inquires of Moses, "If my presence were to go [with you], would I cause you to rest easy?"[12]

For R. Yochanan the mention of God's "face" or "countenance" evokes the image of God's anger, as if God's face is reddened with fury. He reads Exodus 33:14 as a two-part statement: *When* my face will have gone (i.e., when the red in my face that marks my anger passes), *then* I will give you rest. R. Yochanan offers solid pastoral advice for someone faced with a furious person: wait until the person calms down, or at least until the worst of the angry flare-up has subsided, before attempting pacification.

Having established that God prays, that God's purpose in prayer is to achieve self-control over divine anger, and that God seeks help in achieving this goal, the Rabbis now explore the nitty-gritty of the matter: the danger inherent in God's wrath. If God gets angry, how often? When? How long does it last?

> But does the Holy One Blessed be God get angry? Yes, for it has been taught: *God has indignation every day* (Psalm 7:12). And how long does this indignation last? One moment. And how long is one moment? One fifty-eight thousand eight hundred and eighty-eighth part of an hour.

Psalm 7:12 is brought as a prooftext to establish that God's indignation occurs daily. Hence, the potential for danger is ever present.

The question of how long God remains angry is relevant, because during these moments God might unleash divine fury and destruction on humanity. The answer, which is not backed up by a prooftext, perhaps because the Sages do not have one, is that God's anger is momentary.

Strictly speaking, the amount of time they specified is variable because by "an hour" they mean 1/12 of the daylight within a 24-hour period.[13] Hence an hour in the summer is longer than an hour in the winter. If we consider an hour at the spring or autumn equinox, the fraction of an hour specified here is approximately 1/16 of a second—a fleeting moment.

Yet, given the enormity of God's power, even a fraction of a second is long enough to precipitate enormous damage, and so even this tiny interval of time deserves our full attention. The corollary holds true for human beings as well: a fraction of a second of anger, flaring abruptly, can instantaneously place others in danger.

If this is so, why does it matter when this 1/16 of a second of anger occurs?

To help answer this question, the Rabbis now bring Balaam, a gentile prophet, into the conversation. We meet him in Numbers 22 in a story that famously includes a talking donkey. Toward the end of their forty-year journey through the wilderness, the Israelites encamp on the steppes of Moab. Balak, king of Moab, grows alarmed. Aware that Israel has recently emerged victorious in battle with the Amorites, he has cause for concern. In Balak's eyes, the Israelites are like a plague of locusts devouring the land. He therefore hires the prophet Balaam to curse Israel in order to ensure his own nation's victory in the advent of war. Perhaps Balak also hopes that a plague will consume them before they devour the land of Moab.

> And no creature has ever been able to discern precisely this moment except the wicked Balaam, of whom it is written: *who obtains knowledge from the Most High* (Numbers 24:16). He, who did not even know the mind of his animal, how could he know the mind of the Most High? The meaning is, therefore, only that he knew how to discern precisely

this moment in which the Holy One Blessed be God is angry. And this is just what the prophet said to Israel: *My people, remember what Balak king of Moab plotted against you, and how Balaam the son of Be'or responded to him . . . and you will recognize the gracious acts of Adonai* (Micah 6:5).

What does *and you will recognize the gracious acts of Adonai* mean? R. Elazar says: The Holy One Blessed be God said to Israel: See now, how many righteous acts I performed for you in not being angry in the days of the wicked Balaam. For had I been angry, not a single remnant would have been left of the enemies of Israel.[14] And this, too, is the meaning of what Balaam said to Balak: *How shall I damn whom God has not damned, how doom when Adonai has not doomed?* (Numbers 23:8). This teaches us that God was not angry all these days.

Balaam is a puzzling character. On the one hand, he is a prophet-for-hire who will do anything for cash up front. Had he been given the opportunity to exploit his connection with God in order to curse Israel and cash in, he would not have hesitated. On the other hand, Torah acknowledges him as an authentic prophet: God speaks with him directly, and he communicates honestly with God. He obeys God, proclaiming that he cannot (or, perhaps, will not) "damn whom God has not damned . . . [nor] doom when Adonai has not doomed." Yet he is such a buffoon he can neither see nor understand the presence of the angel that his donkey can readily apprehend.

For the Rabbis, Balaam exemplifies God's restraint.

We also witness God's restraint with the Israelites. From the moment they leave Egypt, they give God abundant and repeated reason to be angry. For the next four decades they grumble, whine, complain, and rebel their way through the wilderness. Yet God protects them and supplies them with manna, quail, and a well that follows them wherever they travel. God also ensures their victory over many enemies, from the Egyptians who had pursued them to the shore of the Reed Sea, to the Amorites, whom they defeat just prior to crossing the Jordan River and entering *Eretz Yisrael*. What is more, while both of Israel's enemies, the Egyptians and the Amorites, are not permitted to destroy Israel, neither are they wiped out; they live to fight another day. For forty years Israel and her enemies provoke God time and time again, yet God does not give in to divine anger.

Balaam's example, however, raises another issue: How far might we allow our anger to carry us? What would any of us do if we possessed both the opportunity and capacity to exploit God's power? Would we use it to seek revenge against our enemies?

The Rabbis explore these questions next. First, they presume, we need to know the precise moment of God's anger: the very moment when God is open to the idea of avenging us by destroying another. Balaam's power is in knowing that exact moment when God becomes angry. Presumably he can tap into that anger, siphon some off, and unleash it in the direction of his enemies.

> And how long does God's anger last? One moment. And how long is one moment? R. Avin, and some say R. Avina, says: As long as it takes to say "a moment." Whence do you know that God is angry one moment? For it is said: *For [God] is angry but for a moment, and when [God] is pleased there is life* (Psalm 30:6). Or, if you prefer, you may infer it from the following verse: *Hide but a little moment, until the indignation passes* (Isaiah 26:20). And when is God angry? Abaye says: During the first three hours of the day, when the comb of the cock is white and [the cock] stands on one foot. Why, in each hour it stands this way! In each other hour it has red streaks, but in this moment it has no red streaks at all.

R. Avin (or R. Avina) quantifies the length of time that God is angry, but the Gemara wants a scriptural source. Two prooftexts, one from Psalm 30 and another from Isaiah, then confirm that God's anger is momentary and quickly passes. But precisely when does it occur?

According to a Sage nicknamed Abaye (his real name was Nachmani), who lived in Babylonia in the early fourth century and headed the academy in Pumbedita (he and his childhood friend Rava were considered the finest scholars of their generation), the brief moment of divine anger occurs each day at the same time: when the comb of a rooster changes color during the day's first three hours.

In the talmudic period the day was divided into twelve hours—each, by definition, equal to $\frac{1}{12}$ of the daylight on any given day. However, since these intervals of time were too short to establish with precision, a more feasible division of the day was into quarters: the first three hours, the second three hours, and so on. Hence "the first three hours" means the earliest period of the day, beginning at sunrise.

In the morning, just before the sun rises over the horizon, the sky grows very red and casts a red glow over the earth. The moment the sun peaks, though, there is a stark change; the world seems to lighten dramatically. I suspect this is the moment Talmud has in mind: the very moment the sun peaks over the horizon.

To recap, we now know that God prays for self-control to restrain divine anger because God becomes angry every day for a short interval at the moment the sun peaks over the horizon. Fortunately, God's anger lasts but a short interval, yet even the briefest moment is replete with danger. Were someone to discern the precise moment, he might find a way to take advantage of God's anger and inflict harm on another. Gemara now tells us the story of someone who was provoked and succumbed to the temptation: he tried to harness God's anger to curse his enemy.

> In the neighborhood of R. Yehoshua b. Levi there was a Sadducee[15] who used to vex him greatly with [his interpretations of] texts. One day the Rabbi took a cock, placed it between the legs of his bed, and watched it. He thought: When the moment [of God's anger] arrives, I will curse him. When the moment arrived, he was dozing. [Upon awakening] he said, "We learn from this that it is not proper to act in such a way. It

is written: *[God's] mercy is upon all God's works* (Psalms 145:9). And it is further written: *To punish the innocent is surely not right* (Proverbs 17:26)."

R. Yehoshua b. Levi was an *amora* who lived in the Land of Israel in the first half of the third century. Most significantly here, he was the antithesis of Balaam. He was beloved and admired for being gentle, modest, pious, peaceful, and tolerant — not someone who would be likely to take advantage of God's anger in order to seek revenge.

This is precisely the point: A gentle and righteous soul like R. Yehoshua b. Levi can be provoked to anger he cannot subdue. Even a kind and sweet person can be dangerous when angry.

R. Yehoshua b. Levi plans to exact revenge against an ideological enemy who torments him with sectarian interpretations of Torah or heretical claims against Scripture. Pushing himself to stay awake all night, he employs a rooster tied to his bed as his alarm clock to pinpoint the precise moment of opportunity when he can harness God's anger to curse his enemy. But at the opportune moment, when the rooster's crest changes color, he is asleep. Upon awakening, he realizes that what he planned was improper, and cites two biblical verses that teach us to emulate God's mercy. Even righteous people should not punish others, he says, because their judgment is imperfect, incomplete, and skewed by emotion and bias.

One pressing question remains: Why is God angry every day? Is there a provocation? The answer, unsurprisingly, is yes. We learn from a *baraita* in R. Meir's name that God's anger is, indeed, in response to human behavior.

> It was taught in the name of R. Meir: At the time when the sun rises and all the kings of the East and West put their crowns on their heads and bow down to the sun, the Holy One Blessed be God becomes angry.

Every day, as the sun rises over the horizon, the earthly kings bow in worship of the sun.[16] This enrages God.

Yet God does not *respond* in anger. God tolerates them.

The message is twofold. First, the original premise driving this passage—that we need to worry about God's anger because it endangers us—is proven false. It is human anger, and especially our own anger, that should concern us; day by day, this is a far more imminent danger.

The passage began by focusing on the inherent danger of God's anger. We come to see that our concern is misplaced: human anger is the more potent danger.

Second, just as God tolerates those who offend God, we can and must learn to tolerate people who offend us. God is our role model. Every day, God exhibits self-restraint, controls divine anger, and tolerates insult. Every day, we too can take responsibility for how we behave when we are angry, knowing that doing so is godly behavior.

The Rabbis feared that divine anger would manifest in physical disasters. Human anger sometimes erupts into violence. And even though few of us commit acts of violence when we are angry, many of us do attack others verbally.

The story is told of a young boy who frequently became enraged. In his fury he would lash out with cruel and hurtful words. The lad's father gave him a bag of nails and a hammer and told him that every time he gave in to the temptation to say something hurtful, he was to drive a nail into the fence rimming the backyard.

The first day the boy drove thirty-seven nails into the fence. Over the next few weeks, as he learned to control his anger and hold his tongue, the number of nails he hammered into the fence each day gradually diminished. The boy discovered that it was easier to hold his tongue than to drive nails into the fence.

Finally, the day came when the boy did not lose his temper even once. Soon, he proudly told his father that three days had passed and he hadn't hammered a single nail into the fence.

As he celebrated his son's success, the father suggested that from that point on, every day his son could hold his temper and keep his tongue in check, the boy was to pull out one nail.

Many days passed. Finally, the boy was able to tell his father that all the nails were gone.

Then the father took his son by the hand and led him to the fence. He said, "And now, my son, look at the holes in the fence. The fence will never be the same. When you say things in anger, your words leave a scar just like this one."

Continuing the Conversation

1. Compose Another Prayer for God

This passage addresses the question "What does God pray?" as an entry point for discussing anger.

Can you imagine another prayer God might recite? What would it say? Why might God find it necessary and valuable?

2. Feeling, Expressing, and Suppressing Anger—Should We Display or Hide Our Anger?

Groucho Marx once quipped, "If you speak when angry, you'll make the best speech you'll ever regret."

When and how is it appropriate to show our anger? When is it best not to allow it to show? Many psychologists counsel the importance of expressing anger in order to prevent it from turning inward, into depression. Similarly, U.S. Rep. Maxine Waters has said, "I have a right to my anger, and I don't want anybody telling me I shouldn't be, that it's not nice to be, and that something's wrong with me because I get angry."[17] Waters's anger has fueled her battles against racism and discrimination, though it has also led her to brand her political opponents "demons."

The Rambam (Moses Maimonides, 1135–1204), a physician, philosopher, Torah and Talmud commentator, and community leader, taught in the *Mishneh Torah* that anger is tantamount to idolatry because it is a form of self-worship. He recommended that each person take extraordinary proactive measures to control both emotion and behavior.

Anger is a very bad character trait, and so it is proper for a person to distance himself from it in the extreme, and train himself not to get angry, even regarding something where it is fitting to get angry over that matter. And if he wants to instill fear in his children or the members of his household, or in his community, for instance if he was a *parnas* ['community employee'] and wanted to be angry with them in order to cause them to improve their ways, he should exhibit anger before them in order to redirect them, but his inner posture should be composed, as one who feigns anger at the time of his wrath, though he is not genuinely angry.

The early Sages said: One who becomes angry is like one who worships idols. They also said: Whoever becomes angry, if that person is wise, wisdom will be lost; if that person is a prophet, prophecy will be lost. The life of one who is angry is not truly life.

Therefore, [the Sages] directed us to distance ourselves from anger ... to the extent that we [should] not feel anger even in response to things that provoke anger. This is the good path.[18]

Do you think it is possible to train oneself not to get angry? Could you learn to maintain inner composure during situations in your life that inflame your anger? How would that change your life?

3. Finding Role Models

Do you know someone who refuses to allow anger to drive the controls? For the Rabbis, an even finer immunization against anger is to watch those who have achieved a high degree of self-control. Finding role models for the behavior we want to exhibit (or inhibit) reminds and inspires us that our goals are attainable. Talmud (BT Shabbat 88b) records this teaching: "Those who are insulted but do not insult, who hear themselves reviled but do not answer, and who act through love and rejoice in suffering, of them Scripture says, *Those who love [God] are like the sun rising in might* (Judges 5:31)."[19]

The verse tells us that God is our quintessential role model: When we love God and lean on God for the strength not to respond to those who would ignite our anger, we are like a powerful, brightly shining sun that cannot be diminished by occasional cloud coverings of insults, slander, abuse, or degradation.

Is there someone in your life who is an inspiring role model for you in curbing your anger? If yes, how has this person helped you? Do you—or could you—lean on God when you "hear yourself reviled"?

4. Your Cup, Your Purse, and Your Anger

At age seventy-seven, the American poet, memoir writer, and civil rights activist Maya Angelou reflected, "I've learned that you can tell a lot about a person by the way he/she handles these three things: a rainy day, lost luggage, and tangled Christmas tree lights."

The Talmud expresses it this way: R. Ilai said: "A person's character can be discerned by three things: by *koso* ['his cup'], by *kiso* ['his purse'], and by *ka'aso* ['his anger']."[20]

Do you agree? If others were evaluating you on the basis of how you behave when you drink alcohol, how you spend your money, and how and when you express anger, what would they say? What about when you're cooped up in the house, you've lost your luggage, or your home improvement project has gone terribly awry?

5. Praying God's Prayer—and Your Own

Prayer is another vehicle to gain control over one's emotions. Here are three suggested prayers:

The first prayer reflects the teachings of the Hasidic master Rebbe Nachman of Bratzlav, who encouraged his followers to tame their negative emotions in order to ward off anger and its consequences: "Merciful God, let me experience Your mercy. Save me from pessimism, from bitterness, and from cynicism. Help me overcome my negative feelings; help me avoid every form of arrogance, every hint of greed."[21]

A second recommended prayer is inspired by the one the High Priest Yishmael gave God to pray: "May I have the strength of will and character to approach everyone I encounter today with an attitude of compassion and mercy, and may I suppress my tendency toward judgment, criticism, and impatience."

The third prayer is meant to foster equanimity, the opposite of anger. A Jewish ethical and spiritual tradition called Musar teaches that to diminish a negative trait, a person must practice continually to strengthen its opposite. Rabbi Simcha Zissel Ziv (1824–98, also known as the Alter of Kelm), a foremost student of Rabbi Israel Salanter (who founded the Musar movement), taught: "A person who has mastered *menuchat ha-nefesh* (equanimity, or peace of mind) has gained everything."

Reinhold Niebuhr's serenity prayer has helped many people achieve a greater measure of *menuchat ha-nefesh*: "God, grant me the serenity to accept the things I cannot change, the courage to change the things I can, and the wisdom to know the difference."

Summing Things Up

Proverbs 14:29 advises: *One who is slow to anger has great understanding, but impatience leads to foolishness.*[22]

Anger can be toxic, endangering our health, leading to all sorts of verbal and physical breaches and poisoning our most precious relationships. Yet anger is also so universal that the Rabbis tell us even God experiences it. What's more, it's so instinctual and difficult to control, God also struggles to rein it in.

When we seek to curb our anger before we say or do something we and others may regret, the Rabbis want us to know that we are engaged in the same effort as God. It is a sacred endeavor.

3 Understanding Our Suffering
Babylonian Talmud, Tractate Berakhot 5a–b

R. Meir said: When a human being is in distress, what does the Divine Presence say, as it were? "My head is in pain. My arm is in pain." If the Omnipresent feels distress over the blood of the wicked that is spilled, how much the more so over the blood of the righteous.

—M Sanhedrin 6:5

Why Study This Passage?

It is human nature to ascribe meaning to life experiences. We construct narratives to explain *why* things happen as they do.

This is just as true, if not even more so, for suffering.

Suffering disrupts our sense of order and justice. It compels us to find answers to anchor us in the midst of chaos. "To live is to suffer," writes Friedrich Nietzsche. "To survive is to find meaning in the suffering."

Sometimes "pain" and "suffering" are conflated, but they are not the same. Physical pain is a physiological experience: our bodies' response to danger. Evolutionarily, it is crucial to human survival: if we touch a hot stove, the sharp, burning pain we experience serves to protect us by alerting us to damage happening to our body and induces us to immediately remove our hand to avoid further pain and damage.[1]

Suffering, in contrast, is about how we interpret and ascribe meaning to our experience of pain. The suffering that pain causes may initiate painful emotions, among them anger, anguish, fear, helplessness, or trauma. If we report feelings of pain to medical personnel, we are often asked to rate that pain on a one-to-ten scale. This in itself is an acknowledgement that we can separate our *feelings about* pain from the recognition and measurement of the actual physical sensation.

Our Sages stress the importance of consciously understanding the meaning we ascribe to suffering. They formulated many answers to this meaning conundrum, among them four that Talmud affirms:

> Suffering is punishment for individual or communal sin.
> Suffering tests one's faithfulness to God.
> Suffering is a necessary stop on the path to redemption.
> Suffering is *yissurin shel ahavah* (chastisements of love) from God.
> (For a more in-depth discussion of these answers, see Appendix.)

In addition, Talmud teaches that reward and punishment can be delayed beyond one's lifetime to *olam ha-ba* (the world to come).[2] In other words, those who are not sufficiently rewarded or punished during their lifetimes as commensurate with their deeds will find further reward or punishment awaiting them in *olam ha-ba*.

Tractate Berakhot, the source of this chapter's passage, explores the fourth idea — chastisements of love — which asserts that God sometimes visits painful affliction on innocent, righteous people as an act of love, so as to be able to increase their rightful reward in *olam ha-ba*. The Rabbis thus posit that if we suffer undeservedly in this world, our reward in the *next* world (*olam ha-ba*) will be that much greater than it otherwise would have been.

Such suffering is not something we can choose to experience, however.

It is entirely God's choice, not ours. What is in our hands is whether or not to accept our suffering with love and grace.

Talmud describes the scene as the first-century tannaitic Sage R. Eliezer b. Hyrcanus lies dying. R. Eliezer is considered one of the greatest Sages of his generation: his students describe him as "the Scroll of the Torah," meaning he is not only a student and teacher of Torah, but also a living embodiment of Torah. Visiting him, all his students are distraught to see their beloved teacher wracked with pain and enveloped by suffering. All, that is, except R. Akiva.

R. Akiva's behavior might strike us as peculiar, which is precisely why Talmud records it: so we can probe the narrative for its underlying theological insight.

> Rabbah b. Bar Chana said: When R. Eliezer fell ill, his disciples came to visit him. He said to them, "There is a fierce wrath in the world." They began to cry, but R. Akiva laughed.
>
> They asked, "Why are you laughing?"
>
> He asked them, "Why are you weeping?"
>
> They answered, "Shall the Scroll of the Torah lie in pain, and should we not weep?"
>
> [R. Akiva] replied, "That is precisely why I laugh. As long as I saw that my master's wine did not turn sour, nor was his flax smitten, nor did his oil putrefy, nor did his honey become rancid, I thought, God forbid, that he may have received all his reward in *this* world [leaving nothing for the next world]. But now that I see him lying in pain, I rejoice [because I know he will receive his reward in the world to come]."
>
> [R. Eliezer] said to him, "Akiva, have I neglected anything in the whole of Torah?"
>
> [R. Akiva] replied, "Master, you yourself have taught us, *For there is not a just person on earth who does good and never sins* (Ecclesiastes 7:20)."[3]

R. Akiva observes that throughout his life R. Eliezer has enjoyed great prosperity, presumably recompense for his great learning and deeds. Yet if R. Eliezer has been richly rewarded in *this* world for his righteousness, what is stored up for him in the world to come? The suffering R. Akiva sees assures him that R. Eliezer is accumulating "cosmic capital" that will manifest in abundant reward in *olam ha-ba*.

R. Akiva further reminds his teacher that no person is without sin (Ecclesiastes 7:20 articulates this principle), so perhaps R. Eliezer is also proactively atoning for sin through suffering before he dies. In other words, R. Akiva is saying that a portion of R. Eliezer's suffering is punishment for sin, but because his suffering greatly outweighs his sins, the remainder of his reward will accrue to him in the world to come.

Such an answer to why there is suffering may help those of us who hold God accountable for our pain and therefore find it difficult, if not impossible, to turn to God for strength and comfort. For some, this problem runs very deep, robbing them of the ability to believe in God at all.

Bart D. Ehrman, a scholar and historian of ancient Christianity, describes how this conundrum brought him to faith, and ultimately ripped his faith from him.

> If there is an all-powerful and loving God in this world, why is there so much excruciating pain and unspeakable suffering? The problem of suffering has haunted me for a very long time. It was what made me begin to think about religion when I was young, and it was what led me to question my faith when I was older. Ultimately, it was the reason I lost my faith.[4]

At the same time, embedded in the traditional theology of reward and punishment is an underlying danger: it can be interpreted to give people permission to pass judgment on one another, or on themselves.[5] Witnessing suffering, someone might conclude that the one who suffers deserves the pain. Moreover, those who view their suffering as deserved divine punishment for their crimes and failings can become wracked with guilt and shame.

It is one thing to proffer the theory of *yissurin shel ahavah* (chastisements of love) in the house of study, examine and dissect it in conversation and in writing—all by "taking it out for a spin" in one's mind. It is quite another to lie in bed, stricken with pain, and contemplate suffering as a gift from heaven. In the forthcoming passage from Tractate Berakhot, the Rabbis explore the theology and logic of *yissurin shel ahavah* and then field test it in the real world, permitting us to see how the theory works for several Sages in their sickbeds.

A Broad View to Begin

What should we say and do in the face of human suffering we can neither prevent nor mitigate? At one time or another, we all find ourselves in this situation. How are we to respond to the anger, hopelessness, and negative thoughts a suffering person expresses? How might we help the sufferer make sense of the experience?

To review: A traditional perspective might say, "If God is the Creator of the universe and the author of life, God can both cause and alleviate human suffering. If God rewards goodness and punishes evil, then painful afflictions may be God's payback for your sins." Or, "God might employ suffering to test your faithfulness"—again, God has ordained your suffering. Or, "your suffering may be necessary to effect a future redemption"—thus your suffering is justified on a cosmic scale. Finally, if all these possibilities have been exhausted, one last explanation is offered to find meaning in a terrible reality: "these are *yissurin shel ahavah*—God's chastisements of love."

All four explanations, however, allow an observer to say, in essence, "You're getting what you deserve or what God wants you to experience. Who am I to interfere?"

The Rabbis cannot countenance this type of human judgment. They take us on a difficult journey through the minefield of the humanly constructed theology of suffering in order to teach us how to respond. Our job, they insist, is not to judge, but to heal and comfort.

Exploring the Nooks and Crannies of Our Passage

Our passage opens by walking us through a series of questions that serve as a theological algorithm to analyze the cause of one's suffering. The Rabbis accept the traditional theological notion that God recompenses sin with suffering, but not as quickly or easily as we might suspect.

We begin with a teaching of Rava, or perhaps Rav Chisda, both of whom were Babylonian *amora'im*. Rav Chisda lived in Kafri and died in the second decade of the fourth century CE; his student and later son-in-law, Rava, lived in Machoza.

> Rava, and some say Rav Chisda, says: If a person sees that painful sufferings visit him, let him examine his deeds. For it is said, *Let us search and examine our ways, and turn back to Adonai* (Lamentations 3:40). If he examines [his deeds] and finds nothing [objectionable], let him attribute it to neglect of Torah study, for it is said, *Happy is the one whom You chastise, Adonai, and whom You instruct in Your Torah* (Psalm 94:12).

Question #1: Did the sufferer sin? That is, is the suffering a just punishment for something the sufferer did, or failed to do? Lamentations 3:40 connects the idea of spiritual self-examination with repentance. The Rabbis also presume we are aware of the previous verse, Lamentations 3:39: *Of what shall a living person complain? Each one of his own sins!*

If the sufferer has not committed sins that warrant suffering, we move on to Question #2: Did the sufferer neglect the study of Torah?

Certainly, Torah study is a behavioral matter, and therefore one might argue that Question #1 has already covered it. For the Rabbis, however, Torah study occupies a unique place in Jewish life, and thus warrants special mention. Psalm 94 asserts that the evil people do does not escape God's notice or response. In context, verse 12 tells us that Torah serves to teach us proper behavior, and thereby chastises us when we veer from the right path; here, the Rabbis employ the verse to say that God chastises people for neglect of Torah study by imposing suffering.

If one can respond "No" to these two questions, which is to say that the sufferer's ordeal cannot be explained by sins of either commission or omission, the Rabbis proffer the theory that painful afflictions may be *yissurin shel ahavah*:

> If he did attribute it [to neglect of Torah study], and still did not find [this to be the cause], he can be sure that these are chastisements of love. For it is said, *God rebukes the one whom God loves* (Proverbs 3:12).

In a world in which people understand God to be the source of everything, both good and bad, the concept of *yissurin shel ahavah* simultaneously affirms God as the source of suffering, and—breathtakingly—transforms suffering from divine punishment for sinful behavior into God's gift to a righteous person.

Now, Rava goes further, implying (though not explicitly stating) that God's crushing afflictions are proportional to God's love: the more someone pleases God, the more painful the afflictions may be. Rava presents this teaching with an impressive pedigree and hence credibility: Rav Huna, who headed the famous academy in Sura in Babylonia, is the source.

> Rava, in the name of R. Sechorah, in the name of R. Huna, says: If the Holy One Blessed be God is pleased with a person, [God] crushes him with painful sufferings. For it is said, *But Adonai chose to crush him by disease* (Isaiah 53:10). Now, you might think that this is so even if he did not accept [the afflictions] with love. Scripture therefore says, *If he made himself an offering for guilt* (Isaiah 53:10). Just as the guilt offering must be brought by consent, so also the sufferings must be endured with consent. And if he accepts them, what is his reward? *He will see offspring*

have a long life (Isaiah 53:10). And more than that, his [Torah] learning will endure with him, as it is said, *Through him the purpose of Adonai will prosper* (Isaiah 53:10).

Rava's dramatic theological transformation of suffering from punishment to gift requires a correspondingly dramatic psychological transformation to see suffering in positive terms. Accordingly, the remainder of the passage is devoted to guiding sufferers through a thinking process that enables them to view suffering not as punishment and themselves not as sinners but as an experience that reflects God's desire for them to receive an even greater reward in *olam ha-ba*.

In the age of the Rabbis, there were few analgesics and limited relief from pain. How was one to tolerate it? Perhaps the suggestion "the greater the pain, the greater the person" served as a needed mental or spiritual analgesic. This can only work, however, if the sufferer psychologically "accepts" the suffering. For *yissurin shel ahavah* to have an ennobling effect, the sufferer must receive them with love. In essence, Rava teaches the righteous to offer up physical pain as a sacrifice to God, and assures us that such a sacrifice will be accepted by Heaven and rewarded with prolonged life. Believing great pain to be a reflection of great righteousness may make it easier to bear.

Even in the Rabbis' world, the assertion that suffering can be God's gift to the righteous is riddled with questions that the Rabbis must now tackle. First, they acknowledge an inherent problem: If suffering is a "gift," it makes no sense for God to inflict suffering that prevents a person from doing precisely what God wants that person to do—pray and study Torah. What is more, would God deprive us of the very spiritual disciplines that help us connect to God as a source of comfort and consolation? Therefore, if suffering precludes us from fulfilling our obligations to prayer and Torah study, and thereby from experiencing the Shekhinah (God's abiding presence in the universe), how can we possibly conclude that our suffering is *yissurin shel ahavah*?

> R. Yaakov bar Idi and R. Acha bar Chanina disagree [with regard to the following]: The one says: Chastisements of love are those that do not cause cessation of Torah study, for it is said, *Happy is the one whom You chastise, Adonai, and whom You instruct in Your Torah* (Psalm 94:12). And the other one says: Chastisements of love are those that do not involve the interruption of prayer, for it is said, *Blessed is God who has not turned away my prayer, or God's faithful care from me* (Psalm 66:20).

R. Yaakov b. Idi and R. Acha b. Chanina see this matter differently. One claims that God would not send afflictions that interfere with study; the other claims that God would not send afflictions that interfere with prayer. Perhaps their underlying disagreement concerns the importance of sufferers understanding the source of their suffering (leading to the opinion that God would not cut us off from study of Torah and hence knowledge of the obligations that keep us from sin) versus the importance of receiving succor from God during an ordeal (hence the opinion that God would not impose suffering that precludes one's ability to pray).

The prooftexts are excellent and to the point. We have already seen Psalm 94:12 in this passage. Used here, it takes on new shades of meaning: God's chastisement is accompanied by Torah learning; hence the suffering of one who is unable to engage in Torah study could not be God's chastisement. Psalm 66:20 is interpreted similarly: *God's faithful care* of the sufferer is understood as the *yissurin shel avavah* that will, in due time, benefit the sufferer; and *who has not turned away my prayer* is understood to mean, "who has not made it impossible for me to pray."

But which criteria—inability to study or inability to pray—tells us whether or not suffering is *yissurin shel ahavah*?

> R. Abba, the son of R. Chiyya b. Abba, said to them, "This is what R. Chiyya bar Abba said in the name of R. Yochanan: 'Both of them are chastisements of love, for it is said: *God rebukes the one whom God loves* (Proverbs 3:12).'"

Why, then, does Scripture say *whom You instruct [t'lam'dennu'] in Your Torah* (Psalm 94:12)? Do not read *t'lam'dennu* ['You teach him'] but rather *t'lam'deinu* ['You teach us']. You teach us this thing from Your Torah as a conclusion *a fortiori* from the law concerning tooth and eye. Tooth and eye are only one limb of the person, yet [if they are damaged], the slave obtains thereby his freedom. How much more so with painful sufferings that torment the whole body of a person! And this agrees with R. Shimon b. Lakish, for R. Shimon b. Lakish said, "The word 'covenant' is mentioned in connection with salt, and the word 'covenant' is mentioned in connection with sufferings: 'covenant' is mentioned in connection with salt, as it is written: *[Y]ou shall not omit the salt of the covenant* (Leviticus 2:13). And the word 'covenant' is mentioned in connection with sufferings, as it is written: *These are the terms of the covenant* (Deuteronomy 28:69).[6] Just as in the covenant mentioned in connection with salt, the salt enhances the flavor of [lit. sweetens] meat, so also in the covenant mentioned in connection with sufferings, the sufferings wash away all of a person's sins."

R. Chiyya b. Abba conveys R. Yochanan's teaching that suffering that interferes with either study or prayer is a chastisement of love. He offers a fascinating analogy to an indentured servant. Exodus 21:16–17 tells us that a master who inflicts permanent bodily harm on an indentured servant is obligated to free him. Analogously, since God is our master and we are God's servants, if God causes us to suffer, then God owes us compensation (in the world to come) above and beyond what we would otherwise deserve as a reward for our own good deeds. What is more, beyond physical pain, being deprived of the ability to pray and study Torah compound one's suffering.

Finally, R. Shimon b. Lakish (also known as Resh Lakish) offers an analogy: just as salt lends flavor to meat, thereby enhancing the eating experience, so, too, suffering lends meaning to the experience of God's covenant in our lives. In other words, suffering for the sake of God's covenant deepens one's commitment to God.

Resh Lakish cites a *baraita* (mishnaic-era teaching) of R. Shimon b. Yochai to make the further observation that, historically, suffering accompanied three great gifts God gave to Israel, each of which entailed suffering:

> It has been taught [in a *baraita*]: R. Shimon b. Yochai says, "The Holy One Blessed be God gave Israel three precious gifts, all of which were given only through sufferings. These are: Torah, the Land of Israel, and the world to come." Whence [do we know] Torah [is acquired only through suffering]? Because it is said, *Happy is the one whom You chastise, Adonai, and whom You instruct in Your Torah* (Psalm 94:12). Whence [do we know this concerning] the Land of Israel? Because it is written, *Bear in mind that your God Adonai chastises you just as a householder chastises his son* (Deuteronomy 8:5), and after that it is written, *For your God Adonai is bringing you into a good land* (Deuteronomy 8:7). Whence [do we know this concerning] the world to come? Because it is written, *For the commandment is a lamp, and Torah is a light, and the way of life*[7] *is the rebuke that disciplines* (Proverbs 6:23).

R. Shimon b. Yochai lines up a selection of verses in which a term that means chastise or discipline is associated with Torah and the Land of Israel. The third verse (Deuteronomy 8:7) requires an interpretative stretch: identifying "the way of life" with "eternal life" and hence the world to come. This allows him to claim that in each case, the suffering experienced by the Israelites in connection with the gifts of Torah, *Eretz Yisrael*, and the world to come is "salt" added to "meat" to enhance its flavor, thus making the outcome all the sweeter. Just as people often reflect that a prize hard-won, for which we experienced privation or hardship, often seems commensurately more valuable, Resh Lakish suggests that the more valuable the prize or gift, the more hardship one must experience to acquire it. Knowing this, we can rest assured that suffering is a prelude to a great reward.

Resh Lakish's three examples are communal rewards. Does the principle that suffering enhances the value of the reward hold true for an individual's experience in this world?

To test the idea that God visits suffering on a person in order to justify compensating him or her in the world to come, the Rabbis consider the most incalculable and irredeemable suffering an individual might experience: the loss of a child.

Enter stage right: R. Yochanan, the student of R. Yehudah ha-Nasi and the teacher of Resh Lakish. We learn elsewhere in the Talmud that R. Yochanan's father died before he was born and his mother died in childbirth.[8] If that isn't enough suffering, R. Yochanan fathered ten sons, each of whom predeceased him. As we learn later in this passage, R. Yochanan carried in his pocket a relic (either a bone or a tooth) of his youngest child as a reminder to others of what can be lost and as a symbol of the spirit of resignation and acceptance with which one should approach personal tragedy and suffering. Talmud cites a *baraita* presented before R. Yochanan, followed by R. Yochanan's response.

> A *tanna* recited before R. Yochanan: Whoever busies himself with the [study of] Torah and acts of kindness [5b] and buries his children, all his sins are forgiven him.
>
> R. Yochanan said to [the *tanna*], "I grant you Torah [study] and acts of kindness [cause one's sins to be forgiven], for it is written, *Iniquity is expiated by kindness and truth* (Proverbs 16:6). 'Kindness' means acts of kindness, for it is said, *One who strives to do good and kind deeds attains life, success, and honor* (Proverbs 21:21). 'Truth' means Torah [study], for it is said, *Buy truth and never sell it* (Proverbs 23:23). But whence [does the *tanna* know that the sins of] one who buries his children [are forgiven]?"
>
> A certain elder recited to him in the name of R. Shimon b. Yochai, "It is concluded from [the *gezerah shavah*, which infers a legal decision based on linking identical words in two different verses,] 'iniquity' [and] 'iniquity.' Here it is written, *Iniquity is expiated by kindness and truth* (Proverbs

16:6), and elsewhere it is written, *You . . . visit the iniquity of the parents upon their children after them* (Jeremiah 32:18)."

It is not clear what the *baraita* means by "Whoever busies himself with the [study of] Torah and acts of kindness and buries his children, all his sins are forgiven him." Is the intent that if an honorable person engages daily in Torah study, righteous acts, and generosity, and suffers horrendous loss nonetheless, then whatever sins this person has committed are erased from the record? Or does this presage an increased reward in the world to come? Or some combination of these?[9]

The teaching presented before R. Yochanan is not a perfect fit for the Talmud's conversation, but it serves a purpose. Forgiveness of sins suggests that the sufferer will be absolved of guilt and enjoy greater reward than he would have otherwise, had he not suffered, if only because his soul arrives in *olam ha-ba* sooner. This accords with the promise of greater reward implicit in the doctrine of *yissurin shel ahavah*.

Considering the three acts the *baraita* says mitigate punishment of sin—Torah study, tzedakah (acts of charity), and loss of children—R. Yochanan separates them into two distinct categories. He concedes the points about Torah study and tzedakah—and even provides prooftexts from Proverbs to support the claim. But, R. Yochanan believes, the loss of children is so horrific and cataclysmic he cannot conceive of God imposing such suffering on a person as punishment for sin, to mitigate future punishment for sin, or to warrant greater reward in *olam ha-ba*. Knowing this suffering firsthand—tenfold—he categorically rejects the notion that the loss of a child could ever be God's response to a parent's behavior—and neither could it ever be *yissurin shel ahavah*.

That the loss of a child could be a chastisement of love from God is deeply troubling from yet another moral perspective: the life of an innocent human being—the child—is involved. To claim that God deprives us of our children, cutting their lives short, in order to "gift" us with such colossal suffering that we merit a greater reward in *olam ha-ba* seems an

UNDERSTANDING OUR SUFFERING   53

obscene contradiction even within the theological framework of reward and punishment, because it does not acknowledge that the child is a human being whose life has value and who deserves to be judged on his or her own merit. In such a framework, the child becomes mere chattel (however precious to us) to be given as a gift or taken away by a God. A God who acts in this cavalier way would seem mercurial and cruel, and R. Yochanan rejects the suggestion that God operates with capricious injustice.

The Gemara responds with an argument based on Scripture and inspired by the use of the word "iniquity" in Proverbs 16:6. Note that Jeremiah 32:18 also uses the term "iniquity" and makes the claim that God repays the iniquity of parents to their progeny, visiting the guilt of parents on their children. We are now standing waist-deep in an ancient and classical argument about when, how, and on whom God repays evil. Exodus 34:6–7 famously recounts that after Moses carves two stone tablets to be inscribed by God, God descends on Mount Sinai in a cloud and passes before Moses, saying, "Adonai! Adonai! a God compassionate and gracious, slow to anger, abounding in kindness and faithfulness, extending kindness to the thousandth generation, forgiving iniquity, transgression, and sin; yet [God] does not remit all punishment, but visits the iniquity of parents upon children and children's children, upon the third and fourth generations."[10]

A teaching attributed to R. Shimon b. Yochai contradicts R. Yochanan's opinion by claiming that Scripture affirms that children are, in fact, punished for their parents' sins. If that is the case, might God also choose to make the righteous suffer the loss of children in order to extend to them a greater reward in *olam ha-ba*? While to twenty-first-century readers this idea might sound morally preposterous, in the ancient world it was worthy of sober consideration. Minimally, it suggests that the loss of children might *not* be punishment for sin, thereby subtly and cleverly inverting the original claim of Exodus 34:6–7 as well as the underlying suggestion of the *baraita* presented before R. Yochanan.

Nonetheless, R. Yochanan adamantly rejects the notion that the loss of children is a prelude to future reward. The Gemara cites his teaching that neither skin afflictions nor the loss of children are *yissurin shel ahavah*. This would seem to clinch the argument, but it creates another problem.

> R. Yochanan says, "*Nega'im*[11] and [the loss of] children are not chastisements of love."
>
> But [is affliction from] *nega'im* not [a chastisement of love]? But it was taught [in a *baraita*]: *If a person has one of these four symptoms of nega'im* (M Nega'im 1:1)—they are nothing else but an altar of atonement! They [the four types of *tzara'at*] are an altar of atonement, but not chastisements of love. If you prefer, I can say: This [teaching that says *tzara'at* can be a chastisement of love] applies to us [in Babylonia], and that [saying of R. Yochanan that *tzara'at* is not a chastisement of love] applies to them [in *Eretz Yisrael*].[12] And if you prefer, I can say: This [teaching that *tzara'at* can be a chastisement of love] refers to hidden [skin afflictions], and that [teaching of R. Yochanan that *tzara'at* is not a chastisement of love] refers to exposed [skin afflictions]. But is [the loss of] children not a chastisement of love? How is this to be understood? If you say that [it refers to] one who had children and they died, did not R. Yochanan say, "This is the bone of my tenth child?" Rather, this saying [that loss of children is a chastisement of love] refers to one who never had children, and that saying [R. Yochanan's statement that loss of children is not a chastisement of love] refers to one who had children and they died.

Nega'im, meaning "plague" or "affliction," here connotes *tzara'at*, a constellation of skin diseases discussed in Leviticus 13 and 14 and often erroneously translated as "leprosy." Mishnah includes a tractate devoted to its identification on skin, clothing, and buildings, and rituals for purification from *tzara'at*.

R. Yochanan states that neither *tzara'at* nor loss of children is a chastisement of love from Heaven. The Gemara, however, recalls a *baraita* that appears to contradict R. Yochanan's claim. Quoting a snippet of the first mishnah of Tractate Nega'im,[13] which enumerates four signs of *tzara'at*, the *baraita* terms these afflictions a *mizbach kapparah* (altar of atonement), which the Gemara presumes is equivalent to a chastisement of love. An anonymous voice, though, asserts that an "altar of atonement" is distinct from a chastisement of love.

But is it? If a skin affliction is an "altar of atonement," does this not suggest that one who suffers a skin affliction does so as a sacrifice to atone for sin, which would therefore increase that person's reward in the world to come? The distinction is subtle and difficult to assert with confidence.

We now have two opinions on the table: R. Yochanan's view that *tzara'at* is not a chastisement of love and the Gemara's understanding of the *baraita* that since *tzara'at* is an "altar of atonement," it is therefore a chastisement of love. How are these two views to be reconciled?

Gemara offers two possibilities: The first is R. Yochanan's view that *tzara'at* is not a chastisement of love. The second is the Gemara's understanding of the *baraita* that since *tzara'at* is an "altar of atonement" it is a chastisement of love.

Gemara then offers two possible resolutions, which in itself suggests that neither of the proffered solutions is leakproof. The two options are introduced by "If you like, I can say." The first resolution is that the two teachings apply in different localities: in Babylonia (where this conversation is taking place) *tzara'at* is considered *yissurin shel ahavah*, but in *Eretz Yisrael*, where R. Yochanan lives and teaches, it is not. The second resolution is that the *baraita* refers to skin afflictions that are customarily covered by clothing and hence not visible, whereas R. Yochanan speaks about visible skin afflictions.

Gemara now returns to the larger and more troubling question of children, asking: Can children be considered *yissurin shel ahavah*? Here the text offers a third option for reconciling the contradiction between the *baraita* and R. Yochanan: R. Yochanan was speaking about the death of one's child(ren). After all, he carried a relic of his tenth son in his pocket. He knew from personal experience that the tragedy of losing a child is not a chastisement of love. The *baraita*, Gemara concludes, spoke about a situation in which one suffers infertility: the loss of ever having children. The Gemara thus affirms R. Yochanan's contention that the devastating loss of a child is outside the bounds of what may be considered a chastisement of love.

The concept of *yissurin shel ahavah*, considered in the sober light of the study house, lends at least theoretical meaning to suffering: It comes from a loving God who will compensate the sufferer manifold times in *olam ha-ba*. It is, at least in theory, a modest down payment on an extraordinary eternal reward.

Or so it seems from the perch of the academy. It has been said: In theory, there is no difference between theory and practice; in practice, there is. The length to which the Sages go to find scriptural support for *yissurin shel ahavah*—consider how many verses they have quoted!—is a hint that the doctrine rests on shaky ground.

But even more, in the glaring light of genuine suffering does the theological claim that painful afflictions are God's gift stand up? It's time to take the supposition that God imposes suffering on people for their ultimate benefit out for a test drive. How are *yissurin shel ahavah* received by righteous people?

What follows are the road tests—a series of three short, yet crucially important narratives. All three vignettes are similar in structure, content, and tone. In each case, a Sage who is both an exemplary scholar and a righteous human being lies on a sickbed of pain and suffering. The presumption is that these are all instances of *yissurin shel ahavah*.

Each Sage, in turn, is visited by a colleague and asked a remarkable question: "Are your sufferings welcome to you?" In essence: Do you appreciate the value of *yissurin shel ahavah* and accept your suffering graciously, knowing it will earn you a greater reward in the world to come? After all, as was taught earlier in this passage, one ought to accept one's unmerited suffering as a sacrifice to God, because reward accrues to those who accept what God metes out with an open heart and a willing spirit.

In all three cases, however, the Sage lying on the sickbed responds with a resounding "No!"—and, astonishingly, adds, "Neither they nor their reward." Can you imagine them summoning all their strength to sit up in bed, glare at their visitor in disbelief, and shout: "Are you serious? I didn't choose this; I don't want this; and I'd do just about anything to stop the pain!"

The statement, *"Neither they nor their reward,"* is repeated no fewer than three times, a literary trop that alerts us to the fact that actual pain and suffering undercut the most elaborately erected theological scaffold. And, lest we think that any one of the three accounts is a one-off, an exception to the rule that righteous people unquestioningly accept their suffering with grace and the understanding that their merit in doing so will accrue in the world to come, each scenario repeats the rejoinder: *"Neither they nor their reward."* Gemara places us figuratively at the bedsides of three esteemed Sages schooled in Rabbinic thinking who, in the throes of pain and suffering, offer us wholesale and radical rejection of *yissurin shel ahavah* theology! When the rubber meets the road and suffering is painfully real and no longer theoretical, the value of the promise inherent in *yissurin shel ahavah* may well evaporate into thin air.

In the first scene, R. Yochanan visits R. Chiyya b. Abba, who is ill and suffering.

> R. Chiyya b. Abba fell ill and R. Yochanan went in to visit him. [R. Yochanan] said to [R. Chiyya b. Abba], "Are your sufferings welcome to you?"
>
> [R. Chiyya b. Abba] replied, "Neither they nor their reward."
>
> [R. Yochanan] said to [R. Chiyya b. Abba], "Give me your hand." [R. Chiyya b. Abba] gave him his hand and [R. Yochanan] raised him [up out of his sickbed].

Note both R. Chiyya's rejection of the value of *yissurin shel ahavah* and R. Yochanan's response. R. Yochanan does not encourage R. Chiyya to accept his suffering with grace. He does not attempt to dissuade him from his opinion. Nor does he pull out the relic of his tenth son.

By the same token, R. Yochanan does not applaud R. Chiyya nor voice his personal rejection of what we have, by now, taken to be Rabbinic doctrine on undeserved suffering.

What *does* he do? R. Yochanan reaches out a hand, touches his friend, and raises him out of the sickbed. In other words, the text tells us, R. Yochanan heals R. Chiyya. He actively disrupts and reverses the affliction that God ostensibly decreed for the express purpose of increasing R. Chiyya's reward in the world to come. He does this because R. Chiyya finds his suffering intolerable—no questions asked.

> R. Yochanan once fell ill and R. Chanina went in to visit him. [R. Chanina] said to him, "Are your sufferings welcome to you?"
>
> [R. Yochanan] replied, "Neither they nor their reward."
>
> [R. Chanina] said to him, "Give me your hand." [R. Yochanan] gave him his hand and [R. Chanina] raised him.
>
> Why could not R. Yochanan raise himself? They replied, "The captive cannot free himself from prison."

In the second vignette, R. Yochanan is now ill and R. Chanina visits him. R. Chanina asks R. Yochanan the very same question R. Yochanan asked R. Chiyya b. Abba. We know that R. Yochanan does not accept suffering as a chastisement of love, so we are not surprised when he responds, "Neither they nor their reward." Nor are we surprised when R. Chanina reaches out and heals him, again without attempting to dissuade his suffering colleague. We have learned from the first story that this is the proper response.

In the second vignette, however, a reasonable question is raised: Why doesn't R. Yochanan, who demonstrated that he possesses the power to heal when he visited R. Chiyya, effect his own healing? Gemara supplies an answer: the prisoner cannot free himself from prison. When we are afflicted with pain and suffering, we cannot always act as we normally would. Pain and suffering warp our perspective and diminish our power. We need the help, strength, and support of others. Even though R. Yochanan is a healer, he nonetheless needs R. Chanina to heal him.

> R. Elazar fell ill and R. Yochanan went in to visit him. He noticed that he was lying in a dark room so he bared his arm and light radiated from it. Thereupon he noticed that R. Elazar was weeping, and he said to him, "Why do you weep? If it is because you did not study enough Torah, surely we learned: *The one who sacrifices much and the one who sacrifices little have the same merit, provided that the heart is directed to heaven.*[14] If it is due to lack of sustenance, not everyone has the privilege to enjoy two tables [learning and wealth in abundance]. And if it is due to [the lack of] children, this is the bone of my tenth child."
>
> [R. Elazar] said to [R. Yochanan], "I am weeping on account of this beauty that is going to rot in the earth."
>
> [R. Yochanan] said to [R. Elazar], "For this you should surely weep."
>
> And they both wept. In the meantime, [R. Yochanan] said to [R. Elazar], "Are your sufferings welcome to you?"
>
> [R. Elazar] replied, "Neither they nor their reward."
>
> [R. Yochanan] said to him, "Give me your hand." [R. Elazar] gave him his hand and [R. Yochanan] raised him.

In the third vignette, R. Yochanan visits R. Elazar, who is ill and suffering. The third story echoes the first two, but many revealing details are added. We are told that the room is dark. Why? Is it because light disturbs R. Elazar? Or is it because he is alone and has no one to care for him? Is the dark room to be understood metaphorically as a reflection of his mood and spirit, or as the physical misery of a painful illness, or both?

As R. Yochanan bares his arm, light radiates from it to illumine the room. According to tradition, R. Yochanan is so exceptionally beautiful that his body radiates light.[15] Talmud suggests that R. Yochanan casts two types of light into the room: physical light, to transform this gloomy, depressing room into a cheerier place to elevate R. Elazar's spirits; and metaphorical light, in the form of opening an honest conversation that affords R. Elazar a safe place to share his deepest fears and receive comfort and healing from his colleague.

It is only when both physical and metaphorical light are cast on the room that R. Yochanan realizes his colleague is weeping. Why didn't he hear his weeping before? Was he not listening? Social activist Catherine de Hueck Doherty (1896–1985) has said, "With the gift of listening comes the gift of healing." The light R. Yochanan sheds both reveals and heals.

R. Yochanan asks his colleague why he is weeping. Surely R. Elazar's painful afflictions are more than sufficient to explain his tears. But R. Yochanan is asking more than this. Following the algorithm Talmud has established for analyzing painful suffering, he is asking the source of R. Elazar's suffering. Knowing that R. Elazar observes the mitzvot, R. Yochanan proceeds to Talmud's second question: Is it because you did not study enough Torah? But apparently R. Yochanan poses this question as a straw man—without waiting for a response, he rejects the contention out of hand on general principle: Menachot 110b in the Babylonian Talmud teaches that God does not ascribe merit based on quantity, but rather quality, of study. What God cares about is the sincerity of our efforts. In this way R. Yochanan rejects more than *yissurin shel ahavah*—he rejects a pillar of Rabbinic thinking about suffering: that God would impose suffering to punish a Sage for the failure to study Torah sufficiently. In fact, R. Yochanan claims that God receives all sincere efforts with love and satisfaction, and ascribes it to us as if we had studied even more than we did.

R. Yochanan poses a second question: Do you believe you are suffering because you have not earned enough money to sustain yourself? Perhaps R. Yochanan is suggesting that R. Elazar suffers physically from inadequate nutrition, or perhaps he has in mind psychological and spiritual suffering because R. Elazar was unsuccessful in business and therefore unable to provide adequately for his family. Here, as well, R. Yochanan rejects the possibility, pointing out that not everyone enjoys success in both scholarship and business.

R. Yochanan poses a third question: Are you weeping for lack of children? This time, in contrast with his encounter with R. Chiyya b. Abba, R. Yochanan pulls out the relic of his tenth son. What does he mean in doing this? Is he suggesting that his suffering exceeds that of R. Elazar? Certainly not: He is expressing empathy. If R. Elazar weeps because he either lacks, or has lost, children, R. Yochanan initiates this gesture to express his understanding.

R. Elazar responds that he is weeping because the sight of R. Yochanan—so beautiful that his body emanates light—reminds him that they are both mortal and will eventually die and decompose in the ground. On this account they both weep, though perhaps for slightly different reasons. R. Yochanan is still mourning the loss of his children, as he will for the remainder of his life, and R. Elazar is mourning the lives R. Yochanan and he will one day have to surrender. All suffering, this comment suggests, is a taste of the ultimate loss: death.

Through the ages, various religious and philosophical traditions have wrestled with the question: Is there a purpose to suffering?

Eastern traditions teach that suffering brings wisdom, as well as resilience and compassion. Kahlil Gibran notes: "Out of suffering have emerged the strongest souls; the most massive characters are seared with scars."

In the West, Helen Keller writes that suffering is essential to building desirable character traits: "Character cannot be developed in ease and quiet. Only through experience of trial and suffering can the soul be strengthened, ambition inspired, and success achieved." She also noted: "Although the world is full of suffering, it is full also of the overcoming of it." Swiss philosopher, poet, and critic Henri-Frédéric Amiel (1821–81) wrote, "You desire to know the art of living, my friend? It is contained in one phrase: 'Make use of suffering.'"

The Irish poet William Butler Yeats, however, expresses a different view: "If suffering brings wisdom, I would wish to be less wise."

In one sense, Henri-Frédéric Amiel's words encapsulate the view of our Rabbis, who struggle to "make use of suffering." Yet, where Amiel counsels us to make use of our suffering, the Rabbis teach us: If a person cannot or chooses not to make use of suffering, then whenever and wherever possible, alleviate their suffering. It is not ours to judge; it is ours to mitigate pain and bring relief.

Biblical religion arose in the ancient Near East, and Rabbinic tradition developed in the shadows of Greece and Rome; Judaism is an amalgam of both East and West. The Rabbis leave open the possibility that one might find value in suffering—at least in its reward in the world to come—but they do not insist on it.

Consider Job. As he suffers, he is visited by three acquaintances, each of whom presumes that his sufferings are God's recompense for sin and therefore advises him to determine how he erred and then repent to God. Although Job refers to them as "mischievous comforters" (other translations of Job 16:2 term them "miserable" or "troublesome" comforters), they nonetheless are credited with showing up to support their friend. Their attempts at comfort, however, also earn them disdain because there is no license—and distinct Rabbinic distaste—for preaching to others about the virtues of suffering.

In contrast with Job's visitors, in each of the three sickbed scenes at the end of our passage, the visiting Rabbi responds by extending his hand and raising his friend from his sickbed. This, the Rabbis are saying, is the hand of God in the world, reaching out to love, touch, and heal. Those in dire straits are not healed by someone who tells them why they suffer; they find healing in someone who responds lovingly to the fact of their suffering. The gift of love, caring, and human touch is healing;

it is divine. Each of us is the hand of God, for we are each *tzelem Elohim* (the image of God). Thomas Moore (1779–1852) wrote, "To the soul, there is hardly anything more healing than friendship." R. Yochanan and his colleagues would heartily agree.

Continuing the Conversation

1. *Is There Value in Suffering?*

Positive psychologist Tal Ben-Shahar, who teaches the popular "Happiness" course at Harvard University, writes:

> While it is part of our universal nature to seek pleasure and avoid pain, culture plays a central role in how we deal with suffering. In the West we generally reject suffering. We see it as an unwelcome interruption of our pursuit of happiness. So we fight it, repress it, medicate it, or search for quick-fix solutions to get rid of it. In some cultures, especially in the East, suffering is acknowledged for the important role it plays in people's lives, in the meandering path toward enlightenment.[16]

Which approach—West or East—makes more sense to you? Do you believe that suffering can serve a constructive purpose? Has suffering taught you something of value—have you ever found a proverbial "silver lining" in it?

How does this passage of Talmud inform your thinking about your and other people's suffering?

2. *Passing Judgment on Others*

Torah is grounded in a theology of reward and punishment: God, creator and owner of the universe, establishes the standards for Israel's behavior and intervenes in human history in response to Israel's behavior. Scores of examples of this theology exist, among them the second paragraph of the *Shema* (Deuteronomy 11:13–21), which enumerates the rewards for adhering to God's Covenant and the punishments for violating it; and the *tokhachah* (rebuke) passages of Leviticus 26 and Deuteronomy 28, which detail the blessings and curses that will accrue to Israel for keeping or undermining God's law. Here's a small sample:

> See, this day I set before you blessing and curse: blessing, if you obey the commandments of Adonai your God that I enjoin upon you this day; and curse, if you do not obey the commandments of Adonai your God, but turn away from the path that I enjoin upon you this day and follow others gods, whom you have not experienced. (Deuteronomy 11:26–28)

From this theological perspective God is prepared to inflict great harm and suffering when God judges people to have deviated from the divine path laid out for them.

The Rabbis, wishing to steer people away from indulging in the negative judgment of those who experience unremitting and irremediable suffering, reasoned that a good and compassionate God would only visit suffering on righteous people in order to heap reward on them in the world to come. The effect of this thinking is to explain why "bad things happen to good people."

Another view—which perhaps constitutes the most honest and least judgmental reflection on suffering in the Tanakh—is found in Ecclesiastes: God does *not* reward the righteous and punish the wicked. There is no explanation for why people suffer—at least not one that holds God accountable. Ecclesiastes informs us: *Here is a frustration that occurs in the world: Sometimes an upright man is requited according to the conduct of the scoundrel; and sometimes the scoundrel is requited according to the conduct of the upright. I say all that is frustration* (8:14). All is fleeting and ephemeral, both pain and pleasure, and indeed life itself. Therefore, we humans should focus not on the question of why we suffer, but rather on how to live our lives meaningfully while we can.

Which of these ideas resonates most strongly for you?

Do you consider yourself more judgmental or nonjudgmental? When you see someone who is suffering, are you more apt to construct a rationale for their suffering or to wonder what you might do to alleviate it?

Does this discussion inform your thinking on how best to live?

3. What Kind of God Makes Good People Suffer?

In its subtle rejection of *yissurin shel ahavah*, our passage suggests a different model of God: not the coercive, commanding, passionate, rewarding, and punishing God of the Bible, but an empathetic, nonjudgmental, and compassionate God who teaches us to aspire to these same traits and to become healers of others.

R. Meir describes how God responds to an individual who suffers (M Sanhedrin 6:5; 46a):

> R. Meir said, "When a person suffers, what expression does the Shekhinah [God's indwelling presence in the world] use? 'My head is too heavy for me! My arm is too heavy for me!' And if God is so grieved over the blood of the wicked that is shed, how much more so [is God grieved] over the blood of the righteous."

Another passage describes God's empathy for the People of Israel when they suffer:

> When the Holy One blessed be God recalls God's children [Israel], who are plunged into suffering among the nations of the world, God lets fall two tears into the ocean and the sound is heard from one end of the world to the other—and that is the rumbling of the earth.[17]

Here God is fully identified with both individual and communal suffering. What is the message for us?

Nelson Mandela wrote: "Our human compassion binds us the one to the other—not in pity or patronizingly, but as human beings who have learnt how to turn our common suffering into hope for the future."[18] Do you agree that compassion breeds hope?

Do you believe in God? If so, how would you describe God? Have your ideas about God evolved over the course of your life and, if yes, in what directions?

Has this discussion influenced your view of God? Has it shaped your understanding of God in any way?

4. The Healing Power of Presence and Compassion

Not so many years ago psychologists and neurologists determined that self-centeredness and aggression are innate, fundamental components of the human psyche. More recently neurologists have discovered that our brains are also wired for empathy, compassion, connection, and love. "Mirror neurons," seemingly specially evolved for this purpose, are located in the anterior insula, anterior cingulate cortex, and inferior frontal cortex of our brains. Some neurobiologists hypothesize that these neurons constitute the neurological basis for human self-awareness as well as the biological basis for empathy and compassion.

The fact that evolution has equipped us to be empathetic and shaped us to crave social connection and love suggests that when we are in the presence of someone who is suffering, if we focus on what that person is feeling, our innate empathy will kick in.

For those who worry about what to say to someone who suffers, our passage reassures us that our empathetic presence is healing in and of itself. We need not have the powers of R. Yochanan, a trained physician, or a skilled psychologist to help alleviate another person's suffering.

Similarly, Henri Nouwen (1932–96), the Dutch-born Catholic priest and psychologist who taught divinity students at Yale and Harvard, reflects on his later experiences working at L'Arche Daybreak Community in Ontario, a residential institution dedicated to creating a home and nurturing community for people with mental disabilities:

When we honestly ask ourselves which person in our lives means the most to us, we often find that it is those who, instead of giving advice, solutions, or cures, have chosen rather to share our pain and touch our wounds with a warm and tender hand. The friend who can be silent with us in a moment of despair or confusion, who can stay with us in an hour of grief and bereavement, who can tolerate not knowing, not curing, not healing and face with us the reality of our powerlessness, that is a friend who cares.[19]

The Dalai Lama has often been quoted as saying, "Love and compassion are necessities, not luxuries. Without them humanity cannot survive." The adage, "Showing up is 80 percent of life (or success)" can also speak to being present when someone needs us.

Can you recall a time in your life when someone being present for you made all the difference? What about a time your presence was meaningful and healing to someone else? Having studied this passage, do you feel better prepared to sit with someone who is in pain knowing you cannot cure the illness?

5. Bikkur Cholim: A Healing Presence

Perhaps no mitzvah better capitalizes on the power of human empathy than *bikur cholim*, visiting the sick. In Jewish tradition *bikur cholim* is considered of paramount importance, given that a loving, caring person's presence has the power to bring emotional comfort, physical improvement, and spiritual healing. Scientifically as well, companionship has been demonstrated again and again to boost the immune system — it has a healing effect.

R. Acha b. Chanina taught: "One who visits a sick person removes one-sixtieth of his suffering." Not surprisingly, this was followed by a calculation: "Abaye said to Rava, 'If this is so, then if sixty people were to visit the sick person, he would fully recover!' Rava said, 'Each visitor removes one-sixtieth of the suffering that remains.'"[20]

Long ago, I showed this passage to my two oldest children, both of whom love mathematics, and they drew me a graph depicting the equation implied by R. Acha b. Chanina's statement. It showed a curve (the amount of suffering experienced by the patient) gently sloping downward with each successive visitor. My daughter remarked, "I want to be the first to visit, because I will remove the most suffering." Her brother replied, "It doesn't matter all that much if you're first, because whenever you go, even if you're the one-hundredth visitor, you will alleviate suffering."

Do you feel comfortable or uncomfortable visiting people in the hospital? Some people find *bikur cholim* a difficult mitzvah to perform, because seeing others in pain is disturbing or because hospitals frighten them, and, on top of that, because they doubt their presence will make a difference. Yet Jewish tradition urges us: Don't hesitate to visit someone who is sick. Your presence and compassion are more powerful than you think. Your visit will reduce suffering any time you go.

Summing Things Up

It is difficult to reconcile a good and loving God with the suffering of good and innocent people. The Rabbis suggest the doctrine of *yissurin shel ahavah* to offer comfort and support to those who suffer and to steer us away from equating human suffering with sinfulness. However, this idea appears to work better in theory than in practice—even for the Rabbis, who were steeped in Rabbinic tradition and theology. For us, there are two even more important messages: do not judge people who are suffering, and be present for them. The gift of love and caring is healing; it is divine.

4 Approaching Prayer

Mishnah Berakhot 4:2 and the Accompanying Gemara from the Babylonian and Jerusalem Talmuds

R. Elazar said in the name of R. Chanina, "The disciples of the Sages increase peace in the world, as it is written, *All your children shall be disciples of Adonai, and great will be the peace of your children ['banayikh']* (Isaiah 54:13). Do not read *banayikh* ['your children'] but rather *bonayikh* ['your builders']. *Those who love Your teaching enjoy well-being; they encounter no adversity* (Psalm 119:165). *May there be well-being within your ramparts, peace in your citadels. For the sake of my kin and friends, I pray for your well-being; for the sake of the house of Adonai our God, I seek your good* (Psalm 122:7–8) *May Adonai grant strength to God's people; may Adonai bestow on God's people well-being* (Psalm 29:11).

—BT Berakhot 64a

Why Study This Passage?

Consider for a moment how we typically communicate today. Often, in our haste, when we send an email or text, comment on social media, leave a voice mail, or scribble a note on the kitchen counter, we don't use complete sentences. We leave out words. We may use pronouns rather than names. We may not consider tone (unless we've taken the additional step of adding emoticons). We make typing errors (or miss overriding those perpetrated by the spelling correction software that insists it knows what we want to say better than we do). We may presume that the recipient will understand what we meant to say and in what tone we meant it. But there is no guarantee, is there?

Interpreting texts, including ancient sacred texts, is more similar to understanding modern social communication than we might think. Talmud not only "reads" and "interprets" Torah; it bends it to express what the Rabbis want to say, employing verses as prooftexts to prove their points. This is possible because Torah, as written—especially without vowels and punctuation—does not have one single, objective meaning. Nor does it necessarily have "tone."

The same is true of the Mishnah. Scholars are not entirely sure how Mishnah originally functioned. Mishnah explains itself as a collection of oral traditions and remembrances of the Second Temple period that were written down lest they be forgotten. Scholars have suggested it may constitute the teaching notes of its compiler, R. Yehudah ha-Nasi (for more on this, see the introduction and chapter 1 of this volume). Mishnah is terse, thereby leaving the reader with many questions. Gemara picks up where Mishnah leaves off, filling in "blanks," answering questions, raising more questions, recording discussions and debates, interpolating stories, and wandering into side tangents of thought and discussion.

In this chapter we will discuss a mishnah that briefly comments on the personal prayer custom of R. Nechunya b. HaKanah. In addition, we will look at two interpretations—from the Bavli (Babylonia Talmud) and the Yerushalmi (the Talmud of *Eretz Yisrael*)—that understand the meaning of the Sage's prayers very differently. What they hear may well tell us more about them than about R. Nechunya.

A Broad View to Begin

Prayer has many faces, reflecting diverse motivations that inspire it. For one, prayer can arise from inner spiritual longing and a desire to connect with, and establish coherence with, that which is beyond us (often expressed as "a power above" or "something greater"). Rabbi Chaim Stern expresses the perspective of those who seek spiritual connection with God well:

> Worship . . . is a turning of the whole being toward that which we affirm as ultimately real and valuable. Humble in the face of a spiritual reality whose essence we cannot "know," we speak in metaphors. Our "truth" is a truth of the heart no less than of the mind. The "facts" we assert are those of the hopeful spirit. But we believe that the spiritual reality within us corresponds to a spiritual reality beyond us, and in worship we hope to bring the two realities into communion.[1]

Whether God is perceived as a Being or in more abstract terms, prayer provides access to God as the worshiper perceives and understands God.

A second motivation derives from the understanding that prayer fulfills a mitzvah, a sacred obligation to God. Jewish tradition has deemed prayer a communal ritual and personal obligation—most prayer in Jewish tradition is statutory. The Rabbis determined long ago that prayer would fill the void created by the destruction of the Second Temple, which brought an end to the sacrificial cult. No longer able to serve God through sacrifices, Jews would now serve their Creator by offerings of the heart expressed with the tongue. Over the course of several generations, the Rabbis shaped three daily statutory prayer services (*Shacharit, Mincha, Ma'ariv*), the time parameters within which each set of prayers is to be recited, the themes and order of prayers to be said at each service, and eventually the texts of the prayers themselves. This side of the coin reflects the *keva* (fixed, statutory) aspect of Jewish prayer—a mitzvah uttered to uphold one's covenant with God.

A third motivation is found in the opportunity prayer provides for self-reflection and self-exploration.

For all three ways of thinking about prayer as a religious act, the worshiper's *kavanah* (intentionality, spontaneous quality) is highly prized because it transforms rote prayer into a highly personal expression of the deepest thoughts and feelings of one's heart and mind.

The quality of *kavanah* that characterized the composed prayers complements the *keva* of today's siddur. Rabbi Henry Slonimsky expresses it beautifully:

> I regard the old Jewish *siddur* as the most important single Jewish book—a more personal expression, a closer record of Jewish suffering, Jewish needs, Jewish hopes and aspirations, than the Bible itself. For one thing the Bible is too grand and universal to be exclusively Jewish . . . and for another whatever is quintessentially needed for daily use has been squeezed out of it into the prayer book and so made our daily own. And if you want to know what Judaism is—the question which has no answer if debated on the plane of intellectual argument—you can find it by absorbing that book. The Jewish soul is mirrored there as nowhere else, mirrored or rather embodied there: the individual's soul in its private sorrows, and the people's soul in its historic burdens, its heroic passion and suffering, its unfaltering faith, through the ages. (*Essays*, 1967)

Over time, Jewish statutory prayer evolved from a service organized around an order of prayers in outline form—in which the prayer themes were specified but the precise content, or wording, of the prayers was left to the individual—to the full, robust *siddurim* (prayer books) we have today. At some point, recognizing it was not easy for everyone to create personal prayers thrice daily, the Rabbis commissioned the composition of prayers that everyone could use. In time this liturgy came to be largely fixed, with some minor variations among different Jewish communities—that is, until modernity.

In recent centuries discoveries in science and technology have precipitated huge shifts in the Jewish people's worldview of God and the universe. Thus, modern Jews have revisited the structure and content laid down by the Rabbis, reenvisioning, revamping, and revising Jewish liturgy. In the past century and a half liberal Jewish communities have produced many beautiful and creative prayer books. Their amended prayers speak to contemporary sensibilities, and their new liturgies supplement the traditional prayers, filling in gaps and infusing traditional *keva* with new life and vibrancy.

This chapter's mishnah, however, takes us back to a time before the specific wording of prayers had been determined: a time when *keva* was being formulated and the content of prayer depended on *kavanah*.

It centers around a *tanna* of the latter first and early second century, Nechunya b. HaKanah, a contemporary of Rabban Yochanan b. Zakkai and the teacher of R. Ishmael b. Elisha. We are told that Nechunya b. HaKanah has adopted the practice of offering a personal prayer as he enters the *bet midrash* and another as he leaves, thus bracketing his time in the study house. Since tradition does not prescribe these prayers, the Sages are curious to know their content. The mishnah provides only a headline, not the full text of the prayers.

After reading the short synopsis the mishnah provides, the Rabbis in the academies of Babylonia and *Eretz Yisrael* each propose texts of R. Nechunya's prayers — products of their imaginations. While in some ways the Sages hear the mishnah similarly, in other ways their perspectives diverge, revealing the very different cultural worlds in which they penned their prayers.

Before diving into their prayers, let's consider how the Rabbis of the time conceived of God, because their beliefs about God shaped those prayers. Notably, the Rabbis held differing views and beliefs — which, when we consider the context, is not all that surprising. First, they encountered differing perspectives on God in Torah itself. Torah depicts

God as a cosmic being with will and agency who forged a covenant with a particular people, Israel, and who commands, rewards, and punishes. The God of the Hebrew Bible is anthropomorphic—appearing before people in human bodies (such as the strangers who visit Abraham in Genesis 18 or the man who wrestles with Jacob in Genesis 32)—and also highly anthropopathic, experiencing the full range of human emotions, from deep love and tenderness to extreme jealousy and anger. Hebrew Scripture understands God to be possessed of power far greater than anyone or anything in our world, but God does not impede human free will or force human behavior.

What's more, the trauma of the Second Temple's destruction brought traditional beliefs into question. The Rabbis struggled to make sense of a new world epitomized by human evil, suffering, and the failure of "reward" and "punishment" to line up as they had expected. Where was the God who promised in Scripture to protect and defend Israel from her enemies? After all, Israel's sins, however magnified by the Rabbis, did not rise to the level deserving the suffering and humiliation the Jewish people had experienced in their defeat by Rome in 70 CE. Was God unable to come to Israel's rescue? Unwilling? Or was God simply too distant from this world to become involved? The latter option opened the door to more abstract understandings of God.

Over the ages new and different God-ideas evolved and took root. In order to more fully appreciate this chapter's passage, let's take a moment to consider three highly different God-ideas that Jews have held over the ages. Note that the three ideas cover a broad spectrum, from the earliest, most concrete God-belief to the most abstract, and as such exclude many nuanced Jewish theologies lying between them along the spectrum.

The first God-idea is the traditional notion that God is a cosmic Being with will and agency. Genesis 1 and 2 describe in detail God's Creation of the cosmos and the earth, conveying both God's ownership and sovereignty over the universe as well as God's intense interest in, and commitment to, humanity. Many generations later, when Abraham's family settles in Egypt, grows into a nation, and becomes enslaved by Pharaoh, God rescues them. Scripture tells us that with a powerful show of force — *a strong hand and an outstretched arm* that brought ten plagues and many marvels — God redeems Israel from Egypt to enable the people to worship God. God leads them to Mount Sinai, where they enter into a covenant with God. The Torah spells out the covenantal details and emphasizes God's power, sovereignty, and special attachment to the People of Israel. Torah then goes on to describe how God defends the Israelites against their enemies, including the Egyptians, Amalekites, Amorites, Midianites, and Canaanites. God demands the people's loyalty and obedience, and defends Israel in return. Much of the books of Exodus, Leviticus, and Deuteronomy delineate God's hundreds of ethical and ritual commandments to the Israelites. While most people are familiar with the Ten Commandments, Torah records 613 commandments in all. This passage from Deuteronomy sums things up well:

> And now, O Israel, what does Adonai your God demand of you? Only this: to revere Adonai your God, to walk only in God's paths, to love God, and to serve Adonai your God with all your heart and soul, keeping Adonai's commandments and laws, which I enjoin upon you today, for your good. Mark, the heavens to their uttermost reaches belong to Adonai your God, the earth and all that is in it! Yet it was to your ancestors that Adonai was drawn in love for them, so that God chose you, their lineal descendants, from among all peoples — as is now the case. Cut away, therefore the thickening about your hearts and stiffen your necks no more. For Adonai your God is God supreme and Lord supreme, the great, the mighty, and the awesome God, who shows no favor and takes no bribe, but upholds the cause of the fatherless and the widow, and befriends the stranger, providing him with food and clothing. You too must befriend the stranger, for you were strangers in the land of Egypt. You must revere Adonai your God: only God shall you worship, to God shall you hold fast, and by God's name shall you

swear. . . . Love, therefore, Adonai your God, and always keep God's charge, God's laws, God's rules, and God's commandments. (Deuteronomy 10:12–11:1)

The God described in the Torah is passionate: loving deeply and also enraged when Israel disobeys. To keep Israel in line, God rewards and punishes:

See, this day I set before you blessing and curse: blessing if you obey the commandments of Adonai your God that I enjoin upon you this day; and curse, if you do not obey the commandments of Adonai your God, but turn away from the path that I enjoin upon you this day and follow other gods, whom you have not experienced. (Deuteronomy 11:26–28)

Devoted to Israel and demanding the people's loyalty in return, this God hears prayers and decides whether and how to respond to them.

The second God-idea is an abstract conception of God. Abstract ideas of God evolved slowly in the aftermath of the calamity in 70 CE, when the traditional biblical notion of God no longer seemed to match history and reality. For many, God had grown distant and perhaps even disconnected from Israel. This opened the door to thinking about God in new and different ways.

The Rabbis took the first step through this doorway, treating anthropomorphic and anthropopathic descriptions of God as metaphors to discuss universal human concerns such as anger, jealousy, love, and loyalty (see chapter 2 of this volume), as well as particularistic Jewish issues such as exile and suffering. In the course of time abstract ideas of God gained increasingly greater traction because they did not conflict with the realities of the Jews' historical experience: the biblical God who promised to protect and defend Israel from her enemies "with a strong hand and an outstretched arm" and assured her sovereignty over the land of her ancestors was nowhere evident.

Many abstract conceptions of God took root over the years. In the twelfth century the philosopher and legal codifier Moses ben Maimon (Maimonides) described God in *The Guide for the Perplexed* as the pure thought and reason that undergird the universe.[2] In the twentieth century, the philosophers Martin Buber and Franz Rosenzweig spoke about God from an existentialist framework: God is to be encountered. Buber explained in *I and Thou* that one comes to know God through one's deepest relationships with other people. Rabbi Mordecai Kaplan, founder of Judaism's Reconstructionist Movement, believed that God is the power that makes personal salvation possible. He wrote: "It is sufficient that God should mean to us the sum of the animating organizing forces and relationships which are forever making a cosmos out of chaos. This is what we understand by God as the creative life of the universe."[3]

Common among abstract Jewish notions of God is the conviction that God is not a cosmic being, but a motivating force, principle, or supreme value the worshiper holds dear—such as the force for goodness, pure thought and reason, the source of human free will, the divine spark within humanity, a source of morality, the power that makes salvation possible, that which makes existence possible. Common metaphors in abstract God-ideas include power, force, potential, and energy.

The third God-idea is pantheism, the belief that everything is contained within God, within the divine: God is all, God animates all. Rejecting the traditional belief in religious dualism—that two separate and non-overlapping entities, God and the universe, coexist—pantheism avows that God animates everything, but no one manifestation alone is God.

In Judaism, pantheism derives from Jewish mystical speculation that has existed for at least two millennia. In all its religious varieties mysticism is premised on the belief that what we see and experience in the physical world is transcended by a deeper reality that is far more difficult to discern and is hidden from most of us, but—unlike our "apparent" day-to-day experience of reality—is ultimate reality. Many mystics read Torah as an allegory whose secret meaning reveals the hidden truth about reality. Preferred mystical metaphors include: light/dark, hidden/revealed, finite/infinite. The ultimate truth, for mystical pantheists, is that God encompasses all existence, all being, the entirety of the universe.

The thirteenth-century Ashkenazic pietist Yehudah b. Shmuel of Regensburg (or possibly his father) composed a liturgical song entitled *Shir ha-Yichud* (Song of unity), which includes a verse that encapsulates the pantheistic view: "You surround all and fill all, and when all exists You are in all."[4] The Zohar ("splendor" or "radiance"), the preeminent book of Jewish mysticism that appeared in Spain in the thirteenth century, frequently speaks of God as "filling all worlds" and "surrounding all worlds."

Not surprisingly, the prayers of Jews who hold traditional conceptions of God, abstract views of God, and pantheistic perspectives tend to be very different.

In the traditional view, whereby God is deemed the Sovereign of the universe, prayer is modeled on how one would approach a powerful human sovereign. Praise, petition, and thanksgiving are the major rubrics of prayer to a God who intervenes in nature and in our lives. The worshiper at a typical Jewish prayer service praises and thanks God in part in order to establish a positive relationship with God and in response to God's need or desire to be worshiped. Both prayers of praise and thanksgiving support the worshiper's positive, constructive relationship with God and create a framework into which the worshiper can insert petitions in the hope that God will respond positively. Petitions acknowledge that God is powerful, the source of many blessings that God can choose to bestow or withhold: the worshiper hopes that these prayers will reach God and merit a favorable response.

Worshipers who hold abstract conceptions of God may understand the activity of prayer differently: as deep self-reflection and introspection in order to understand oneself better. They may plumb the prayers for moral and spiritual guidance, and inspiration for living.

For pantheists, prayer serves to focus the mind on their religious understanding that all is within God and on the proper behavior that flows from this realization.

Exploring the Nooks and Crannies of Our Passage

The scene is set in the *bet midrash*, where Sages gather to study, debate, and determine what halakhah requires and forbids. Historically, the Rabbis were a small and initially only modestly influential movement within the broader Jewish community. In their minds, however, their mission was of cosmic significance because they were discussing, debating, and ultimately determining the will of God for the Jewish people. It is no surprise, then, that they took their responsibility seriously and repeatedly expressed concern about "getting it right."

> **Mishnah Berakhot 4:2**
>
> R. Nechunya b. HaKanah would offer a short prayer upon entering the *bet midrash* and upon leaving. They said to him, "What is the nature of this prayer?" He told them, "Upon entering, I pray that no mishap should occur because of me; and upon leaving, I give thanks for my portion."

As simple as this mishnah seems from the outset, there are many questions to ask.

The Sages frame their question as follows: *Mah makom li-tefillah zo?* (What is the place of this prayer?). In context, the term *makom* (place) seems to mean "purpose" or "propriety," but because *makom* is not generally used in this way, the meaning is unclear. Are they asking, Why does R. Nechunya pray at these junctures? Or, perhaps, What does R. Nechunya pray?

The rationale for his prayers, as the mishnah reports them, seems innocuous enough. First, he wants to avoid any halakhic misstep—which ostensibly refers to rendering an incorrect decision concerning Jewish religious practice that would thereby cause others to err. Second, he is grateful for his *chelek* (portion).

Yet the term *chelek* also raises questions, because of its dual associations with weightiness and one's reward in *olam ha-ba* (the world to come). According to the Talmud, R. Nechunya is wealthy: Is he therefore expressing gratitude for his material fortune? Perhaps, instead, he is speaking of his gravitas as a respected Sage, in which case he gives thanks for being able to spend his days in the *bet midrash*, rather than engaged in manual labor or some other endeavor he would find less meaningful and prestigious. Or maybe he is eluding to the reward he expects to receive in *olam ha-ba*.

Here is how the Sages of the Bavli (Babylonian Talmud) discuss the matter.

> **Babylonian Talmud — Gemara to Berakhot 4:2 (28b)**
> Our Rabbis taught [in a *baraita*]: Upon entering what does he say? "May it be Your will, my God, that no mishap may occur because of me, and that I may not stumble in a matter of halakhah [such] that my colleagues may rejoice over me; and that I may not declare something *tame* ['ritually impure'] to be *tahor* ['ritually pure'] or something *tahor* to be *tame*; and may my colleagues not stumble in a matter of halakhah and I rejoice over them." Upon leaving [the *bet midrash*] what does he say? "I thank You, Adonai my God, that You granted me a portion to be among those who sit in the *bet midrash*, and You granted me a portion not to be among those who sit on street corners. For I rise early and they rise early, but I rise early for words of Torah while they rise early for frivolous talk. I labor and they labor, but I labor and receive a reward while they labor and do not receive a reward. I run and they run, but I run to life in the world to come while they run to life in the pit of destruction [i.e., *Gehinnom*].

The Rabbis in Babylonia read the mishnah as a headline ("R. Nechunya reports: May I not make a mistake; I am thankful to God") that requires elaboration and commentary. For the Bavli, R. Nechunya's first prayer has a three-part chiastic structure:

(1) May I not err in a halakhic determination, thereby giving my colleagues an opportunity to experience schadenfreude (pleasure derived from someone else's misfortune) and rejoice in my error.
(2) May I not err in determining what is ritually pure and ritually impure.
(3) May my colleagues not err in their halakhic determinations, providing me an opportunity to taste schadenfreude and rejoice in their error.

Jeffrey Rubenstein, scholar of Rabbinic literature, who has written extensively on the culture of the academies in Babylonia, notes that they thrived on competition for status and positions of authority. In this competitive environment verbal insults were not uncommon.[5] He writes:

> The highly competitive, even combative ethos prevails within the academy. The sages attempt to excel in dialectic argumentation, in the constant probing of traditions by propounding objections and providing solutions. . . . Debate is simultaneously the means to greater status and even rank. . . . The verbal sparring sometimes takes an unfortunate turn from healthy, competitive debate to insults and hostility, which can make the academy feel like a violent arena. A sage's constant fear is that he will be unable to answer attacks upon his position and suffer public humiliation. This is a grave danger, for the sages experience shame as a type of social death, and the failure to perform may also jeopardize their positions within the hierarchy. Yet, inasmuch as the victim suffers from being shamed, so the perpetrator risks divine punishment for shaming a fellow sage. To achieve academic success is therefore an extremely delicate task.[6]

According to the Rabbis in Babylonia, R. Nechunya's first prayer is directed at his colleagues and their relationships with one another in the *bet midrash*. As he enters the house where he will likely spend the day in study, discussion, and at times rancorous debate, his colleagues and the various relationships within the *bet midrash* are on his mind.

Upon leaving the *bet midrash*, however, R. Nechunya's prayer is said to be directed at those he will encounter outside the house of study: people who conduct business in the street, as well as people who idle there, perhaps chitchatting, perhaps begging, but to his mind all wasting precious time when compared with how he has spent his day engaged in Talmud Torah. Thus, in R. Nechunya's second prayer he compares himself with them: While both he and they rise early in the morning, he engages in holy words of Torah while they partake in idle words of gossip and meaningless nonsense. While both he and they work hard, his holy work will be rewarded by God, while theirs will not. While his energies are directed toward earning himself a portion in *olam ha-ba*, theirs are directed at unworthy endeavors that will secure them a spot in *Gehinnom* (purgatory).

Note that in other passages in the Bavli, R. Nechunya is portrayed as humble and forgiving.[7] Indeed, from reading just the original passage in the mishnah, one might conclude that he is both humble and grateful. Yet as the Rabbis of Babylonia understand or imagine his prayers, R. Nechunya appears arrogant, superior, and condescending.

Are the Rabbis of Babylonia projecting their own experiences in the *bet midrash*—and the anxieties arising from those experiences—onto R. Nechunya's prayers?

What do the Sages in *Eretz Yisrael* think R. Nechunya prayed each day? We turn to the Yerushalmi's answer.

Jerusalem Talmud—Gemara to Berakhot 4:2; 33a

Upon entering, what does he say? "May it be Your will, Adonai my God and God of my ancestors, that I not be impatient and arrogant with my colleagues and that my colleagues not be impatient and arrogant with me; that we do not declare *tame* that which is *tahor* and that we do not declare *tahor* that which is *tame*; that we do not forbid that which is permitted and that we do not permit that which is forbidden; for then I would find myself humiliated in this world and in the world to come." And upon leaving, what does he say? "I give thanks to You, Adonai my God and God of my ancestors, that You granted me a portion among those who sit in the *bet midrash* and in the synagogues, and that You did not grant me a portion in the theaters and taverns. For I labor and they labor, I am diligent and they are diligent, [but] I labor to inherit the Garden of Eden while they labor to [and will inherit] the pit of destruction (i.e., Gehinnom), as it is said, *Because You will not abandon my soul to She'ol; You will not allow Your pious one to see destruction* (Psalm 16:10).

A cursory reading might lead one to mistakenly conclude that the Bavli and Yerushalmi provide two nearly identical elaborations of R. Nechunya's prayers. In both accounts the prayer upon entering the *bet midrash* concerns what will transpire there and R. Nechunya's relationships with his colleagues; upon leaving, the focus is redirected toward people in the world outside the *bet midrash* and the difference between his life and theirs. Commonalities also appear in some of the details and language: a concern to correctly determine that which is *tame* and that which is *tahor* (matters of purity were a major preoccupation of the Rabbis), God's role in granting "portions," people laboring diligently in different endeavors, and the afterlife destinations (Paradise or *Gehinnom*).

Nothing could be further from the case.

In the Yerushalmi's version, R. Nechunya's prayer upon entering the *bet midrash* has four parts:

1. He prays that he and his colleagues treat one another with patience and consideration. The use of the term *akpid/yakpidu* (may I not be/they not be impatient and arrogant) evokes the Talmud's contrast of Hillel, who was *anav* (humble), and Shammai, who exhibited *kapdanut* (impatience and arrogance).[8] While both accounts imagine R. Nechunya as focused on the collegial interactions that

will transpire this day in the *bet midrash*, the R. Nechunya of the Bavli does not want anyone to stumble in halakhic analysis because he presumes that one who stumbles provides his colleagues with an opportunity to gloat, whereas the R. Nechunya of the Yerushalmi seeks patience and goodwill among his colleagues. His attitude is to foster collaboration rather than competition.
2. The Yerushalmi, like the Bavli, has R. Nechunya express concern about correctly determining what is *tame* and what is *tahor*.
3. The Yerushalmi adds to the *tame/tahor* distinction another related concern: what is permitted and what is forbidden. But whereas the Bavli couches R. Nechunya's prayer in the first-person singular (that *I* may not declare), the Yerushalmi renders Nechunya's concerns about *tumah/tahara* (ritual impurity/ritual purity) and *asur/mutar* (forbidden/permitted) in the first-person plural (that *we* do not declare ... that *we* do not forbid). In other words, the R. Nechunya of the Yerushalmi seeks to be on fine terms with his colleagues and to work collaboratively with them toward the communal good.
4. And, should he err, R. Nechunya expresses concern in his prayer that he would be humiliated both in this world and in the world to come. He does not presume that others should be humiliated. He feels it is his responsibility to participate in the *bet midrash* in such a way that he does not lead his colleagues to the wrong halakhic conclusions; doing so would be crushing and humiliating to him.

Upon leaving the *bet midrash*, R. Nechunya gives thanks that he can spend his days in the house of study, rather than occupied by the diversions of theaters and taverns prevalent in the Greco-Roman world. Remarkably, he acknowledges that all people, whether engaged in the holy enterprise of Talmud Torah or in the secular and decadent endeavors of Roman society, work hard and diligently. Unlike the R. Nechunya of the Bavli, however, he does not excoriate those whose lives and values differ from his by disparaging them as "idle" and their talk as meaningless. Rather, he asserts his belief that God rewards those who dedicate their lives to Torah, whereas those who invest their time and effort in the theaters and taverns can expect a place in *Gehinnom*. A careful reading reveals that this is not because these individuals possess inherently flawed characters (such as idleness or a preoccupation with trivial talk), but because they have not engaged in the requisite effort to earn the reward R. Nechunya anticipates for himself.

The Rabbis' imagining of R. Nechunya's prayers opens a small window into the cultures of the academies in Babylonia and *Eretz Yisrael*. Perhaps the Bavli's version of R. Nechunya's prayers is a product of the fierce competition within their academies, competition that itself is an outcome of their success: Babylonia boasted numerous academies that considered their level of learning to be far beyond that of *Eretz Yisrael*. Babylonian scholars of Torah saw their studies not as an adjunct to their lives, but as the focus of them; and because the Jewish community in Babylonia was wealthier, many scholars devoted themselves to the academy full-time. The academies of Babylonia were socially and culturally insular: Those who attended often left home and family for years at a time and devoted themselves entirely to their teachers and studies. Indeed, the academy was a surrogate family. In contrast, the academies of *Eretz Yisrael* were smaller and fewer, the surrounding community less wealthy, and many attendees supplemented Torah study with work that brought in an income. Perhaps as a result, the culture of their *batei midrash* (houses of study) may have been more collaborative and respectful, and they themselves may have been less judgmental toward those who did not study Torah.

Rubinstein, however, proffers another theory, drawing on the current thinking concerning how the Babylonian Talmud was redacted. He explains that there are two strata evident in the Bavli. The earlier amoraic stratum, completed by the early decades of the fifth century CE, features traditions attributed to named Sages and comprises approximately half the Bavli. The later stammaitic[9] stratum consists of anonymous material produced by unnamed redactors who inherited the amoraic material, constructed discussions and arguments leading to the conclusions of the *amora'im*, and ordered and shaped the material into the Talmud we now have. Rubinstein writes:

> The essential tradition . . . was preserved and transmitted during Amoraic times. The Stammaim, however, attempted to reconstruct the argumentation that produced the conclusions and to preserve it for posterity. . . . The innovative argumentation of the Bavli and the intellectual shift it represents likewise should be identified with the transition from the Amoraic to Stammaitic periods. The Stammaim subjected Amoraic traditions to an extended and heavy-handed redactional process that created a *talmud* substantially different from that which had existed before, a process to which Palestinian traditions were not subjected."[10]

In summary, there are two possible ways to account for the starkly different perspectives on R. Nechunya's prayers, as expanded by the Bavli and the Yerushalmi. It may be that cultural differences between Babylonia and *Eretz Yisrael* explain why the academies of Babylonia were more competitive and those of *Eretz Yisrael* more collegial. Alternatively, the difference may lie in the historical fact that the Talmud of Babylonia underwent an extensive redacting process in which debates and arguments were fashioned by the editors to explain the conclusions they inherited, whereas the Yerushalmi underwent very little redacting.

This talmudic passage can also open a window into how personal experiences and judgments can affect how we interpret terse communication.

Continuing the Conversation

1. The Advantages and Disadvantages of Statutory Prayer

Is a prayer book with a fixed liturgy an advantage or a disadvantage?

Having a fixed liturgy has relieved Jews of the considerable pressure to compose prayers three times daily to fulfill their prayer obligations. However, if the goal of prayer is to infuse *keva* (the fixed form and content of Jewish prayer) with *kavanah* (intention, focus, and feeling), there is an inherent danger in repeating the same prayers time after time. The prayers may become calcified through rote recitation.

On the one hand, Rabbi Abraham Joshua Heschel, a leading twentieth-century Jewish theologian, writes in *Man's Quest for God*:

> How grateful I am to God that there is a duty to worship, a law to remind my distraught mind that it is time to think of God, time to disregard my ego for at least a moment! It is such happiness to belong to an order of the divine will. I am not always in a mood to pray. I do not always have the vision and the strength to say a word in the presence of God. But when I am weak, it is the law that gives me strength; when my vision is dim, it is duty that gives me insight.[11]

Yet in the same book Heschel reflects on the downside of *keva*:

> In reality . . . the element of regularity [*keva*] has often gained the upper hand over the element of spontaneity [*kavanah*]. Prayer has become lip service, an obligation to be discharged, something to get over with. "This people draw near, with their mouth and with their lips do honor Me, but have removed their heart far from Me and their fear of Me is a commandment of Me learned by rote" (Isaiah 29:13).[12]

Do Heschel's words reflect your experiences? How might you take advantage of the benefits of a standardized liturgy while avoiding the potential pitfalls?

2. Other Potential Traps of "Fixed" Prayer

Another mishnah in Tractate Berakhot includes this teaching attributed to R. Eliezer b. Hyrcanus: If one "makes their prayers fixed, their prayers lack [genuine] supplication."[13]

R. Eliezer appears to be concerned that "fixed" prayer can overwhelm *kavanah*. It is not obvious what "fixed" means in this context, so the Gemara[14] offers four possible understandings:

1. R. Yaakov bar Idi in the name of R. Oshaya says that "fixed" prayer feels like a burden to say. This suggests that prayer has become a chore or obligation to be checked off one's to-do list.
2. The Rabbis say that prayers are "fixed" when one does not recite them with a heartfelt sense of supplication. This view allows for statutory prayer to feel like a burden, but if the prayers are nonetheless sincere supplication to God, they are not "fixed."
3. Rabbah and Rav Yosef say that when you do not add something "new" to the statutory prayers, your prayer is "fixed," suggesting that reciting the siddur text alone is insufficient. Worshipers need to go beyond the words printed on the page, whether in their minds or aloud, with additional words that express what is in their hearts.
4. Abaye bar Avin and R. Chanina bar Avin say that when people do not go the extra mile to pray at the most propitious times, their prayers are "fixed." Relegating prayer to a more "convenient" time suggests that prayer is not one's highest priority.

These four opinions touch on challenges many people face as they try to make regular prayer a part of their lives. Which apply to your experience? How do you think you might be able to overcome them?

3. Spontaneous Prayer

Rabbah and Rav Yosef (see above) encourage us to add something "new" to our prayers. The Gemara records the personal prayers some of the Sages added after reciting the *Shemoneh Esrei*. Also called the *Amidah*, this is the central prayer in a Jewish prayer service, composed of blessings of praise, petition, and thanksgiving. The Gemara offers:

R. Elazar b. Azariah (first-century *tanna*): "May it be Your will, Adonai our God, to make present among us love, comradery, peace, and friendship. Increase the number of our disciples, make us successful, give us purpose and hope, and grant us a portion in the Garden of Eden. May we enjoy good companions and good intentions. May we arise early to find our hearts' aspiration to hold Your Name in awe, and may the fulfillment of our needs appear before You as worthy." (BT Berakhot 16b)

Rav (Abba Arika, third-century *amora* who established the yeshiva at Sura in Babylonia): "May it be Your will, Adonai our God, to grant us long life, a life of goodness, blessing, sustenance, health, fear of sin, a life free from shame or humiliation, a life of wealth and honor, a life filled with love of Torah and awe for You, a life in which You fulfill our heart's desires for good." (BT Berakhot 16a–b)

Rav Safra (fourth-century Babylonian *amora*): "May it be Your will, Adonai our God, that You establish peace in the heavens above and here below, and between the students who are engaged in [the study of] Your Torah, whether for its own sake or not. And may it be Your will that all who engage in [the study of] Torah not for its own sake, engage in Torah for its own sake." (Consider this prayer especially in light of what R. Nechunya's prayers reveal about life in the Babylonian academies.) (BT Berakhot 16b–17a)

R. Alexandri (*amora* from *Eretz Yisrael*): "May it be Your will, Adonai our God, to let us stand in an illuminated corner and not in a dark place, and may our hearts not be pained nor our eyes dimmed." (BT Berakhot 17a)

Which of these prayers do you find meaningful? What gives them meaning for you?

If you pray, what do you typically pray for?

If you were to add something new to your prayers, what would you want to say? Try composing your own prayer.

4. To Whom Are We Praying, and Therefore What Are We Saying?

Jews who do not know what they believe about God (including many with a strong Jewish identity) often have a difficult time making prayer work for them. After all, to whom are they praying?

Earlier in this chapter we discussed three of the many ways Jews understand God: (1) a cosmic Being with a will and agency; (2) abstract conceptions (such as a force for goodness, pure thought and reason, the source of human free will, the divine spark within us, the source of morality); (3) the sum total of everything that exists (pantheism). Each idea provides a lens through which to interpret the prayers in the siddur and to compose our own prayers.

It can be valuable to "try on" different ideas. How would you interpret the following three prayers through the lenses of these three God-ideas? Keep in mind that prayer is poetry, metaphors abound, and we are free to understand the words (such as "soul," "create/creation," "parent," and "sovereign") in our own way.

> The soul that You have given me, O God, is pure. You created it, you formed it, you breathed it into me, you guard it within me.

> You illumine the earth and its inhabitants with mercy. In your goodness, you renew Creation each day. How great are your works, Adonai; with wisdom you made them. The earth is filled with your creations.

> Deep is your love for us, Adonai our God, and great is your compassion for us. Our parent and sovereign, for the sake of our ancestors who trusted in you, and whom you taught the laws of life, now graciously teach us.

5. Who Needs Prayer: Jews or God?

A story is told of the Besh"t, the Baal Shem Tov, founder of Hasidism:

Once, when he was about to enter a synagogue to pray, he paused at the threshold and said, "I cannot enter. This synagogue is filled with prayers."

His disciples assured him there was plenty of room in the synagogue for him and them to pray, but the Besh"t said, "There is no room here because the space is filled with words of prayer."

Now his disciples were confused: If their teacher was speaking of the synagogue in complimentary terms, why was he refusing to enter?

The Baal Shem Tov explained: "The synagogue is filled with prayers that cannot fly to heaven because they were not uttered with love and joy and sincerity. And so they fill this space, going nowhere."

The Besh"t thus taught that our prayers need *kavanah:* they need to be uttered sincerely and meaningfully to take wing to heaven. Only then will they be valuable to God.

Does this story speak to you?

The question of whether we pray for God's sake, because God needs our prayers, or for our own sakes, because we need to pray, has been discussed and debated for centuries. Which perspective resonates with you?

Summing Things Up

R. Nechunya b. HaKanah made it a habit to recite two additional personal prayers that arose from his mind and heart; they reflected his ideals and guided how he lived.

How the Sages in Babylonia and *Eretz Yisrael* interpreted these prayers gives us insight into their respective cultures.

Today, many Jews struggle to find styles and modes of prayer that express what is in their hearts and minds. Understanding the various ways Jewish tradition views God and prayer, as well as reflecting on the challenges inherent in balancing *keva* and *kavanah,* may open us up to experimenting with prayer. Our tradition provides stories and role models that can help each of us experiment and find our way.

PART 2 **FIRST SPHERE**
Family Relationships

5 Honoring Our Parents
Jerusalem Talmud, Tractate Pe'ah 1a, 5b–6b

Our Rabbis taught: There are three partners in the creation of a human being: the Holy Blessed One, the father, and the mother. When a person honors their father and their mother, the Holy Blessed One says, "I ascribe merit to them as though I had dwelt among them and they had honored Me."
—BT Kiddushin 30b

Why Study This Passage?
For most of us, our relationships with our parents are the first, most intense, and longest relationships of our lives, beginning at the moment of birth and riding the roller coaster of our lives.

The mitzvah (religious obligation) of *kibbud av va-em* (honoring father and mother) is so fundamental, such an essential principle of Jewish ethics, that it is one of the reigning Ten Commandments (Exodus 20:12 and Deuteronomy 5:16) and is stressed yet again in Leviticus 19:3.

Notably as well, within the Ten Commandments this mitzvah is number five; lying on the boundary between the first four, which address the honor of God, and the last five, which address human relations, it thereby serves as a vital bridge between divine-human relations and human-human relations. As the Rabbis see it, the parent-child relationship mirrors our relationship with God—both God and parents are creators, nurturers, teachers, and judges; consequently, our relationship with God provides a model for our relationship with our parents.

Gerald Blidstein, scholar of Jewish thought, emphasizes the deep connection and reciprocity between honoring parents and honoring God.

> [T]he honor and reverence of parents becomes a basis of the Jewish ethos, as weighty as the honor and reverence of God; indeed, God Himself, as it were, is honored or dishonored in man's relationship with his parents: honor shown them is for that reason shown God, for it acknowledges as valid and binding His claim as well. The human relationship takes on added urgency because it is patterned on and reveals the divine; and God is brought close as He is assimilated to the warmth and immediacy of the family. . . .[1]
>
> For by acknowledging parents, man admits that he is not the source of his own being, that he owes existence itself to forces beyond his own personal reality. This can remain a most abstract, intellectual perception, to be sure; it is difficult to jar the certain sensation of self-sufficiency. But the religious consciousness demands the awareness of a greater source of reality beyond. The issue of origins, then, is paradigmatic of the choice between radical self-centeredness and acknowledgement of the Other.[2]

While we would hope for peaceful and mutually nurturing relationships with our parents, sometimes they are tumultuous and challenging. Many (if not most) people find their relationship with their parents to be complex and multifaceted, evoking deep and sometimes conflicting emotions: in the best cases love, gratitude, trust, and devotion; at times anger, resentment, insecurity, and sometimes even betrayal.

Further complicating the picture, toward the end of their parents' lives adult children may find themselves caring for their parents in a number of difficult, inconvenient, and uncomfortable ways. A parent's physical or mental decline may necessitate help with managing finances, making appointments, and getting help with the activities of daily living such as dressing, bathing, and toileting. Moreover, this may occur at a phase of life when adult children are "burning the candle at both ends"—working and raising their own children. Often called the "sandwich generation," they may also be caught between the ideal vision of the parent-child relationship—encompassing spending quality time with their parents—and the struggle to fulfill *kibbud av va-em* given many other pressing life commitments.

The root of *kibbud* (honor) means "weighty," and indeed *kibbud av va-em* is a weighty obligation. But just how weighty is it?

Although the Torah does not set boundaries as to what is required to fulfill the mitzvah of honoring one's parents, the Talmud attempts to do just that. The Rabbis ask: How far must we go to fulfill this mitzvah? The Rabbis do acknowledge that it is difficult to set a standard, because honor encompasses not only deeds, but also attitudes—and these, among them respect, gratitude, and obedience, can be difficult to maintain unwaveringly in emotionally turbulent situations. Midrash notes that *kibbud av va-em* is, in fact, the most difficult of the difficult mitzvot we are obligated to fulfill (Genesis Rabbah 6:2).

Therefore, recognizing that the ideal cannot always be realized, the Rabbis also ask: Are there ever mitigating emotional circumstances to the fulfillment of *kibbud av va-em*? Talmud addresses both questions as the Rabbis try to help us navigate a path through the ideal and the real.

A Broad View to Begin

The realms of Jewish thinking and values are firmly grounded in the world of Jewish doing. Mitzvah, usually translated "commandment," is a covenantal obligation to God, although the behavior required may be directed toward another human being. Torah stipulates many mitzvot that God requires and forbids—613 in all—and the Rabbis enlarged on these, exploring, explaining, and expanding Torah to accommodate life in a post-Temple world. They were particularly interested in elaborating on the mitzvot they believed would strengthen family and society, protect the most vulnerable, and generally improve the world.

The Sages considered many pragmatic questions surrounding the performance of mitzvot: *Who* is obligated? *What* precisely is entailed in performing a given mitzvah? *When* should this mitzvah be done? *Where* must it be done? And how does the doer know when the mitzvah is done sufficiently—in other words: *how much*?

For many mitzvot, including honoring one's parents, Torah did not establish a minimum and maximum amount, nor did it delineate the details of its performance. Presumably, people were to use common sense, as well as their sense of decency.

Recognizing the emotional complexity of fulfilling this difficult mitzvah, the Sages devoted several *dapim* (folios) in the Bavli, the Babylonian Talmud, to a discussion of challenging parent-child relationships and situations. To begin, the Rabbis pointed to a discrepancy in the wording of the three Torah texts directing us to honor our parents. While Exodus 20:12 and Deuteronomy 5:16 each instruct us to *honor (kabbed) your father and your mother*, Leviticus 19:3 tells us, *You shall each revere (tira-u) his mother and his father*. The Rabbis therefore wondered: What is the difference between honor (*kavod*) and reverence (*yir'a*)?

They taught: "Reverence means: one does not stand in their place nor sit in their place, nor contradict their words, nor side against them [in public]. Honor means: one feeds them and provides them drink, dresses and clothes them, leads them in and out [i.e., provides transportation]."[3] Honor, in other words, comprises attending to physical needs, whereas reverence means attending to the parent's dignity and psychological needs as related to position and status. Honor requires the child's time and energy; reverence requires humility. Both necessitate patience and sensitivity.

As the conversation in the Bavli proceeds, the Rabbis discuss the potentially contentious issue of who is responsible for funding elderly parents' care. At first, the Rabbis disagree: Rav Yehudah says the child should pay for the parents' care; R. Natan bar Oshaya holds that the parents' resources should fund their own care. And so this potentially volatile conundrum is referred to another Sage to settle. He determines that the parents' own funds should be used to pay for their care.[4]

Even here, the decision is challenged. A *baraita* (an oral teaching from the mishnaic period) juxtaposes the mitzvah to honor one's parents with *Honor Adonai from your wealth* (Proverbs 3:9): If honoring God requires that we expend funds to fulfill the mitzvah, then surely honoring our parents does as well.

The Rabbis' final resolution entails a beautiful compromise: The parents' funds are to be used to pay for their care, because their children's increased expenditures of time diminish their ability to earn money. Therefore, caring for parents translates to expending funds (or time) for their care. Throughout their discussion of *kibbud av va-em*, the Rabbis help us navigate a path through the real with an eye toward the ideal.

Exploring the Nooks and Crannies of Our Passage

The mishnah that serves as the inspiration for our passage stands on its own as an important text.

> These are the things that have no measure: the corners of the field [*pe'ah*], first fruits [*bikkurim*], appearing [in the Temple on festivals; *re'a'yon*], acts of loving-kindness [*gemilut chasadim*], and Torah study [*talmud torah*]. These are the things whose fruits a person eats in this world but the principal remains intact [to enjoy] in the world to come: honoring father and mother [*kibbud av va-em*], performing acts of loving-kindness, bringing peace between two people [*hava'at shalom ben adam l'chavero*]. And Torah study is equal to them all. (M Pe'ah 1:1; 1a)

When the Rabbis say that a mitzvah "has no measure," this means there is no minimum or maximum quantity required to fulfill it. Consider, for example, the mitzvah of *pe'ah* (corner), a form of charity. Torah specifies that a farmer may not harvest all the way to the corners of the field.[5] Some produce is to be left for poor people to come and gather what they need as their due from God, who is the true owner of the land. Torah does not specify precisely how large a corner area to leave. Similarly, Torah instructs farmers to bring *bikkurim* (the "first fruits" of their harvest) to the Temple for a ceremony of thanksgiving[6] but does not stipulate the amount.

Deeds of loving-kindness are even more ambiguous, since the precise acts are not quantifiable.

The mishnah further informs us that, in the cases of honoring one's parents, acting with loving-kindness, and making peace, not only does one enjoy a reward in this world (the "fruit"), but a full reward in *olam ha-ba* as well. While fulfilling these mitzvot brings immediate benefit in the form of enhanced relationships with others, the Sages assert that it also brings future rewards in the afterlife. (For those who do not subscribe to a belief in the world to come, one can think of the "reward" as the continuing positive ripple effects of significant good deeds.)

Finally, the mishnah asserts that study of Torah is in a class by itself—a statement sometimes interpreted to mean that since Torah study leads to the practice of all the mitzvot, those who study Torah diligently will reap the reward for all the mitzvot (because their intensive study will motivate them to fulfill the mitzvot).

In the Gemara for this mishnah, which discusses at length the mitzvah of honoring one's father and mother, the Rabbis ask: "How much must I do to fulfill this mitzvah?" In other words: "When have I done enough?"

As we will soon see, there is more at play here than quantity (how much time, how many chores, how much housework). Further still: Does the parent's treatment of the child factor into the obligation?

The Gemara (5b–6b) begins with the account of an exemplary son who is the epitome of filial devotion, thereby setting the bar very high.[7]

Honoring father and mother. R. Abbahu said in the name of R. Yochanan, "They asked R. Eliezer, 'To what extent must one go to honor father and mother?' He said to them, 'Why do you ask me? Go and ask Dama ben Netina.'"

Dama ben Netina was the head of the city councilors. Once his mother hit him in front of his entire council, and the slipper with which she hit him dropped from her hand. He bent down and picked up the slipper for her so that she should not be troubled to do so. R. Hezekiah said, "He was an Ashkelon gentile who was head of the town council. During his entire life, he never sat on the stone seat on which his father would sit. When his father died, he treated the stone as his god."

R. Eliezer offers what he considers the finest model of honoring one's parents: Dama ben Netina, a civic leader living in Ashkelon who accepted his mother's public abuse and humiliation of him in order to avoid violating her sense of honor. We might have expected R. Eliezer to cite one of his Rabbinic colleagues or a Jewish communal leader, but R. Eliezer's apogee of morality is not even Jewish, suggesting that no special religious, social, or learning credentials are required to be a paragon of *kibbud av va-em*.

In the second story, the Yerushalmi as well records that Dama ben Netina honored his father, treating with reverence the place where his father was accustomed to sit. (Recall that the Babylonian Rabbis consider this an essential aspect of honoring one's parents, as we saw above in BT Kiddushin 31b: "One does not stand in their place nor sit in their place.")

These two brief anecdotes prepare us for the primary story R. Eliezer wants to relate about Dama ben Netina, concerning a time when he stood to profit handsomely by selling the Rabbis a gem needed for the High Priest's breastplate.[8]

> Once the jasper stone representing the tribe of Benjamin in the High Priest's breastplate was lost. [The Rabbis] said, "Does anybody have a gemstone to replace it?"

They said, "Dama ben Netina has one."

[A contingent of Rabbis] went to him and agreed with him on a price of one hundred *dinarim*.⁹ [Dama] went and wanted to bring [the jewel] to them, but found his father sleeping. Some say the key to the chest [in which the jasper stone was stored] was attached to his father's fingers, and some say his father's leg was resting on the chest.

Dama returned and said to them, "I cannot bring the stone to you."

[The Rabbis] said [to one another], "Perhaps he wants more money." They raised [their offer] to two hundred *dinarim*. [He declined.] They raised [their offer] to one thousand *dinarim*. [He declined.]

The Rabbis offer Dama one hundred gold *dinarim*—a substantial sum totaling approximately two thousand times the average daily wage in the first century—to purchase the stone needed for the High Priest's breastplate. Dama agrees to the amount and goes to fetch the stone, but he cannot secure it without disturbing his father, who is napping on the chest in which the gem is stored. Therefore, Dama returns to the Rabbis and reports that he is unable to sell them the stone.

The Rabbis misconstrue Dama's refusal to sell them the stone; they think he is trying to haggle over the price. Since they need the stone, they double their offer. Dama declines. Desperate, the Rabbis offer one thousand *dinarim*, an exorbitant sum that far exceeds the market value of the stone. Dama's answer remains the same. His concern is not price but rather his father's comfort.

As we read the story, we might wonder: Why didn't Dama simply explain that he cannot sell the Rabbis the gem *at this time*, but will sell it to them in an hour or two when his father wakes up?

When [Dama ben Netina's] father awoke from his sleep, he went down and brought them the gem. They wanted to give him the amount of money that they had offered him at the end [i.e., one thousand *dinarim*]. [Dama] would not accept it from them. He said, "Shall I sell you my father's honor for money? I won't benefit even slightly from honoring my father."

Eventually Dama's father wakes from his nap. Dama retrieves the gem from the chest and delivers it to the Rabbis. They recall that their last offer was one thousand *dinarim* and give that amount to him, but he refuses to accept it. Dama agreed to one hundred *dinarim* and therefore that is as much as he consents to accept. To take more would be to act dishonestly and purchase the additional profit at the cost of his father's honor. In other words, Dama honors his father so deeply that he will forego a profit made disingenuously through his act of honoring his father. For Dama, doing so would diminish and tarnish his father's honor. This also explains why Dama did not explain the situation to the Rabbis. They had every right to leave his shop and search out a merchant who could deliver the gem immediately. Dama was unwilling to manipulate the transaction in any way that might (in his own eyes) compromise his father's honor, such as blaming his inability to produce the gem on his elderly father's need to nap.

> How did the Holy Blessed One reward [Dama ben Netina]? R. Yose b. R. Bun said, "That very night his cow produced a red heifer and all Israel paid him the cow's weight in gold to buy the cow." R. Shabbetai said, "It is written, *[God] is great in power and justice and abundant in righteousness; [God] does not delay* (Job 37:23). The Holy Blessed One does not delay paying the reward to a gentile who performs a religious duty."

The Rabbis note that heaven richly rewards Dama ben Netina for honoring his father, even though he is not Jewish, and therefore, strictly speaking, the Toraitic mitzvah of *kibbud av va-em* is not incumbent on him.[10] And so, in selecting Dama ben Netina as the exemplar of honoring parents, the Rabbis are saying that this responsibility is even more than a mitzvah to be practiced by Jews: it is a universal obligation of all humanity.

R. Yose b. R. Bun supplies an addendum: Heaven rewarded Dama ben Netina in a manner the Rabbis often term *middah k'neged middah* (measure for measure). As Numbers 19 explains, the ashes of a pure red heifer were needed for ritual purification after contact with a corpse. Ritual purification was essential to the smooth running of the sacrificial cult in the Temple. Red heifers are exceedingly rare; consequently, they command a high price. Because Dama ben Netina chose to forego enormous profit to protect his father's honor, God compensated him through the highly profitable sale of his exceptionally valuable red heifer.[11]

Next, the Rabbis tell two stories of Rabbinic Sages who accorded their parents abundant honor. If Dama ben Netina's situation was complicated by his father's physical need to nap, these situations are complicated by the emotional needs of parent and child.

The first example is the *tanna*, R. Tarfon, and his mother:

> R. Tarfon's mother went down to take a walk in her courtyard on Shabbat [and her slipper fell off[12]]. R. Tarfon went and placed his two hands under the soles of her feet, so that she could walk on them until she got to her bed.
>
> Once R. Tarfon became ill and the Sages came to visit him. [His mother] said to them, "Pray for Tarfon, my son, who pays me altogether too much honor."
>
> They said to her, "What does he do for you?"
>
> She repeated the story to them.
>
> They said to her, "Even if he were to do a million times as much, he still would not have paid [you] half the honor of which Torah speaks."

R. Tarfon's mother walks all over him — literally. But we find that this is not her demand; rather, it is his desire to honor her in this way. She herself believes R. Tarfon goes to excessive lengths to accord her honor, suggesting she would prefer he not treat her in this manner; yet the Sages hyperbolically declare that she is due even more. This suggests that her needs and desires are not in themselves what determine the proper manner in which to honor a parent.

Does that make sense? If R. Tarfon's mother is not experiencing her son's attention as honor—but rather as uncomfortable excess—is it truly honor? If R. Tarfon allows his mother to walk all over him, why do his colleagues deem his efforts insufficient to fulfill his obligation to her? Both stories appear to serve the Rabbis' agenda of proving there is "no measure"—no limit—of the honor that should be accorded a parent.

The Babylonian Talmud includes a different version of the R. Tarfon story that may shed additional light on the unexplained peculiarities of the version we find in the Yerushalmi.[13] In the Bavli's version, R. Tarfon allows his mother to use him as a step stool to ascend into bed and descend to the floor, but then boasts to his colleagues in the *bet midrash* of his meritorious actions. Since it is R. Tarfon—and not his mother—who reports his "admirable" behavior to the Rabbis, the Rabbis view his behavior as self-promoting and accordingly censure him: "You have not reached half the honor [you owe her]." They also mention an incident not recounted in the Yerushalmi version: when R. Tarfon's mother throws money into the sea, he shames her. The latter incident is particularly strange. Why would anyone throw money away? Perhaps R. Tarfon's mother is suffering from dementia, in which case his disrespectful behavior in response is reprehensible. Or perhaps she is of clear mind but, annoyed by his boasting, she throws money into the water to provoke him into showing his true colors. It is also possible that the story is a fiction, a "constructed story" written in service of the Rabbis' criticism of R. Tarfon, or possibly to conjecture that were his mother to cause him financial loss, R. Tarfon would not exercise proper restraint; he would dishonor her. Real or fictional, the account of R. Tarfon's response to his mother throwing money away is marshaled here to bolster the Rabbis' disapproval of R. Tarfon's treatment of his mother. His colleagues accuse R. Tarfon of not truly honoring his mother because his actions were designed to improve his own image; hence he did not "reach half the honor" he owed her.

The version in the Bavli may help explain the Yerushalmi's version of the story, including why his mother is annoyed by his gestures and why the Sages are unimpressed by them. If R. Tarfon treated his mother with exceptional deference in order to promote his image in the eyes of his colleagues, but they knew his true motivation and chided him for failing to treat her with genuine honor, then the Yerushalmi's conclusion that his efforts were insufficient to fulfill the mitzvah of *kibbud av va-em* makes far more sense.

The anecdote about R. Tarfon and his mother raises another question: How much is enough?

The Rabbis now consider a doubly inverted case: a parent who believes far more honor is due from a child, but in a strange manner that no one else would consider to be honoring her. The second example concerns R. Tarfon's contemporary, R. Yishmael, and his mother.

> The mother of R. Yishmael came and complained about him to our Rabbis. She said to them, "Rebuke Yishmael, my son, because he does not treat me with honor."
>
> At that moment [i.e., upon hearing this] the faces of our Rabbis turned red. They said [to one another], "Is it possible that R. Yishmael does not treat his parents with honor?" They said to her, "What did he do to you?"
>
> She said, "When he leaves the *bet midrash* ['study house'], I want to wash his feet in water and drink the water [in which his feet were bathed], but he does not let me do it."
>
> They said to [R. Yishmael], "Since that is her desire, that is the honor due her."
>
> R. Mana said, "The millers are so right when they say, 'Everyone's merit is in his own basket.'"
>
> The mother of R. Tarfon said this to [the Rabbis], and they responded thus [i.e., saying that R. Tarfon could never pay his mother the full honor

due her], and the mother of R. Yishmael said this to them and they responded thus [i.e., that she was due the honor she wanted for herself].

R. Yishmael's mother is the third mother we have encountered in this series of stories. Dama b. Netina's mother hit her son with her slipper in public. R. Tarfon's mother, in sharp contrast, felt her son paid her far too much honor. Now, R. Yishmael's mother complains that her son does not accord her sufficient honor, apparently because the act she believes will give her honor he believes will dishonor her.

At first, R. Yishmael's colleagues are shocked to hear a negative report from his mother, but upon querying her they soon learn that what she wants is the opposite of what anyone but she would consider honor: for her, it is a very great honor to treat her illustrious son as if he were a king or a priest or a god and she his lowly servant.

The Rabbis cite this example to teach us that according parents honor is not a precisely defined set of behaviors, because what one person considers honor, another may view as a burden. They conclude that the only way to judge whether a parent is being properly honored is if the parent *feels* honored: R. Tarfon's mother felt sufficiently and even excessively honored, but R. Yishmael's mother did not—despite the lengths to which both sons went to accord their mothers honor. The mitzvah of honoring one's parents is thereby a mitzvah without measure—not only because there is no set amount of respect that satisfies the obligation, but also because one cannot fulfill it without knowing the individual sensibilities of the particular parent.

Missing from the discussion in the Yerushalmi, but found in the Bavli, is the question of honoring an abusive parent. We saw that Dama ben Netina's mother slapped him with a slipper, but it is unlikely that this episode inflicted great pain or injury. How is one to revere parents who have more deeply hurt their children?

The Sages do not consider examples of parents who physically or sexually abuse their children (for this, see other Jewish sources later in the chapter), but they do weigh issues concerning emotional abuse. For example, the Bavli records, in a report attributed to R. Dimi, that Dama was once sitting with a group of Roman nobles when his mother physically attacked him, ripping off his shirt, striking him on the head, and spitting on his face. Dama did not respond to his mother's provocative, humiliating, and abusive behavior.[14]

Why? Tosafot, a medieval commentary on the Talmud, frames the account this way: She was suffering from *meturefet mi-da'ata* (a torn mind), in other words, some form of dementia. Hence her abusive behavior was not intentionally cruel and disrespectful to Dama. His tolerance of her is therefore admirable.

The Bavli then tells another story concerning Rav Assi, a third-century Babylonian *amora*, whose mother's behavior disturbs him to the point that he flees Babylonia to get away from her.

> Rav Assi had an elderly mother. Said she to him, "I want jewelry."
> He made [jewelry] for her.
> [She said,] "I want a husband."
> [He replied,] "I will look for one for you."
> "I want a husband as handsome as you."
> He left her and went to [live in] *Eretz Yisrael*. When he heard that she was coming after him, he went before R. Yochanan and asked, "May I leave *Eretz Yisrael* for abroad?"
> [R. Yochanan said,] "It is forbidden."
> "But what if [I leave in order] to meet my mother?"
> [R. Yochanan] said to him, "I do not know."
> [Rav Assi] waited a short time and went before [R. Yochanan] again. [R. Yochanan] said, "Assi, you have made up your mind to go; may God bring you back in peace."
> Then [Rav Assi] went before R. Elazar and said to him, "Perhaps, God forbid, R. Yochanan was angry?"
> [R. Elazar] said, "What did he say to you?"

[Rav Assi] said, "'May God bring you back in peace.'"

[R. Elazar] said to [Rav Assi], "Had he had been angry, he would not have blessed you."

Meanwhile, [Rav Assi] heard that [his mother's] coffin was coming. Rav Assi said, "Had I known, I would not have left *Eretz Yisrael*."[15]

This story raises many questions: Is Rav Assi justified in leaving Babylonia to avoid his mother and thereby his obligation to honor her? Is her behavior and are her demands sufficiently inappropriate so as to justify his actions? Is her desire for a husband as handsome as her son a hint that her relationship with him crossed a sexual boundary, at least in her mind? The story suggests that parents who do not respect appropriate boundaries with their children risk not only driving them away, but also foregoing the right to be honored in the manner they wish.

Furthermore, halakhah assures us that the obligation to honor one's parents does not extend to violating Torah: "Even if one's father or mother tells him to transgress one of the commandments of the Torah, he should not obey, as Torah says, *[One should revere his mother and his father] and keep My Sabbaths; I am Adonai your God* (Leviticus 19:3). You are obligated to honor Me."[16] The juxtaposition of reverence for parents with Shabbat suggests that, to the Rabbis, our obligations to God, our divine parent, outweigh those of honoring our human parents when the two are in direct conflict.

R. Tarfon and R. Yishmael may have found themselves in emotionally complicated relationships with their mothers, but adult children who do not have the opportunity to fulfill the mitzvah of *kibbud av va-em* because their parents are no longer living also face a quandary. Recall that the mishnah told us: "These are the [mitzvot] whose fruits a person eats in this world but the principal remains intact [to enjoy] in the world to come." The mitzvah of *kibbud av va-em* is therefore understood as a mitzvah that will garner a significant reward in *olam ha-ba*. R. Zeira, a third century *amora* living in *Eretz Yisrael*, is an orphan and therefore lacks the opportunity to fulfill the mitzvah and earn its rewards: neither "the fruit" in this world nor the reward that accrues for *olam ha-ba*.

> R. Zeira had been distressed, saying, "Would that I had a father and a mother, whom I might honor, and so inherit the Garden of Eden." But when he heard these two teachings [about R. Tarfon and R. Yishmael], he said, "Blessed be the Merciful One, that I have no father and mother. I would not be able to act as R. Tarfon did, nor could I bear what R. Yishmael did."
>
> R. Avun said, "I am exempt from honoring father and mother." They said [explaining R. Avun's statement]: When his mother conceived, his father died; and when his mother gave birth to him, she died.

Given the heavenly reward Mishnah promises for honoring one's parents, it is no surprise that R. Zeira would lament his status as an orphan. What is astonishing is R. Zeira's assessment that, given the stories he has heard, he finds it preferable to be off the hook for this obligation and hence ineligible for the rewards. Similarly, the Bavli reports that R. Yochanan, orphaned from birth, once remarked, "Happy is the one who has not seen them," suggesting that the mitzvah of honoring one's parents is so complex and difficult to fulfill, for him as well it is preferable to be exempt.

Like R. Zeira and R. Yochanan, R. Avun is also an orphan. In contrast to R. Zeira's highly emotional and freighted observation, however, his response is emotionally neutral: he merely notes that he is exempt from the mitzvah. Perhaps the Rabbis include R. Avun's less emotional viewpoint to encourage people whose parents are no longer alive to frame their situation as R. Avun does or to make the point that even with difficult parents there are multiple ways of viewing that relationship.

The Rabbis have elucidated that given the complexity of the mitzvah of *kibbud av va-em*, it is not possible to stipulate a simple minimum or maximum. Even more, attempting to specify actions that fulfill the mitzvah can be stymied by the complexities of a parent's emotional needs. While we might be tempted to rely on parents' subjective experience as the criterion to determine whether or not they are genuinely honored, in certain situations in life, even this criterion is insufficient. Therefore, Talmud ends the discussion of *kibbud av va-em* by pointing out that in times of duress our obligation to honor a parent may require behavior that ostensibly appears to be the antithesis of honor. In this situation, what appears to be disrespect and abuse is actually protection.

> There is a person who feeds his father fattened birds but inherits *Gehinnom* ['purgatory'], and there is a person who puts [his father to work] grinding at the millstone and inherits the Garden of Eden.
>
> How does one feed his father fattened birds and inherit *Gehinnom*? There was a man who fed his father fattened hens. Once, his father said to him, "My son, where did you get these?" [The son] said to [his father], "Old man, old man, eat and be quiet just as dogs eat and are quiet." Thus, we find that one can feed his father fattened hens and yet inherit *Gehinnom*.
>
> How does [a son] put [his father to work] grinding at the millstone and inherit the Garden of Eden? There was a man [grinding] at the millstone [when] a [military] draft came to the grinders [to conscript one person from the family of each grinder]. [The son] said to [his father], "Father, come and grind in my place. If shame comes [to those drafted to do the king's work], better it should [come] to me than to you; if lashes come, better to me than to you." Thus, we find that one can put [his father to work] grinding at the millstone and inherit the Garden of Eden.

In the ancient world rulers often conscripted people for both labor forces and armies, generally by taking one person per household. In the situation above, the king's officer comes to the grinders either to conscript people to grind for the king or, more likely, to conscript soldiers for the king's army. The son offers himself for the draft so that his father will not be drafted. The point of this passage is that without knowing the finer details of the situation, we would be inclined to think that feeding one's parent luxurious food is a deed God would reward ("inherit the Garden of Eden"), and compelling an elderly parent to engage in strenuous labor is a deed God would punish ("inherit *Gehinnom*"). Our perspective, however, is reversed when we view the full picture. Treating a parent with disdain and disrespect is a greater sin than the fine food is a good deed, and protecting a parent from shame and physical harm is great good even if it comes at the cost of subjecting that parent to physical labor.

The ultimate criterion for successfully fulfilling the obligation of *kibbud av va-em* is attending to the parent's well-being, and this depends both on the parent's subjective experience and on circumstances. Commonly accepted standards, such as "Feed your parent the finest food available," or "Protect your elderly parent from having to engage in arduous and dangerous physical labor," do not operate in a vacuum. The son who feeds his father haute cuisine but treats him with undisguised contempt, equating his father's value to that of a dog, fails to honor his father because the father's well-being is diminished far more by the son's scorn and derision than it is raised by the quality of the food placed before him.[17] Conversely, in times of grave danger, when life is topsy-turvy, what would normally be considered deeply disrespectful behavior may prove to be soul saving and even life saving. The Rabbis imagine a son who puts his elderly father to work at a millstone to prevent him from being drafted into the king's army, where he might be compelled to engage in immoral activities or perish.

In short, there are no simple rules or criteria for observing the mitzvah of *kibbud av va-em* that apply in all cases. We are continually called on to make sensitive judgments based on the circumstances and the individuals involved.

Continuing the Conversation

1. Obedience and Honor

Obeying is not the same as honoring, although there is certainly overlap. Mark Twain famously quipped: "Obey your parents—when they are present." One can easily imagine the royal wink as King Edward VIII of England said: "The thing that impresses me most about America is the way parents obey their children."

While the Babylonian Rabbis assert that a parent's demand that requires a child to violate Torah is to be disregarded, how that child expresses refusal to comply with the parent's demand is also important.[18] The manner of communication can spell the difference between honoring and dishonoring the parent.

Where do you believe obedience and honor overlap? How would you delineate the boundaries between them?

2. Honor versus Reverence

How are we to understand the differences between honor and reverence? Both versions of the Ten Commandments instruct, *Honor your father and your mother* (Exodus 20:12 and Deuteronomy 5:16), yet Leviticus 19:3 commands, *You shall each revere your mother and your father*. Furthermore, Leviticus reverses the order of father and mother.

Rashi explains why the father is mentioned first with respect to honor, and the mother is mentioned first with respect to reverence: "*You shall each revere your mother and your father*: Here, [Torah] mentions the mother before the father because it is evident to God that a child reveres his father more than his mother. But, regarding honor, [Torah] mentions the father first because it was evident to God that a child honors his mother more than his father because she wins his favor with kind words."

According to Rashi, children naturally honor their mothers more than their fathers because of their close emotional bonds to their mothers, and innately revere (since fear can be a component of reverence) their fathers more than their mothers because they fear their fathers' power. Torah therefore seeks to balance nature with the ideal vision that we should honor and revere both parents.

Does Rashi's observation of human nature apply to parental roles and parent-child relationships in the twenty-first century? Does it comport with your experience? How would you differentiate between "honor" and "revere"? Do you believe you have fulfilled both mitzvot in your relationship with your parents?

3. How Much Is Too Much?

Moses Maimonides wrote in Mishneh Torah, *Hilkhot Mamrim* 6:8–9 (quoting Shulchan Arukh, *Yoreh De'ah* 240:19):

> Even though [children] are commanded [to dutifully show their parents much honor and reverence], parents should not place too burdensome a yoke upon them or be too exacting with them in matters pertaining to their honor for fear that they may cause them to sin [by dishonoring them]. They should forgive their children and close their eyes, for parents have the discretion to forgo the honor due to them. Parents who strike their grown child are excommunicated because they violate the biblical prohibition, *You shall not place a stumbling block before the blind* (Leviticus 19:14).

Do you believe parents have a responsibility to set reasonable limits in order to relieve children of a possibly taxing burden? How might a parent and child come to a mutual understanding of what is reasonable and how much is too much?

How is one to fulfill this mitzvah in emotionally charged cases without specified limits? When might a child honorably conclude, "*Dayenu*; I have done all I can"?

4. Honoring Elderly Parents

Other people's behavior influences what we do, and in turn our behavior influences what others do. When we see others perform the mitzvah of *kibbud av va-em* with generosity and graciousness, we may be likewise inspired. Similarly, when we treat parents and elders with honor and reverence, we may be teaching our children, by example, how best to treat us.

A folktale set in a wide variety of cultures and variously attributed to both Leo Tolstoy and the brothers Grimm tells of an old man who came to live with his son and daughter-in-law.[19] He thought he would be happy there, surrounded by their love.

> The first morning, the old man tried to make himself breakfast, but when he tried to break eggs into a bowl, he dropped them on the floor.
>
> "Your hands are trembling," his son said. "Let me do that so I don't have to clean up the mess."
>
> Later, to be helpful around the house, the old man tried to take the garbage out to the road. But he dropped a bag, it split open, and its contents scattered on the driveway.
>
> "Dad, please don't bother," his daughter-in-law said. "It takes me longer to clean up the trash than to take it out myself."
>
> The following year, the couple had a baby. The old man could see that the new parents were nervous about allowing him to hold the baby, lest he drop the infant.
>
> As the child grew, so did the old man's tremors. He began to drool. Occasionally he dropped a dinner plate on the floor and it shattered. His son and daughter-in-law gave him a wooden bowl because it wouldn't break if dropped.
>
> One day some years later the son and daughter-in-law found their son sitting on the front steps whittling away at a chunk of wood.
>
> "What are you making?" they asked.

The boy replied, "I'm carving bowls for you when you grow old."

Does this story encapsulate a truth about our lives?

Here is the classical ending of the story:

> The parents were speechless. Tears welled up in their eyes. That evening, they lovingly led the old man to the family dinner table and placed their best china before him. When he spilled liquid, they quietly wiped it up. When he drooled, they discretely wiped his chin. Never again did they show concern for dishes and glasses that broke, tablecloths that were stained, or utensils that fell on the floor. The old man lived very happily in their home for the remainder of his days.

Is this how you imagined the story would end? If not, what ending would you compose and why?

5. Limits to Honoring One's Parents

Torah and Talmud assume that parents are due honor from their children in principle. But are all parents deserving of honor? Are children who have been physically, emotionally, or sexually abused or neglected by their parents obligated to honor them?

Jewish tradition is divided on this issue. The mystic and legalist rabbi Joseph Karo (1488–1575) wrote the Shulchan Arukh (Set table), long considered an authoritative code of Jewish law for Sephardic Jews.[20] Rabbi Moses Isserles (1520–72; also known as the Rema), a renowned Polish Ashkenazic legal authority, wrote a gloss to the Shulchan Arukh called the Mappah (Tablecloth) that delineates where Ashkenazic halakhah and custom differ from Karo's rulings.

The Shulchan Arukh holds that "even if one's parent is an evildoer and violator of the law, one must honor and show reverence for that parent."[21] Parents are due honor and reverence by virtue of bringing the child into life—regardless of their subsequent actions. Karo seems to have based his uncompromising view on Moses Maimonides.[22] Several of the images he employs come from either the Bavli's or Yerushalmi's discussions of *kibbud av va-em*.

> To what degree does the mitzvah of honoring one's parents extend? Even if one's parent takes his purse of gold and throws it into the sea in his presence, he should not embarrass them, shout, or vent anger at them. Instead, he should accept the Torah's decree and remain silent. To what degree does the mitzvah of revering one's parents extend? Even if one were wearing fine garments and sitting at the head of the community, if one's father and mother came, ripped his clothes, struck him on the head, and spit in his face, he should not embarrass them. Instead, he should remain silent and revere the Ruler of rulers who commanded him to conduct himself in this manner.

Do you agree with the Rambam? Do you think his standards are realistic?

How do you think children whose parents embarrass or humiliate them should balance their self-respect with the obligation to honor their parents?

Rabbi Moses Isserles disagreed with Karo. He noted in his gloss, "Some say that one is not obliged to honor one's wicked parent unless that parent has repented." Isserles thereby exempts a child from the mitzvah of *kibbud av va-em* (including the care and maintenance of parents and showing respect for their status and position) but upholds the prohibition against causing parents physical pain and distress.

A parent's due can be limited in another way. Rambam recommends that parents set boundaries on their own expectations: "A person is forbidden to impose too heavy a yoke on his children, to be too exacting with them in matters pertaining to his honor, lest he cause them to stumble. Rather, he should forgive and disregard [their actions]; for a father has a right to forgo the honor due to him."

Which view, and under what circumstances, strikes you as most reasonable, and why?

If, as Isserles opines, parents' evil behavior—which is not necessarily directed toward their children—compromises their right to honor and reverence from their children, what can we say about parents who physically and/or sexually abuse their children? Rabbi Mark Dratch, noting that abusive parents are in the category of *rasha* (wicked) and therefore are no longer due parental honor, writes: "respect and reverence are not automatic[ally due an abusive or wicked parent]; they are earned by merit and only if parents show signs of repentance and have made amends to their children."[23]

Psychotherapist Beverly Engel writes that in extreme cases it can be unhealthy and even damaging to remain in a relationship with such parents:

> Why isn't there a commandment to "honor thy children" or at least one to "not abuse thy children"? The notion that we must honor our parents causes many people to bury their real feelings and set aside their own needs in order to have a relationship with people they would otherwise not associate with. Parents, like anyone else, need to earn respect and honor, and honoring parents who are negative and abusive is not only impossible but extremely self-abusive. Perhaps, as with anything else, honoring our parents starts with honoring ourselves. For many adult children, honoring themselves means not having anything to do with one or both of their parents.[24]

Dratch further notes that abused children are exempt from the obligation to mourn and say *Kaddish* for their abusers. They do not need to sit shivah (the seven days of mourning) either in order to honor the deceased. And if they happen to be sitting shivah out of their own sense of obligation or for their other parent's sake, they are not obligated to mourn the deceased.

How might Dama ben Netina have responded to Engel's ideas? How might R. Assi have responded? How do you think the Rabbis might have responded?

Summing Things Up

The Rabbis liken the mitzvah of *kibbud av va-em* to honoring God. They consider the mitzvah essential to maintaining the structure of the family and community, and hence civilization itself. Yet they teach that *kibbud av va-em* is a mitzvah "without measure," meaning that one cannot establish a minimum performance, leaving us to make sensitive judgments of when, how, and how much is required to fulfill the obligation. In a series of stories told in the Jerusalem Talmud (as well as stories in the Babylonian Talmud), the Sages acknowledge how complicated parent-child relationships can be, and hence how difficult and even burdensome it can be to fulfill an obligation that calls on the best in us. The Talmud thus opens an honest and ongoing conversation about how to appropriately honor our parents.

6 Affirming Our Sexuality

Babylonian Talmud, Tractate Nedarim 20a–b

Rabbah b. Bar Chana said in the name of R. Yochanan, "It is as difficult for God to make matches as it was to part the Reed Sea."

—BT Sotah 2a

Why Study This Passage?

The Rabbis discuss *everything* in the Talmud, even topics as sensitive and intimate as sex.[1]

Given the Rabbis' major concern—appropriate human behavior within the Jewish covenant with God—they ask a fundamental question: What kind of sex acts between a husband and wife does Torah sanction? For example, are there permitted and impermissible positions for lovemaking? May one fantasize about another person while making love with one's spouse? In general, what does sex, Torah style, look like?

Much of the Rabbis' discussion of sex in the Talmud concerns heterosexual marital unions between two married cisgender people (those who, in modern parlance, identify with the gender assigned to them at birth); the Rabbis did not consider gay and lesbian marriages or marital partnerships involving people who are not cisgender. Judaism is not, as constituted in the ancient world, a monogamous religion—Abraham had three wives, Jacob had four wives—and therefore halakhah permits a man to have more than one wife. The Rabbis did discuss premarital and extramarital sex, both complex halakhic topics beyond the purview of our chapter's Talmud text. The Rabbis, who are deeply committed to the institution of marriage and family and, we will see, considered procreation a mitzvah, have a special concern for the relationship between a husband and wife. What is more, because the Talmud was written by, and for, men, it therefore most often explores and expresses ideas from a man's perspective. This, however, does not mean the Rabbis are never sensitive to women's concerns, as our passage will demonstrate.

Today many of us have broadened our understanding of marriage and family. We accept, in ways earlier generations did not, that few families resemble those in *Ozzie and Harriet* or *Leave It to Beaver*. Contemporary marital partnerships may be heterosexual or homosexual, the partners may be cisgender or transgender, and the children may be, as the old expression goes, any combination of "yours, mine, and ours"—or none at all.

Moreover, regardless of the kind of marital partnership, the sexual component of a marital relationship is not always idyllic. One's sexual desires and preferences do not always align with those of one's partner, and a misalignment can cause strain, dissatisfaction, and unhappiness.

The Rabbis place great importance on loving and sexually satisfying marital relationships. Today we would apply the principles they deduce as leading to healthy, safe sex within marriage to all marital relationships and indeed all intimate relationships (worth noting since in our day people tend to marry later or not at all, yet still engage in intimate relationships). The values that undergird and inspire the chapter's passage—and ultimately form the substance of what it teaches us—are key.

A Broad View to Begin

The answer to the question, "What kind of sex does Torah permit?" emerges in the first chapter of Genesis. In describing God's creation of various life forms, Torah emphasizes the inherent capacity of each species to procreate in order to replicate itself. Concerning plant life: *God said, "Let the earth sprout vegetation: seed-bearing plants, fruit trees of every kind on earth that bear fruit with the seed in it"* (v. 11). Concerning sea creatures and birds: *God blessed them, saying, "Be fertile and increase, fill the waters in the seas, and let the birds increase on earth"* (v. 22). Similarly, concerning people: *God blessed them and God said to them, "Be fertile and increase, fill the earth and master it; rule the fish of the sea, the birds of the sky, and all the living things that creep on earth"* (v. 28).

Although it is clear from the context that the phrase *Be fertile and increase* is descriptive, highlighting the nature and capacity of all life to replicate itself in God's self-sustaining world, the Rabbis choose to read Genesis 1:28 prescriptively: as a mitzvah to procreate. When reading the biblical text as a commandment, several questions naturally follow: Is everyone obligated to procreate? How many children is one obligated to produce? What happens if one is unable to have children?

Mishnah Yevamot 6:6 answers these questions.

> No man may abstain from keeping the law, *Be fertile and increase* (Genesis 1:28), unless he already has children: according to the Bet Shammai (the School of Shammai), [he is obligated to procreate until he has] two sons; according to Bet Hillel (the School of Hillel), a son and a daughter, for it is written, *Male and female God created them* (Genesis 5:2). If he married a woman and lived with her ten years and she did not bear a child, he is not permitted to abstain [from fulfilling the mitzvah of procreation]. If he divorced her, she may be married to another, and the second husband may live with her for ten years. If she had a miscarriage, the interval [of ten years] is measured from the time of the miscarriage. The duty to be fruitful and multiply falls on the man, but not on the woman. R. Yochanan b. Baroka [dissents from this view and] says: [Procreation is incumbent on both men and women because] of them both it is written, *God blessed them and God said to them, "Be fertile and increase"* (Genesis 1:28).

Many people are troubled by this mishnah, particularly the notion that an infertile couple should divorce for lack of children, regardless of their love for one another. (So were many of the Rabbis; they address this concern elsewhere, but it is not the focus of the talmudic text in this chapter.)[2] Beyond this real issue, the mishnah makes it abundantly clear that, for the Rabbis, sexual intercourse is an essential aspect of married life because it is necessary for reproduction, which God requires to maintain human life on earth.

At the same time, the Rabbis recognized that sexual intercourse plays another important role in human life: pleasure. Exodus 21:10 establishes women's conjugal rights: *If a man marries another [woman, a second wife], he must not withhold from this one [the first wife] her food, her clothing, or her conjugal rights.* Since the Rabbis only consider the man's obligation to procreate (they reject R. Yochanan b. Baroka's minority opinion in the mishnah above), the conjugal rights they afford a woman can only be for purpose of pleasure.

In the Gemara accompanying the above mishnah (BT Yevamot 62b), the Talmud elaborates on a man's duty to pleasure his wife: R. Yehoshua b. Levi teaches that a man who fails to fulfill his conjugal duties is called a "sinner," especially if he embarks on a trip but did not first provide her with pleasure before leaving. Notably, the Sages even discuss how a man is to pleasure his wife. Close bodily contact (without clothing) is important.[3] Attending to the woman's emotional and physical needs is necessary.[4] Moreover, men are to see that their wives climax first, to ensure their satisfaction.[5]

The passage in this chapter answers a different question: What sex acts does Torah permit?

The passage comes from Tractate Nedarim, which discusses vows (*neder* means "vow"), and is located in the Order Nashim (Women). Long ago, many promises and contracts were executed by verbal oaths rather than by written documents. In our time, people are often cautious before signing a document that encumbers them with a legal obligation, but tend to be less wary about the words that emanate from their mouths, even if these words establish a commitment. Apparently not much has changed over the centuries. The Rabbis were keenly aware that in the heat of anger or in moments of fear or desire people make vows they cannot, should not, or do not intend to keep. Therefore, the Sages discouraged all vow making and sought ways to release people from vows they should not have made.

Our passage opens with a phrase from M Nedarim 2:5 that presents three examples in which someone verbalized a vow in public and subsequently denied having entered into the vow, claiming to have meant something altogether different. R. Meir holds that if the one who made the vow lacks a convincing explanation he is to be penalized and treated stringently. The Sages, however, overrule R. Meir, because they wish to find a legal solution—"an opening from another place"—to release the person from his unwise vow.

Exploring the Nooks and Crannies of Our Passage

The Rabbis discourage the making of vows and oaths because, having often been uttered with little forethought and being difficult to keep, they are often broken. To support this contention, they quote a *baraita* (mishnaic-era teaching) that advises men to avoid four unrelated behaviors that lead to trouble. The first of these behaviors is making vows, which is why we find the *baraita* in a tractate that discusses vows. The fourth behavior mentioned in the *baraita*—conversing excessively with a woman—launches a lengthy discussion about sex and sexuality that we examine in this chapter.

> But the Sages say: We make for them an opening from another place. A *tanna* taught [in a *baraita*]: At all times, you should not make a habit of making vows because ultimately you may transgress the prohibition against oaths. And you should not make a habit of spending time with an ignorant person because he might eventually give you *tevel* ['untithed

produce'] to eat. And you should not make a habit of spending time with an ignorant *kohen* ['priest'] because he might eventually give you *terumah* ['the priest's portion of the sacrifices'] to eat. And you should not converse excessively with a woman, because you might eventually come to lewdness.

R. Acha, the son of R. Yoshiyah, says, "Whoever looks at women will ultimately come to sin; and whoever gazes [even] at the heel of a woman will have children lacking good character." Rav Yosef said, "This refers to when his wife is a menstruant."

R. Shimon b. Lakish said, "The heel that the *baraita* mentions is [a metaphor for] the unclean place that is opposite the heel."

This *baraita* advises Jewish men not to make vows, not to socialize with someone who is ignorant of halakhah (because that person might provide food to eat that has not been properly tithed[6] and eating it would violate the Torah), and, similarly, not to socialize with an ignorant priest (because this could lead one to eat his *terumah*, the portion of tithes set aside exclusively for priests and their families).

In the fourth item on the *baraita*'s list—do not converse excessively with a woman—we encounter the *baraita*'s presumption that extended conversation can lead to emotional closeness and the desire for inappropriate sexual contact.

Reading the *baraita* with twenty-first century eyes, we might suspect that we have entered the realm of extreme conservatism. And there would be a grain of truth to that, but the Gemara moves in another direction with R. Acha's rejoinder to the *baraita*. He tells us: Forget conversation! A man should not even *look* at a woman, because that is enough to send him spiraling into uncontrollable sin. R. Acha adds yet another stern warning: One who gazes at a woman's heel will beget children of bad character.

The concern expressed about the character of offspring subsequently conceived—subsequent to what?—signals us that the Rabbis are no longer talking about casual human contact, such as spending time with an ignorant person or an uneducated priest. The conversation R. Acha imagines is not in the marketplace or courtyard; it is in the bedroom. He has shifted the conversation to the danger of talking to one's wife during coitus. Rav Yosef confirms this, explicitly stating that the woman in question is one's wife, but attempts to constrain the harshness of R. Acha's restriction by limiting it to the period of the wife's menses, since the couple is not permitted to enjoy sexual relations during this time. Perhaps Rav Yosef's concern is that the husband will cause himself undue frustration, but it is difficult to imagine how he could live in the same house with her and avoid looking at her for more than a week. Even this strikes R. Shimon b. Lakish as excessively strict and likely unrealistic for a man and woman living under the same roof, and he therefore explains that R. Acha's words are not to be taken literally; rather, "heel" is a euphemism for female genitalia.

Despite Rav Yosef's and R. Shimon b. Lakish's efforts to mitigate the severity of R. Acha's pronouncement, two potentially peculiar and troubling concerns have been raised. First, R. Acha presumes that the manner in which one engages in coitus is a matter of morality and hence will affect the moral character of a fetus conceived through that act of sex. This reflects the ubiquitous Rabbinic belief of *middah k'neged middah* ("measure for measure," retributive justice), the notion that "what goes around comes around" because Heaven—poetically or symmetrically—rewards or punishes people in like manner to what they do.[7]

Second, until R. Acha was brought into the conversation, the passage concerned people out in the world, perhaps in the field or marketplace. R. Acha, particularly as understood by Rav Yosef and R. Shimon b. Lakish, redirects the conversation away from the public sphere and into the private realm of a married couple's bedroom. The presumptively forbidden behavior—according to R. Shimon, looking at a woman's genitals—applies to a man looking at his own wife in the privacy of their bedroom.

R. Acha, Rav Yosef, and R. Shimon have, in short order, turned the corner of this discussion from a warning about "excessive conversation" with women in public to a prudish prohibition against a man looking at his own wife's genitals in the context of their private bedroom. A question looms large: why does the Talmud redirect the conversation?

The Rabbis next make a pious pitch for modesty that arises from bashfulness.

> It was taught [in a *baraita*]: [Moses answered the people, "Be not afraid; for God has come only in order to test you, and] in order that the fear of [God] may be ever with you, [so that you do not go astray] (Exodus 20:17). This refers to shame. *So that you shall not go astray*—this [teaches] that shame leads to fear of sin. Based on this, they said: It is a good sign if person is bashful. Others say: Anyone who is bashful does not hurry to sin. And if someone is not "shamefaced" [i.e., bashful], it is known that his ancestors did not stand at Mount Sinai.

Gemara quotes Exodus 20:17 to laud the trait of bashfulness because it can frighten one away from committing sexual sins. The mention of the "ancestors that stood at Mount Sinai" suggests that all the Israelites in Moses's generation who were present when Torah was revealed either were saints before the revelation or were made so by the giving of Torah, and that their saintliness is marked by innate modesty in sexual matters. What is more, their descendants possess the very same trait. Hence, anyone lacking sexual modesty could not be descended from those who stood at Mount Sinai. This is a surprising claim, given that this same generation built the Golden Calf and, in ensuing years in the wilderness, rebelled against Moses time and again. The Rabbis have elevated sexual modesty to a vaunted level and established it as a criterion to judge whose lineage can and cannot be traced back to Sinai.

Perhaps, however, the Rabbis' real purpose in placing the *baraita* here is to tie it to the end of the passage (to follow). For now, Gemara returns to the primary thrust of its discussion concerning what is, and what is not, permitted in the marital bed.

> Yochanan b. Dahavai said, "The ministering angels told me four things: Why are people are born lame? Because they [i.e., their parents] overturned their table. Why are people born mute? Because they kiss that place. Why are they born deaf? Because they converse during sexual intercourse. Why are they born blind? Because they look at that place."
>
> But this contradicts [the claim concerning conversation during sexual intercourse]. They asked Ima Shalom, "Why are [20b] your children so exceptionally beautiful?" She replied to them, "[Because] he [R. Eliezer b. Hyrcanus, her husband] 'converses' with me neither at the beginning nor at the end of the night, but [only] at midnight. And when he 'converses,' he uncovers a handbreadth and [immediately] covers up a handbreadth, and it is as though he were compelled by a demon. And when I asked him, 'What is the reason for this?' he replied, 'So that I will not set my eyes on (i.e., think about) another woman, lest my children be like *mamzerim* ['bastards'].'"
>
> There is no contradiction: This [Ima Shalom's testimony that teaches permission to talk during sexual intercourse] refers to conjugal matters; the other [R. Yochanan b. Dahavai's prohibition against talking during intercourse] refers to other matters.

If you thought that R. Acha was severe, allow me to introduce you to R. Yochanan b. Dahavai, who is downright puritanical (note H. L. Mencken's definition of Puritanism: "the haunting fear that someone, somewhere, may be happy"). R. Yochanan b. Dahavai claims that no less than the ministering angels, God's right-hand assistants, personally told R. Yochanan that parents who engage in certain sexual practices will produce offspring with physical disabilities that mirror the immoral behavior of their parents. This is, again, *middah k'neged middah* (measure for measure).

AFFIRMING OUR SEXUALITY 131

The expression "overturn the table" is not entirely clear from context, except that we can surmise from the "measure for measure" consequence of lameness that it connotes penile penetration: "feet" is a common biblical euphemism for male genitalia.[8] "Overturn the table" could mean sex when the woman is on top, the man enters the woman from behind, or anal intercourse. Many scholars believe the expression is a euphemism for anal intercourse, there being nothing unusual about the first two options.[9]

Following the pattern of *middah k'neged middah*, according to R. Yochanan b. Dahavai, if the parents engage in oral sex (expressed as "kiss that place"), the child will be unable to use his or her mouth to speak. If the parents converse with one another while making love, the child will be deaf. If the parents look at one another's genitals, the child will be blind. R. Yochanan b. Dahavai is a real fun guy.

His claim that these prohibitions come directly from the ministering angels is immediately challenged with a story about Ima Shalom, the wife of R. Eliezer b. Hyrcanus. R. Eliezer, a first-century *tanna*, was one of Rabban Yochanan b. Zakkai's primary disciples. He was a strict, no-nonsense, pious man; his teacher compared his mind to a plastered cistern that never leaked a drop.[10]

When Ima Shalom says that R. Eliezer "conversed" with her, she is using the term as a polite substitute for sexual intercourse. She tells us that her husband would engage in sexual intercourse only at midnight, indulging neither the moment they went to bed nor as soon as he awoke. Further, he would uncover only a small part of her body at a time, to catch only a small glimpse of her, in order to exhibit restraint, because he had the sexual appetite of a demon.[11]

In bringing Ima Shalom's story, the Sages choose to read "converse" not as she intended, but according to its literal meaning. In this way it illustrates the claim they wish to make: if R. Eliezer "conversed" with his wife while making love, then certainly it is permitted.

Ima Shalom's account adds another verse to the *middah k'neged middah* litany: Apparently, R. Eliezer believed that even thinking about an impermissible act during intercourse could have physical repercussions for a child conceived at the time. If a man thought about having sex with another woman (which, if it actually occurred, would be adultery) while having intercourse with his wife, then the child conceived with his own wife would nonetheless be tainted with the status of *mamzerut* and be considered a bastard.[12]

Talmud has uncovered a glaring contradiction: R. Yochanan b. Dahavai claimed that conversation during sex is not permitted, yet Ima Shalom's story testifies that no less than the great Sage R. Eliezer b. Hyrcanus engaged his wife in conversation during lovemaking. How is this contradiction to be resolved? One common talmudic method is to assign the application of a problematic viewpoint or principle to one narrow realm, rather than allow it to stand as a general rule. R. Eliezer's permission to talk during sex, we are told, applies to conversation *about* sex. R. Yochanan b. Dahavai's prohibition pertains to all other conversation.

This resolution is an exceedingly clever reconciliation of conflicting views. At first glance, it appears that R. Eliezer's more "liberal" perspective has been limited to discussion about sex, while R. Yochanan b. Dahavai's more "conservative" viewpoint is made to apply to all other conversation. However, at second glance, it becomes clear that the Rabbis are issuing an invitation, even an encouragement, to engage in conversation *about* lovemaking with one's partner during sex—to ask one's partner what he or she wants, how things feel, and so on. Mundane conversations (the kids, the shopping list, doctor's appointments, chores) are to be set aside to focus on lovemaking.

Ima Shalom's story is not the only one the Rabbis might have brought into this conversation. In Tractate Berakhot we find a humorous story about R. Kahana, the student of Rav (also called Abba Arika), who established the great academy of Sura in Babylonia.

> R. Kahana once went into [Rav's house] and hid under Rav's bed. [Later that night] he heard him chatting and joking and making love [with his wife].
>
> [R. Kahana] said to [Rav], "One would think that Abba's mouth never tasted the dish before [meaning: one would think this was Abba's first time engaging in sex]!"
>
> [Rav] said to him, "Kahana, are you here?! Get out of here. This is not the way of the world (i.e., you are being rude)."
>
> [R. Kahana] said, "It [i.e., sexual relations] is Torah and I need to learn."[13]

As charming as this story is, it would not have served the Rabbis' purpose of drawing a distinction between the viewpoints of R. Yochanan b. Dahavai and R. Eliezer because the conversation between husband and wife is incidental to the main point: learning to make love to one's wife is an essential element of living a life of Torah. Nonetheless, it reinforces the Rabbis' essentially positive view of marital sex and supplies an example of a great Sage who engaged not only in conversation while making love, but, it appears, joking and idle chatter as well.

R. Yochanan's fourfold teaching remains a problem to be overcome. Its rigidity and puritanical flavor is at odds with the Rabbis' generally favorable view of the pleasures of sexual intimacy. They cannot allow it to stand.

We might ask why they include it at all. Perhaps it had gained sufficient currency in the Rabbinic community that it could not be ignored. In that case, it could be far more dangerous to allow it to circulate orally and influence people than to confront it directly and dismantle it entirely. The Rabbis next proceed to do just that.

> Yochanan [b. Nafcha] said, "The above is the view of R. Yochanan b. Dahavai, but our Sages said that the halakhah is not according to R. Yochanan b. Dahavai. Rather, a man may do whatever he pleases with his wife [during sexual intercourse]."

A parable concerning meat that comes from the abattoir: if he wants to eat it salted, roasted, cooked, or seethed, he does. So too fish from the fishmonger.

Ameimar said, "Who are the 'ministering angels'"? The Rabbis. For should you say they are literally the ministering angels, why did R. Yochanan say the halakhah does not follow R. Yochanan b. Dahavai, seeing that the angels are more expert concerning the formation of the fetus than we are? And why are they designated "ministering angels"? Because they are so distinguished.

Step one in demolishing R. Yochanan b. Dahavai's teaching is to state unequivocally, as does the third-century Sage R. Yochanan b. Nafcha, that his view is not accepted as halakhah. In fact, R. Yochanan asserts, Torah does not in any way limit what a husband and wife do alone in the privacy of their bedroom.

Gemara supplies an analogy to meat and fish that may strike modern readers as crude, but it is unlikely that it came across as crude to the Sages; rather, it was clear and unequivocal. The butcher does not tell customers to roast their chicken but not grill it; those who purchase meat or fish may prepare and eat it any way they desire.

For step two, recall that R. Yochanan ben Dahavai makes his claim on the authority of the ministering angels and not on his own. Ameimar tells us that in saying "ministering angels," R. Yochanan b. Dahavai merely intends some Rabbis. (We might well have surmised this because we know from R. Yochanan b. Nafcha that halakhah does not follow R. Yochanan b. Dahavai.)

Step three: There might be residual concern that R. Yochanan b. Dahavai is correct, since the ministering angels are privy to an insider's view (so to speak) of fetal development. Gemara therefore asserts that R. Yochanan b. Dahavai did not mean "ministering angels" in a literal sense, but rather used the term as an honorific title for the Rabbis whose opinion he conveys.

Gemara next provides two brief illustrations of revered Sages who ruled on halakhah in accordance with R. Yochanan b. Nafcha's explanation and in contradiction to R. Yochanan b. Dahavai's view. This confirms R. Yochanan b. Nafcha's interpretation as the correct and authoritative opinion.

> A woman once came before Rabbi [Yehudah ha-Nasi] and said, "Rabbi, I set a table for my husband, but he overturned it." Rabbi replied: "My daughter, the Torah has permitted you to him. What, then, can I do for you?"
>
> A woman once came before Rav and said, "Rabbi, I set a table before my husband but he overturned it." Rav replied, "How is this different from fish?"

In both cases, a woman presents a query to a Rabbinic authority. She says that while she consented to sex with her husband, and even prepared the bedroom accordingly, her husband wanted anal intercourse. She asks if this is permitted (most likely because she does not want to engage in anal intercourse). Both Rabbis affirm that not only is anal intercourse permitted, but, more significantly, Torah does not legislate the sexual acts in which a husband and wife may engage in the privacy of their bedroom.

Why does the Gemara tell virtually the same story twice? Doing so makes ironclad that Torah does not forbid particular sexual acts. R. Yehudah ha-Nasi, a *tanna* from the Land of Israel who served as president of the Sanhedrin and compiled the Mishnah, is considered the most authoritative Sage of his day. Rav, an *amora* who established the great academy of Sura in Babylonia, was the foremost Sage of his day. The two men are the greatest voices in the creation of the Mishnah and the Gemara. Between them, R. Yehudah ha-Nasi and Rav speak for both the *tanna'im* (Rabbis of the Mishnah) and the *amora'im* (Rabbis of the Gemara), as well as for the Sages in the Land of Israel and Babylonia.

It might seem that no base has been left uncovered in opening the door to sexual acts between a husband and wife in the privacy of their bedroom, but a question implicit in the two scenarios (those of R. Yehudah ha-Nasi and Rav) has not been made explicit: Must a woman consent to a sex act she finds objectionable because the man desires it?

The Rabbis will address the question of consensual sex next, as soon as they clear up another question that might have crossed the minds of some readers: a man's sexual fantasies about a woman other than his wife.

> *Do not seek after your own heart* (Numbers 15:39). On the basis of this Rabbi [Yehudah ha-Nasi] taught: One may not drink out of one goblet while setting his eyes on [i.e., thinking about] another. Ravina said, "This [restriction] is necessary only when both are his wives."

Recall that Ima Shalom told us that her husband, R. Eliezer, believed that if he thought about another woman while having sex with his wife, the resulting child could be branded a *mamzer*, because the very thought of engaging in adultery at the time of intercourse could convey the status of *mamzerut* to the fetus conceived through that act of sex. This is a dangerous notion, both for a child that could be so branded for life and for the health of the marriage, given that sexual fantasies arise naturally and unbidden.[14]

To mitigate these dangers, the Rabbis engage head on with the claim that fantasizing is forbidden. They quote an authority no less than R. Yehudah ha-Nasi who forbids it, and then overlay the clarifying view of Ravina, to teach that the prohibition against fantasizing about another woman while making love with your wife applies only if the subject of the husband's fantasies is also his wife: a second wife. Ravina's caveat alone takes the sting out of R. Yehudah ha-Nasi's opinion: Given that most Jews had long been monogamous by the time this ruling was promulgated, it appears a clever way to render the prohibition essentially mute. Hence, fantasizing during lovemaking is permissible.

Still unanswered, and perhaps the most difficult question to address, is whether a husband may do as he pleases even if his wife objects. Does Torah weigh in on whether marital sex must be consensual? The Sages recognize a clear and present danger: marital rape. They now proceed to close any lingering gap that could be construed to permit this.

And I will purge from among you the rebels and those who transgress against Me (Ezekiel 20:38). R. Levi said: This [verse] refers to children belonging to the following nine characteristics—children of A-S-N"T M-Sh-G-A"Ch [a mnemonic for the following]: children of fear; violent force; a hated wife; [a man who is] under a ban; an exchanged woman; strife; intoxication [during intercourse]; emotionally divorced; mingling; and of a brazen woman.

On the basis of a verse from the prophet Ezekiel that speaks of purging rebels and transgressors from among the Jewish people, R. Levi supplies a list of nine *middot* that render sex between a husband and wife, legally joined in marriage and alone in their bedroom, nonetheless impermissible by halakhah. The term *middot* generally connotes character traits, but here the "nine characteristics" speak to the emotional situation of the couple: the state of mind of the husband and wife. The Rabbis' concern is *not* the act (i.e., *how* the couple engages in sex) but whether they may be intimate at all.

R. Levi attaches to the prohibition a severe warning that children born of intercourse under these nine conditions will be damaged; they will become "rebels ... who transgress against [God]."

Upon examination, it appears that the "nine characteristics" are the conditions, or states of mind, that are likely to generate physical and emotional abuse, and even marital rape. From this we see that the Rabbis' underlying and overriding concern is for the woman's safety and well-being.

Let's examine them:

"Children of fear" means a situation in which the woman is afraid of the man. Her fear is a signal that he may be dangerous.

"Violent force" speaks to the situation in which a man compels his wife to engage in sexual intercourse if she does not want to. (Here the text is talking about sexual intercourse, but halakhah would extend the principle to all sexual acts.)

"A hated wife" is one who is the object of her husband's animosity and contempt. He is unlikely to treat her with gentleness and compassion; in fact, quite to the contrary, he is dangerous to her.

"[A man who is] under the ban" refers to a man who, because he has been excommunicated, is forbidden from having sexual intercourse, even with his wife. Given the state of mind expected of one who is excommunicated, he could be a danger to her.

"An exchanged wife" is the wife who is mistaken for another wife. In the case of a polygamous marriage, if the husband intends to have sexual intercourse with one wife, he may not have sexual intercourse with another.

"Strife" means that there is significant discord between the husband and wife. Under such conditions, sex will not be an expression of love and may become dangerous.

"Intoxication" during intercourse may strike us as surprising because a moderate amount of alcohol can promote sexuality. However, alcohol also lowers inhibitions, which can lead to rough or dangerous behavior.

"Emotionally divorced" refers to a situation in which the man has decided that he will divorce his wife and is therefore no longer emotionally committed to her. The Rabbis feared that his emotional distance and lack of commitment might result in rough or callous behavior.

"Mingling" refers to a situation in which a woman has had sex with another man in the past three months. The most likely scenario is that her first husband died and she is now in a second marriage.

Sexual intercourse with the second husband is prohibited until a full three months have passed to ensure that if she is pregnant, the identity of the father will be clear. While at first glance, it may seem that this condition does not fit R. Levi's list, it is appropriate here because a woman carrying another man's baby for perfectly legitimate reasons might evoke strongly negative emotions on the part of her husband.

"A brazen woman" is one who seduces her husband.

Did you wonder why "a brazen woman" is #10 on the list of R. Levi's nine *middot*, or states of mind, that preclude a man from engaging in sexual intimacy with his wife? In fact, #10 was tacked on precisely so that it can be discussed, refined, and affirmed:

> [Concerning the last item on the list:] But is this so?! For R. Shmuel b. Nachmani said in the name of R. Yonatan, "Any man whose wife summoned him to his marital duty will beget children such as were not to be found even in the generation of Moses, for as it is said, *Pick from each of your tribes men who are wise, discerning, [and experienced, and I will appoint them as your heads]* (Deuteronomy 1:13), and it is written, *So I took your tribal leaders, wise and experienced men* (Deuteronomy 1:15), but "discerning" is not mentioned. But it is also written, *Issachar is a large-boned ass* (Genesis 49:14), while elsewhere it is written, *And of the children of Issachar, who were discerning about the times* (1 Chronicles 12:33)? This is when her seduction is pleasing.

Before delving into R. Shmuel b. Nachmani's teaching, which lauds women who seduce their husbands, it is significant to point out that in Tractate Eruvin, we find R. Shmuel b. Nachmani's teaching preceded by this succinct ruling:

> Rami b. Chama citing R. Assi further ruled: A man is forbidden to compel his wife to the [marital] obligation, since it is said in Scripture,

And he who acts impetuously with his feet sins (Proverbs 19:2). R. Yehoshua b. Levi said, "Whoever forces his wife to engage in marital relations will have children who are not of good character."[15]

As we have pointed out, the Rabbis often use "feet" as a euphemism for the male member. Acting impetuously implies sexual coercion or force. It is strictly prohibited.

R. Shmuel b. Nachmani, in the name of R. Yonatan, asserts that not only is a "brazen woman" *not* prohibited, but a woman who seduces her husband is a many-splendored thing. He boldly claims that a child conceived when a woman seduces her husband will be of the finest caliber, even superior to those in Moses's generation who received the Torah at Mount Sinai. He accomplishes this by comparing verses from Deuteronomy concerning the Israelites in the wilderness. In Deuteronomy 1:13, Moses tells the Israelites to choose from among themselves leaders possessed of three traits: *chakhamim* (wise), *n'vonim* (discerning), and *vidu'im* (experienced). However, two verses later we learn that the selected leaders possessed only two traits: *chakhamim* (wise) and *vidu'im* (experienced)—Torah does not say they were *n'vonim* (discerning). R. Shmuel concludes that the leaders of the generation of Moses were not ideal because they lacked discernment. However, children conceived when a woman seduces her husband, according to R. Shmuel, will possess all three attributes, and hence exceed the generation of Moses in character.

Gemara expresses skepticism: Perhaps it is not always the case that children conceived after a wife seduces her husband turn out so well? In making its argument, Gemara cites two verses concerning Issachar, one concerning the son Leah conceived after seducing Jacob and the second referring to the eponymous tribe of Issachar.[16] Jacob, blessing his children prior to his death, says, "Issachar is a strong-boned ass, crouching among the sheepfolds" (Genesis 49:14)—not an especially favorable assessment. However, through the second scriptural verse, the Gemara concurs that Issachar's descendants were *yod'ei vinah*, *men who knew how to interpret the signs of the times, to determine how Israel should act* (1 Chronicles 12:33). They were endowed with *binah* (discernment), a quality lacking even among the generation of Mount Sinai.

What, then, distinguishes a positive from a negative outcome when a wife seduces her husband? What ensures that children so conceived will be human beings of high moral caliber? The answer: when the husband is pleased to be seduced. Mutual pleasure and respect are key.

Continuing the Conversation

1. Men's Perspective — Women's Perspective

The Talmud's voice is the voice of men living in a homosocial world: they spend their days engaged in study and conversation with men about topics of importance to men. This passage is clearly written from the perspective of men talking to other men about sex. If women had gathered in their own study house to discuss "what sex does Torah permit and not permit," what specific concerns do you think would have been raised? What decisions, wisdom, and advice might have been promulgated?

2. When Is It Marital Rape?

Rape is variously defined, but in general the term refers to unwanted intercourse or penetration (vaginal, anal, or oral) obtained by force or threat of force. For most of U.S. history, laws deriving from seventeenth-century British common law exempted husbands from the charge of marital rape. The British jurist Matthew Hale writes in *The History of the Pleas of the Crown*: "But the husband cannot be guilty of rape committed by himself on his lawful wife, for by their mutual matrimonial consent and contract the wife hath given up herself in this kind unto her husband, which she cannot retract."[17]

This attitude prevailed in American law and throughout much of American society until the 1970s, when people began asking: What constitutes marital rape? How should the boundaries be drawn between permissible and impermissible sex in marriage? Some legislators who sought to change American law consulted talmudic experts, because Judaism had always outlawed spousal rape thanks to the passage in this chapter and Moses Maimonides, who writes in his law code *Mishneh Torah*: "A husband should not be overly jealous of his wife; nor should he compel her to have sex against her will, but only with her agreement, and amid conversation and joy."[18] By 1993, marital rape was a crime in all fifty states.

One remaining question, and not yet firmly a part of the definition, concerns the situation in which the wife is unable to consent. Some states still exempt the husband of a mentally or physically impaired wife (or one who is unconscious, asleep, or legally unable to consent) from the charge of rape. How do you think the Rabbis would have responded to the propriety of intercourse under such conditions?

3. Who Owes Whom Sex?
The Rabbis considered sex a gift from God to be enjoyed within the prescribed boundaries of permitted relationships. Yet they taught that sex is also a right: the husband is obligated to give his wife sex regularly and in a manner she finds pleasurable and satisfying. A wife, however, does not owe her husband sex.

Do you think sex in marriage is an obligation? If so, who owes whom, and why? Why do you suppose the Rabbis did not specifically obligate wives as they did husbands?

4. Sex as Glue
It has frequently been claimed that sex is the glue that strengthens relationships and holds marriages together. At the same time, sexual incompatibility or dissatisfaction is often cited as a leading contributor to divorce. A closer look at the shoals on which marriages founder, however, reveals more nuanced factors—communication problems, a power imbalance, problems with "roles" and unmet expectations, loss of intimacy, and the inability to resolve conflicts—all of which affect a couple's sexual relationship.

Consider these factors with respect to R. Levi's nine *middot*: Could they result in the *middot* R. Levi delineates? Given that sex can be either the glue or the shoals, does the Rabbis' view of sex promote one or the other?

5. A Blessing for Sex?

Jewish tradition provides blessings to say before performing a mitzvah to acknowledge that what we are about to do is in fulfillment of a religious obligation. In addition, we are given many blessings of thanksgiving to say, such as when we eat or drink, see the ocean, survive a dangerous situation, buy a new garment, witness a rainbow or lightning, or see a head of state. But there is no blessing to recite for having sex. Why do you think this is? If you were to write a blessing to say before making love, what would it be?

Summing Things Up

When the Rabbis consider the sexual relationship between a husband and wife, they ask, "Which sex acts are permitted and which are forbidden?" In pursuing the answer, they begin with an exceptionally conservative and restrictive opinion—no doubt held by many—and then proceed to dismantle it through a series of arguments, scriptural interpretations, and interpreted stories. In the end, they conclude that while procreation in the context of marriage is the primary purpose of sex, pleasure is an important and worthy secondary purpose. Therefore, Torah does not de facto prohibit specific sex acts between a married couple in the privacy of their bedroom. Rather, Torah is concerned with the emotional environment of their relationship. Husbands are to see to their wives' pleasure and are forbidden to engage in sex when their emotional state might be dangerous to their wives. Talmud paints a picture in which marital sex takes place under the conditions of love, respect, and mutual consent.

7 Balancing Family and Study
Babylonian Talmud, Tractate Ketubot 61b, 62b–63a

> Be careful to honor your wife because blessing enters the house only because of the wife.
>
> —BT Bava Metzia 59a

Why Study This Passage?

For women, balancing work, marriage, and children has never been easy. In 1983 a large billboard advertising *Redbook* magazine featured a young and fit, smiling and energetic woman effortlessly juggling a briefcase, frying pan, and diaper bag. The 1980s ushered in the era in which women were supposed to be able to "have it all." Before, and since, women have been keenly aware that in the real world time, energy, and resources are not limitless, and so one must set priorities. Often the conflict is between equally high priorities, with enormous implications for relationships at work and at home. Unsurprisingly, such choices can be difficult and painful to make.

In the ancient world women had few options—and most women had no options. Whether wealthy or poor, their lives were determined by economic necessity and cultural norms. What is more, the Rabbis taught that in addition to raising children and supporting their families, they were duty bound to promote their husbands' Torah study.

Rav said to R. Chiyya, "Whereby do women gain this merit [of Torah study]? By making their sons go to the synagogue to learn and their husbands go to academy to study the teachings of the Rabbis, and by waiting for their husbands until they return from the academy.[1]

Today, men often face the same dilemmas as women: choosing between time invested in work or in family. More than ever before, men have genuine options, because their wives are working outside the home, too.

During the talmudic period, men had few options, especially if they were not wealthy. Thus, the teaching of Rabban Gamliel, the son of R. Yehudah ha-Nasi (who lived in the first half of the third century) speaks to the desirable balance between Torah study and gainful employment, rather than between work and home life.

Rabban Gamliel the son of R. Yehudah ha-Nasi said, "The study of Torah is commendable when combined with a gainful occupation, for when one toils in both, one forgets sin. Study alone, without an occupation, leads to idleness and ultimately to sin."[2]

Nonetheless, the challenge of attaining work-study balance was ever present. Talmud envisions and describes a world in which *talmidei chakhamim* (students of Torah) not only can find financial support to study full time, but can even travel far from home for extended periods to sit at the feet of great Sages and imbibe their wisdom.

Is this envisioned world actually true? What do we know of the historicity of the Sages' stories recounted throughout the Talmud, and in this passage in particular? Nineteenth-century academic scholars of Judaism (*Wissenschaft des Judentums*) accepted the talmudic stories preserved in the Bavli and Yerushalmi as reflecting historical nuggets about the lives and activities of the Sages, despite the many conflicts and contradictions found in various story versions. In the modern era, the religious historian Jacob Neusner revolutionized scholarship in the field by demonstrating that we lack a way to distinguish history from fiction in talmudic stories. For example, often a story about a first-century Sage, or *tanna*, is recounted by someone who lived several centuries later in Babylonia, and the Talmud containing it was redacted yet another several centuries later. Not infrequently, the Bavli and Yerushalmi preserve several irreconcilable versions of the same story. Neusner concluded that although we cannot ascertain whether talmudic stories about the Sages contain historical kernels, we can recognize that they served a didactic function, conveying a theological idea, emphasizing Rabbinic values and priorities, supporting a sacred myth, or forging group identity. Hence, while we cannot study these stories to learn history, Neusner averred, we can examine them to understand the process of transmission and the meaning the Rabbis extracted from them (or perhaps infused into them).[3]

With this in mind, we can ask: Did the academies the Talmud describes exist at that time, or were they a figment of the Rabbis' imaginations? Consider, for example, the story in volume 2, chapter 2, of *The Talmud of Relationships*: Rabban Gamliel so severely restricted access to the *bet midrash* that, following his deposition, Abba Yosef b. Dostai reported it was necessary to add four hundred benches and the Rabbis claimed seven hundred more benches were required to accommodate the flood of potential students who wanted to enter. Whether four or seven hundred benches, that would amount to an increase of well over one thousand people, a paltry sum when compared with the twelve thousand, and later twenty-four thousand disciples of R. Akiva we will encounter in this chapter's passage.

A brief passage from Tractate Ketubot sheds light on the question of these hyperbolic numbers. The Talmud knows two types of students: those who devoted themselves to full-time learning and those who attended yearly Rabbinic study gatherings, after which they returned home to their families and jobs (much like the distinction today between those who study year round and those who attend a yearly conference).

Consider this description of the academies in the first four generations of Babylonian *amora'im*:

> When the Rabbis [who came for the yearly gathering] departed from the academy of Rav, twelve hundred Rabbis still remained [to study full-time with Rav]. [When the Rabbis departed] from the academy of Rav Huna, eight hundred Rabbis remained. . . . When the Rabbis rose [to depart] from the academies of Rabbah [bar Nachmani] and Rav Yosef [b. Chiyya], four hundred Rabbis remained, and they called themselves "orphans." When the Rabbis departed from the academy of Abaye—some say from the academy of Rav Pappa and some say from the academy of Rav Ashi—two hundred Rabbis remained and they called themselves "orphans among orphans."[4]

The claim that there were twelve hundred full-time students in the first generation of *amora'im* is clearly hyperbolic and contrasts starkly with the precipitously decreasing enrollments over the four generations of Rav, Rav Huna, Rabbah and Rav Yosef, and Abaye (Rav Pappa and Rav Ashi, in fact, are fifth- and sixth-generation *amora'im*, respectively).[5] As Jeffrey Rubenstein, scholar of Rabbinic literature, summarizes, "The tradition essentially offers an exaggerated and nostalgic vision, romanticizing the halcyon days when study of Torah took place on a colossal scale. And while the numbers taper over the course of the Amoraic period, consistent with the generally pessimistic Rabbinic historical view, they nevertheless assume an institution of significant proportions."[6] Here Rubenstein, like Neusner, is not focused on the magnitude of the numbers, but rather on their *meaning*, and hence the numeric sequence is important.

Historian David Goodblatt understands the academy to be "an institution which transcends its principles. It has a staff, curriculum, and, most important, a life of its own, a corporate identity. Students come and go, teachers leave and are replaced, the head of the school dies and a new one is appointed—the institution goes on."[7] However, Goodblatt claims, large and established academies arose *after* the talmudic period (in the gaonic period). He concludes: "The organization of rabbinic instruction in Sasanian Babylonia [during the talmudic period] was rather different from the way it has been described in medieval and modern accounts. The large Talmudic academies . . . did not exist in Amoraic times. Instead, disciple circles and apprenticeships appear to have dominated academic activity."[8] Hence students would "sit before" their master, studying either in his home or in a shaded public space. Those who traveled from afar to study would often lodge with the teacher and his family.[9]

We do not know historically how many, and to what extent, men absented themselves from home: perhaps the Talmud's description is more reflective of the Rabbis' idealized world than historical reality. But even as an ideal it had to have been riddled with real-world pitfalls, potentially affecting the quality of the men's marriages.

Jewish tradition prizes marriage, which is, first and foremost, for companionship. Torah conceives of the creation of women for this purpose: *The God Adonai said, "It is not good for man to be alone; I will make a fitting helper for him"* (Genesis 2:18), and *Hence a man leaves his father and mother and clings to his wife, so that they become one flesh* (Genesis 2:24). The secondary purpose of marriage is procreation, as the Rabbis learn from the Torah: *God blessed [humanity] and God said to them, "Be fertile and increase"* (Genesis 1:28). Hence finding a loving partner, establishing a home, and raising children are deemed fulfilling for the individual and good for the community.

The home is also essential to transmitting Judaism from generation to generation. In 1989 the Dalai Lama met with six Jewish leaders at a Buddhist monastery in New Jersey. His goal was to learn the "Jewish secret" for spiritual survival in exile. Jews, he reasoned, had nearly two millennia worth of experience living in a diaspora; Tibetan Buddhists, exiled from their home by Communist China, faced a similar challenge. Referring to the many Jewish observances and celebrations that occur at home, Blu Greenberg of the National Jewish Center for Learning and

Leadership told the leader of Tibetan Buddhism, "The Jewish family kept the Covenant and the Torah alive. That, no doubt, is one of our secrets."[10] Many Jewish rituals, practices, and holiday celebrations—including Shabbat, the Pesach seder, kashrut, and tzedakah—are instilled and sustained in the home.

The locus of intense Torah study is the academy, but the home is the core of Jewish life. What happens when the demands of two domains come into conflict? Romantic notions of love and marriage, family and children, sooner or later give way to the reality that there is not enough time in a day to keep a briefcase, a frying pan, and a diaper bag in the air simultaneously. And, for the Rabbis, yet another challenge interfered with their juggling act: Much as they may have loved their wives, they were also infatuated with Torah study. What happens when there is not enough time to fulfill both passions?

A Broad View to Begin

Our passage is found in the Tractate Ketubot, which discusses the relationship and financial commitments of marriage. The Rabbis understood marriage as a *brit*, a covenant between a man and a woman, just as Torah is a *brit* between God and the Jewish people. Both covenants were considered commitments of love and loyalty. Often the Rabbis felt torn between the two *britot* (covenants)—marriage and Torah—that defined their lives, as if they were caught between two lovers.

Jeffrey Rubenstein frames the dilemma this way:

> To eschew marriage and embrace celibacy—a remedy available to Greek and Roman philosophers and demanded of the Church Fathers—was not an option for the rabbis. Marital sex and procreation were *mitsvot*; consequently rabbis could not withdraw completely from female society out of a singleminded devotion to Torah. Moreover, Babylonian sages believed that without a legitimate sexual outlet, men would inevitably transgress the law. Marriage was the only way

to avoid sin (illicit sex, adultery, masturbation) or "thoughts of sin" (lust, sexual fantasies). Even widowers who had fulfilled the obligation to procreate were encouraged to remarry. The sages therefore faced a fundamental systemic tension, in that competing commandments pulled them in opposite directions. For many, it was undoubtedly difficult to find the right balance.[11]

When the Rabbis consider the sexual relationship between a husband and wife, they begin with a verse in the Torah that they interpret as establishing a wife's conjugal rights. Because it serves as the foundation for Talmud's discussion of husbands who leave home for long periods to study Torah, it is important to understand the verse. Torah stipulates that a man who marries a Hebrew slave and subsequently takes a second wife retains obligations to the first wife: *If he marries another, he must not withhold from this one* [i.e., the first wife] *her food, her clothing or her conjugal rights [onah]* (Exodus 21:10).

The Rabbis understand the term *onah* to mean conjugal rights. While scholars have suggested alternative translations of *onah*,[12] Rabbi Michael Gold expresses the dominant view that *onah* means "conjugal rights" when he writes:

> The Torah considers the obligation of *onah* (regular sexual relations) to be *a man's duty and a woman's right*. The Torah teaches that a man should not withhold his wife's food, clothing, and sexual rights (Exodus 21:10). This is precisely the opposite of Western norms which see sexual relations as a man's right and a woman's duty.[13]

Understanding *onah* as conjugal rights is a remarkable recognition of women's sexual desires. Mishnah records the statement of R. Yehoshua b. Chananiah that "a woman prefers a *kav*[14] [of food] and physical intimacy to nine *kabin* [nine measures of food] and abstinence."[15] This was likely not meant as a compliment—R. Yehoshua is saying that women

BALANCING FAMILY AND STUDY   151

are foolish enough to prefer sex even when it entails starvation rather than to forego sex and eat—but it is nonetheless acknowledgement of women's desire for sexual intimacy with their husbands.[16]

From the husband's perspective, long absences from home might prevent him from fulfilling his obligation to procreate, so let us consider that obligation. Mishnah Yevamot 6:6 asserts, "No man may abstain from keeping the law, *Be fertile and increase*."[17] In the Gemara following this mishnah, R. Eliezer makes the startling declaration that one who does not engage in procreation "is as though he sheds blood." R. Yaakov makes an equally hyperbolic claim: one who does not procreate "is as though he has diminished the divine image." Ben Azzai, a Torah scholar who chose not to marry and have children, tells us that both drastic statements are true. Not surprisingly, his colleagues turn to him and say, "Some preach well and act well; others act well but do not preach well. You, however, preach well but do not act well!" In essence, the Rabbis accuse him of hypocrisy. Ben Azzai replies, "But what shall I do, seeing that my soul is in love with the Torah?" Ben Azzai understands that devoting his time, physical attention, and spiritual energy exclusively to Torah study precludes being a good husband and father. All the more so if Torah study requires a husband to travel far from home for an extended period of time.

During the talmudic period people traveled to visit family, to fulfill work obligations, and to study Torah. Travel was slow and arduous, but facilitated by a network of Roman roads constructed for military and administrative purposes. Trips for business, study, or personal reasons might take days, weeks, or even months depending on the distance and nature of the work involved. Therefore, those who traveled to study Torah might stay with their teachers for an extended period.[18] This inspires the question: How long may a husband stay away from home, depriving his wife of her companion and sexual partner?

Our passage begins with the mishnah's discussion of how long a husband may leave his wife and segues into seven stories of Rabbis who absented themselves from home for long periods of time to study Torah.

To fully appreciate the power of this passage, it is important to recognize that when the Rabbis tell stories, their intent is to illustrate or confirm a point in an emotionally compelling manner, rather than to recount a historical event. Talmudic stories are carefully crafted and strung together like pearls to convey a message. The passage in this chapter comprises seven stories, ordered and linked together to form a beautiful literary commentary about Rabbis who were so besotted by Torah learning that they neglected their wives and children—at great cost, and with increasingly devastating consequences.

Exploring the Nooks and Crannies of Our Passage

Exodus 21:10 establishes that a husband is obligated to provide his wife with food, clothing, and sexual intimacy, but does not stipulate minimums of time or quantity for any of the three. In the case of conjugal rights the mishnah therefore asks: How long may a man deprive his wife of her conjugal rights? The mishnah's answer is presented in three parts.

Mishnah 5:6; 61b

If a man forbade himself by vow to have intercourse with his wife: Bet Shammai ruled that [she must consent to the deprivation for] two weeks. Bet Hillel ruled one week.

Students may go away to study the Torah, without the permission [of their wives for a maximum of] thirty days. Laborers: one week.

The times for conjugal duty prescribed in the Torah are [as follows]: For men of leisure: every day. For laborers: twice a week. For donkey drivers: once a week. For camel drivers: once in thirty days. For sailors: once in six months. These are the words of R. Eliezer.

According to the Rabbis, there were two reasons why a husband would abstain from sex with his wife. The first was an ancient notion that by eschewing sexual intercourse a man could preserve his energy for other endeavors. Jewish men could therefore sidestep their conjugal obligation for a limited period of time by making a vow, using a common verbal formula by which they created a religious obligation to refrain from enjoying sex for a period of time.[19] In the first section of the mishnah, the schools of Shammai and Hillel disagree (as they characteristically do) on the length of time a woman may be compelled to tolerate the lack of intimacy that such a vow would create for her.

The second reason a husband would abstain from sex was pragmatic necessity: a man who has traveled away for business is obviously unavailable to his wife. But how long may he travel, thereby denying his wife intimacy? The Rabbis begin with the occupation that most concerns them—Torah study—and the presumption that Torah study undergirds the purpose and continuing existence of the universe. R. Elazar is quoted in the Bavli as saying, "Great is Torah, for were it not for it, heaven and earth would not endure, as it is written, *[Thus said Adonai:] As surely as I have established my covenant with day and night—the laws of heaven and earth* (Jeremiah 33:25)."[20] (R. Elazar reads the verse from Jeremiah to say that God sustains natural laws for the sake of God's covenant with Israel.) As Rabbi Aharon Lichtenstein has pointed out, "the role of *talmud Torah* is conceived in cosmological and mystical terms, bordering, in some formulations, on the magical. From this perspective, it attains continuous cosmic significance as a metaphysical factor affecting the fabric of reality—indeed, as that which supports and sustains the very existence of the universe."[21] The value of Torah for the Rabbis cannot be underestimated.

The second section of the mishnah stipulates that a man may stay away from home for a full month to pursue Torah study.[22] In contrast, a laborer, whose work is far less cosmically consequential, may be away for only one week.

In the third section of the mishnah, the Rabbis report a teaching of R. Eliezer b. Hyrcanus, a disciple of Rabban Yochanan b. Zakkai, who established limits for men who do not work, donkey drivers, camel drivers, and sailors. The permitted intervals of abstinence are proportional to the amount of time someone in these professions would reasonably need to be away from home. The husband who does not work is expected to respond whenever his wife desires him, since he is always at home. Laborers need to take only short trips for work. Donkey drivers are usually away longer, but generally no more than a week, while camel drivers travel farther and are therefore away longer.[23] Sailors are gone for many months once their ships set sail and are therefore permitted a six-month absence from their wives.

Six months is a long time for a woman to be alone, provoking the question: Does Jewish law truly permit a husband to be away for half a year? The Gemara begins with, and focuses on, the answer to this question.

Gemara (62b–63a)

For sailors: once in six months. These are the words of R. Eliezer. Rav Beruna said Rav said, "The law follows R. Eliezer." Rav Ada b. Ahava said Rav said, "Those are the words of R. Eliezer [alone], but the Sages say that students [of Torah] may depart for Torah study for two or three years without the consent [of their wives]." Rava said, "The Rabbis relied on the words of Rav Ada b. Ahava and acted accordingly at the cost of their lives."

R. Eliezer's permission for a sailor to be away for half a year generates discomfort. Gemara offers two proposals concerning how to understand R. Eliezer's statement. The first proposal, offered by Rav Beruna in Rav's name, is that R. Eliezer's opinion is accepted halakhah. However, Rav Ada b. Ahava, also in Rav's name, offers an alternative proposal: he claims to have heard from the same teacher, Rav, that this is merely R. Eliezer's personal opinion, and not established law. How often do two people listen to the same lecture or read the same essay but hear a different message?

The Gemara next cites the opinion of "the Sages." The Rabbis permit a man undertaking Torah study to leave home for two to three years, thereby depriving his wife of sexual intimacy for a far lengthier period than the thirty days Mishnah stipulated. The Sages have raised the ante considerably. This would seem to render Rav Beruna and Rav Ada b. Ahavah's disagreement concerning the status of R. Eliezer's opinion moot.

Rava responds to the claim that the Rabbis permitted men to deprive their wives of sexual intimacy for two, and even three, years by issuing a sober and stern warning: This is dangerous and can result in disaster! Men who choose this course of action have died!

Rava tells us that the Rabbis grounded their surprising permission in the words of Rav Ada b. Ahava—and not in the words of Rav Beruna. Recall that Rav Ada b. Ahava said that R. Eliezer was merely expressing his personal viewpoint whereas Rav Beruna had claimed that R. Eliezer's view was accepted halakhah. Rava's claim that R. Eliezer's permission is *not* established halakhah and should not be understood as such opens space for rejecting it. Given the apparent danger associated with long absences from home (to be amply illustrated shortly), it is far easier to undercut the Rabbis' granting permission for two to three years by establishing R. Eliezer's view as merely his own personal opinion.

Is Rava correct that leaving home for an extended period of time—even for the purpose of Talmud Torah—is dangerous? The Gemara proceeds to recount seven stories of Sages who left home to study with their masters, leaving wives and children behind for long periods. (For the sake of clarity, I am numbering them below.) Let's see how it turned out for them.

> (1) Thus, Rav Rachumi, who frequently [studied at the school of] Rava in Machuza, used to return home on the eve of every Yom Kippur. On one occasion, he was attracted by [his] studies [and forgot to return home]. His wife was looking out [in anticipation of his return, saying], "He is coming soon! He is coming soon!" He did not come. She became distressed and tears flowed from her eyes. [Rav Rachumi, at this very moment,] was sitting on a roof. The roof collapsed under him and he died.
>
> What is the conjugal obligation for scholars? Rav Yehudah, in the name of Shmuel, replied: Every Friday night. *Which yields its fruit in season*

(Psalm 1:3). Rav Yehudah, and some say Rav Huna, and some say Rav Nachman said that [this means] one who has sex every Friday night.

Rav Rachumi is gone for a year at a time studying in Machuza at the academy of Rava—the very same Rabbi who warned of the danger of extended absence from home. Rav Rachumi limits his absences to a year's duration, well within the parameter of two to three years that the Gemara suggests is acceptable.

Rav Rachumi's wife misses him terribly; her excitement at the prospect of his return is palpable. We cannot but wonder if her anticipation at their reunion is reciprocated, given that he customarily arrives home each year on the eve of Yom Kippur, a day when enjoying sexual intimacy is prohibited.[24] What is more, this choice seems to belie his name: Rachumi comes from the root meaning "compassion" or "mercy"—where is his compassion for his wife?

For Rav Rachumi it appears that Torah is more exciting and enticing than his wife. One year he is so enthralled with his studies that he does not return home at all. This causes his wife such deep disappointment and heartache that he is punished by heaven: at the very moment her tears fall, the roof where he sits engaged in Torah study collapses. The disaster Rava warned against has come about: Rav Rachumi dies.

As a result of this incident Rav Yehudah teaches in Shmuel's name that Torah learning should not come at the expense of marital intimacy. Torah is about life, nurturance, meaning, and a loving relationship with God. What could mirror that better than a loving and sexually fulfilling marriage? Therefore, scholars should be home with their wives every Shabbat—a time especially propitious for intimacy.

On to the second story.

(2) Yehudah b. R. Chiyya, the son-in-law of R. Yannai, went and sat in Rav's house of study, but he would return home every [Friday eve at] twilight. Whenever he would come, people would see a pillar of fire

[going] before him. One day his studies so captivated him that he did not come [home]. Because they did not see that sign, R. Yannai said to them, "Overturn his bed, for were Yehudah alive, he would not have neglected the performance of his marital duties." It was *as an error committed by a ruler* (Kohelet 10:5), and his [Yehudah's] soul departed.

Yehudah goes away to study, but dutifully adheres to Shmuel's standard of weekly visits home. He returns imbued with passion: the pillar of fire is a clear phallic symbol. But is his passion for the Torah he has been learning or for the wife who awaits his arrival? On the occasion Talmud recounts, Yehudah's passion for Torah outweighs his passion for his wife, and he does not return home for Shabbat. His father-in-law, aware of his commitment to returning each Shabbat, concludes from Yehudah's absence that something dreadful must have happened to him along the way. Only death, he presumes, would prevent Yehudah from returning home to his wife. His bed is therefore overturned, because that was the custom when a person died.

Gemara comments that R. Yannai's declaration that his son-in-law, Yehudah, must have died may be compared with "an error committed by a ruler," meaning that once uttered it cannot be retracted. As a result, Yehudah died. The Gemara is suggesting that R. Yannai's premature conclusion that Yehudah was dead (rather than that he forgot to return home) was made real by its utterance, but we know from the first story that his death came about because he broke his wife's heart.

On to the third story.

(3) Rabbi [Yehudah ha-Nasi] was planning for his son's [marriage] into the family of R. Chiyya. As he was about to write the ketubah, the girl died. Rabbi said, "Is there, God forbid, a blemish [in her lineage]?" They sat down and investigated the families. [They found that] Rabbi descended from Shephatiah, the son of Avital [the wife of King David]. R. Chiyya descended from Shimi, the brother of [King] David. [R. Yehudah ha-Nasi] said, "Were there not a problem, she would not have died."

[R. Yehudah ha-Nasi] went and planned for his son's [marriage] into the family of R. Yose b. Zimra. They agreed that [Rabbi's son] would go and study for twelve years in the academy. They passed [R. Yose's daughter] before [Rabbi's son]. He said, "Let it be six years." They passed her before him again. He said, "Let me consummate the marriage and then I will go." He was ashamed before his father. [R. Yehudah ha-Nasi] said to him, "My son, you have your Maker's inclination. At first it is written, *You will bring them and plant them in Your own mountain, [the place You made to dwell in, Adonai, the Sanctuary* ['Mikdash'], *Adonai, that Your hands established] (Exodus 15:17). But then it is written, Let them make me a Sanctuary* ['Mikdash'] *that I may dwell among them* (Exodus 25:8)."

He married her. He went and sat in the academy for twelve years. By the time he came back, his wife had become barren. Rabbi said, "What will we do? Should he divorce her? People will say, 'That poor woman waited in vain.' Should he marry another? People will say, 'This one is his wife; that one is his whore.'" He prayed for her and she recovered.

The first match R. Yehudah ha-Nasi arranges for his son is unsuitable. The prospective groom is a descendant of King David and his wife Avital (according to 2 Samuel 3:4) and the prospective bride is a descendant of Shimi, the brother of David; hence, whereas Rabbi and his family are direct descendants of the royal dynasty of King David, R. Chiyya's family is not. We are to understand that the prospective bride's death prevents an unsuitable match from being consummated. This is but prelude to the successful match that is suitable and eventually consummated.

From this story onward, the intervals of time mentioned in the story are noteworthy because they become a motif for the stories that follow. The numbers six and twelve will repeat almost rhythmically, and the intervals of time will oscillate as the benefits and risks of leaving home for long durations is explored through the seven anecdotes Talmud presents.

Rabbi chooses a new bride for his son, but wants him to go away to study for twelve years before marrying her. The prospective bride is expected to wait the twelve years. Once Rabbi's son catches a glimpse of her, however, he is decidedly disinclined to wait that long. He negotiates for six years. When he sets eyes on her a second time, he realizes six years would be unbearable. He wants to marry her immediately.

The transparently sexual urge of Rabbi Yehudah ha-Nasi's son embarrasses him before his father, but to his credit Rabbi responds with compassion couched in a beautiful Torah teaching. Rabbi quotes two verses (Exodus 15:17 and 25:8) that refer to the *Mikdash* (Sanctuary). The first verse tells us that the *Mikdash* is located *in Your own mountain*; this refers to the Temple in Jerusalem; the second verse refers to the wilderness Tabernacle. When the Rabbis speak of the wilderness Tabernacle and the Jerusalem Temple, they frequently comment on the metaphorical marriage of God and Israel at Mount Sinai, a relationship that was "consummated" through the rituals performed in the Tabernacle and Temple.[25] On this basis, Rabbi reads Exodus 15:17 as saying that originally God planned to wait until Israel settled in *Eretz Yisrael* and built the *Mikdash* (Temple) in Jerusalem, which would have postponed consummation of the marriage consecrated at Mount Sinai. Rabbi reads Exodus 25:8 as saying that God subsequently commanded Israel to build a *Mishkan* (Tabernacle) in the wilderness to enable God to consummate the marriage with Israel sooner and not have to endure the long wait. Rabbi tells his son: You are doing just what God did, my son.

The wedding takes place immediately, Rabbi's son consummates the marriage, and then he leaves to study for twelve years. Recall Rava's prediction that long absences would have terrible consequences. Rava's prediction is here confirmed: by the time the groom returns, his wife is unable to conceive. Rabbi attributes her infertility to the long separation.

The situation places Rabbi's son in a difficult position: His wife is unable to facilitate his fulfillment of the mitzvah of procreation. If the couple were to be forced to divorce so that Rabbi's son could marry a woman who would bear him children, or if he were to marry a second wife in order to father children, he would be solving his problem at enormous emotional expense to his wife who had endured twelve years without him. Such a solution would be immoral. Therefore, Rabbi pleads with God, and God restores his daughter-in-law's fertility in response to his prayer.

Note that the time intervals are growing, and in the fourth story a Sage is, like Rabbi's son, away for twelve years.

> (4) As R. Shimon b. Yochai's wedding celebration was winding down, R. Chananiah b. Hakhinai got ready to leave for Rav's academy. [R. Shimon] said to him, "Wait for me and I will go with you." He did not wait for him. He went and sat in Rav's academy for twelve years.
>
> By the time [R. Chananiah b. Hakhinai] returned, all the streets of his town had changed, and he did not know the way home. He went and sat on the bank of a river. He heard them calling to a certain girl, "Daughter of Hakhinai, Daughter of Hakhinai, fill your pitcher and come along." He said, "That means this girl is ours." He followed after her. His wife was sitting and sifting flour. He attracted her eye. She saw him. Her heart swelled. Her spirit flew away. He said before God, "Master of the universe, this poor woman, that is her reward?" He requested mercy for her and she was revived.

Following his friend's wedding, R. Chananiah b. Hakhinai is so eager to return to Rav's academy in Sura that he cannot even wait for his friend to join him on the journey. By the time he tries to return home, following twelve years of study, the town has changed so much he does not recognize enough to find his way. And that is not all, or even the worst of it: overhearing someone refer to a girl as "Daughter of Hakhinai," he realizes she is his own daughter, whom he did not recognize. Perhaps she had been a toddler when he left and has now grown into adulthood—he missed her childhood. R. Chananiah has effectively abandoned his wife and child for twelve years.

Ben Hakhinai now follows his daughter home. His wife immediately recognizes him. His appearance in the doorway is like a bombshell, and she dies of shock. What a catastrophe! R. Chananiah pleads with God that her death is unjust, and God restores her life.

In summary, the consequences of leaving for extended periods might be death of the scholar, infertility, or death of the scholar's wife from grief or shock.

The fifth story includes two elements of the previous story—twelve years away and its alienating effect—as well as an attempt to obviate the potentially disastrous consequences. This story is set in three brief scenes: the academy, a *bet midrash* in the scholar's hometown, and his home.

(5) R. Chama b. Bisa went and sat for twelve years in the academy. As he [prepared] to come [home], he thought: I won't do as the son of Hakhinai did.

[R. Chama] went and sat in the academy [of his town] and sent word to his home. R. Oshaya, his son, came and sat before him. He [R. Chama b. Bisa] asked him about his studies. He saw that his studies were sharply honed. He became distressed, thinking: If I had been there, I could have had a son like this one.

He entered his house. His son entered [after him]. He [R. Chama b. Bisa] rose before him because he thought that he [the son] wanted to question him about his studies. His wife said to him, "Was there ever a father who rose in front of his son?" Rami b. Chami applied to him the verse, *A threefold cord is not readily broken* (Ecclesiastes 4:12)[26]—this applies to R. Oshaya, son of R. Chama b. Bisa.

R. Chama b. Bisa is determined to learn from the errors of R. Chananiah, but he repeats the mistake of absenting himself from his family for a ruinously long period of time and thereby faces other consequences: he cannot recognize his own son, he can no longer teach his own son, and, what is more, his son's learning is superior to his own. The reader cannot help but wonder: since there was an effective teacher of Torah in the area, why did R. Chama b. Bisa need to leave home to study in the first place?

It would seem that, despite the imperative of studying Torah, an extended hiatus from home is disastrous. The sixth story, about R. Akiva and his wife, presents the exception that proves the rule. The story is presented in four scenes.

> (6) R. Akiva was the shepherd of Ben Kalba Savua. His daughter saw that he was modest and upright. She said, "If I become betrothed to you, will you go to the house of study?" He said to her, "Yes." She was betrothed to him in secret and sent him off [to study]. Her father heard. He threw her out of the house and swore that she should have no benefit from his property.
>
> [Akiva] went and sat for twelve years in the academy. When he returned, twelve thousand students came with him. He heard a certain old man say to [R. Akiva's wife], "How long will you lead the life of a widow?" She said to him, "If he listened to me, he would stay another twelve years." [Akiva] thought: Then I am doing this with her consent! He went back and sat for another twelve years in the academy.
>
> When he returned, twenty-four thousand students came with him. His wife heard and went forth to greet him. Her neighbors said to her, "Borrow something to wear and adorn yourself." She said: "*A righteous man knows the life of his beast* (Proverbs 12:10)." When she approached him, she fell on her face and kissed his feet. His attendants pushed her away. He said to them, "Leave her be. What is mine and yours is hers."
>
> Her father heard that a great man had come to town. He thought: I will go to him; perhaps he can release me from my oath. When [Ben Kalba Savua] came to [R. Akiva], [R. Akiva] said, "Did you swear knowing that [your daughter would marry] a great man?" He said to him, "Had he known but one chapter or one law [I would not have sworn the vow]." He said, "I am he." [Ben Kalba Savua] fell on his face and kissed [R. Akiva's] feet and gave him half his money. The daughter of R. Akiva did the same for Ben Azzai. Thus goes the proverb: "Ewe follows ewe; a daughter's acts are like those of her mother."

Finally, Talmud supplies proof that Torah scholars *can* leave home for a long duration without dire consequences.

R. Akiva's case, however, is different from the five previous examples in a significant way: R. Akiva's wife, Rachel, not only consents to his long absences from home in order to study Torah, she has engineered them.[27] Recognizing his unique potential, Rachel agrees to marry Akiva on condition that he will study to fulfill his promise as a Torah scholar. Even after twelve years, during which time Rachel lives in destitute poverty, having been disowned by her father and having a husband who could not support her, she continues to believe in her husband's potential as a scholar. She rejects the suggestion that he has abandoned her to a "living widowhood" and asserts that she would have him stay away another twelve years to study. Overhearing her comment, R. Akiva complies with her wish and reverses course, heading back to the academy—apparently without even visiting her. When he returns again after another twelve years away, Rachel's neighbors encourage her to dress up for the reunion, but she responds that this is unnecessary to curry his attention, approval, affection, and appreciation. Rachel likens herself to a "beast" (quoting Proverbs 12:10), to her mind a term of pride. She does not feel neglected or deprived, because she chose her sacrifice to serve a greater purpose. And, indeed, she is correct: R. Akiva rebukes those who push her away, telling them that both he, and all his students, owe their learning to her sacrifice.

While many have interpreted the account of R. Akiva and Rachel to affirm that an arrangement whereby husbands leave their wives for prolonged periods can work under the right circumstances, I would suggest a different message: Rachel and R. Akiva are the exception to the general rule that long absences from home *do not work* and are inappropriate. As has been pointed out, Rachel conceived and approved her husband's time away to study. Just as significantly, however, R. Akiva is *not* comparable to the other Rabbis. He is a second Moses (as we saw in chapter 1 of this volume). If Moses is the Giver of Torah, R. Akiva is the Giver of Oral

Torah, the shaper of halakhah and, to a large extent, midrash. For such a unique, rare, and singular mind, the Rabbis are telling us that sacrifice is warranted. And not merely for twelve years—for twice that long. But not for anyone else. R. Akiva is the exception that proves the rule that Torah scholars should not leave their wives for an extended period.

Why, then, does Talmud include a seventh story? Will this one resolve the tension between the ideal of going away to pursue one's love of Torah and the reality of needing to be home with one's wife and lover?

> (7) Rav Yosef b. Rava [was sent] by his father to the academy of Rav Yosef [b. Chiyya]. They [the families] agreed [to support him financially] for six years. After three years, when the eve of Yom Kippur approached, [Rav Yosef b. Rava] thought: I will go to see my family. His father heard. He took an axe and went forth to meet him. He said to him, "Did you remember your whore ['zonat'kha']?" Others say that he said: "Did you remember your dove ['yonat'kha']?" They quarreled and neither one ate the last meal before the fast.

Twelve years away (let alone the twenty-four that R. Akiva's wife endured) is now off the table. Rav Yosef b. Rava is sent away for half that length of time in the hope that he will succeed as a Torah scholar yet not bring disaster on his family. Rav Yosef loves his wife so dearly that he cuts short his intended period of study to return home after three years. His father's reaction is aggressively hostile. Believing that Torah should be his son's one true lover, he likens his daughter-in-law to a whore (*zonah*), a corrupting distraction. But to Rav Yosef his wife is a dove (*yonah*), the focus of his affection and longing.

While Rav Yosef b. Rava's time away does not result in disaster, neither does it end well. There is no resolution to his quarrel with his father over his relationship with his wife. We leave father and son quarreling outside on the eve of Yom Kippur, the sacred day devoted to forgiveness and reconciliation. They have missed the last meal prior to the fast, and there is no sign they will reconcile. They must live with the tension, as must we all, when our hearts pull us in multiple worthy directions in a world of finite time and energy.

Continuing the Conversation

1. Rabbinic Procreation Reconsidered

This chapter's passage suggests a comparison of the teacher-disciple relationship with the marital relationship. Indeed, the Rabbis created an insular, homosocial world in the academy. A student often lived with his master, eating in his home and spending most of his time with his master—an intensity of relationship that facilitated the growth of the Rabbinic movement and the writing of the Talmud. Scholar of Rabbinics Howard Eilberg-Schwartz points out that in the Rabbinic world, Rabbis teaching their disciples Torah "was also a form of reproduction that could do without women. . . . [I]n the rabbinic form of reproduction, women are altogether dispensable. Males could now reproduce homosexually. If husbands inseminated women, Sages disseminated Torah to their male students."[28]

Do you hear echoes of Eilberg-Schwartz's thesis in the stories of this passage and in the case of R. Chama b. Bisa in particular? What is the most impactful and meaningful relationship you have had with a teacher or with a student? What are the advantages and dangers of intense teacher-disciple relationships?

2. I Wanted It All to Work Out!

Do you find the lack of a resolution at the end of the passage comforting or disconcerting? We all like happy endings, but Talmud often does not give us that. It is, above all, deeply steeped in the reality of our lives; and in reality, for many life dilemmas, there is no neat and clean solution. Ultimately we must live with the tension—and try to do so with integrity.

Is Talmud's assertion that even fundamental challenges in life find no easy resolution comforting and affirming of your experience, or disconcerting and disturbing because it shatters the dream of the ideal?

3. What Role Should Parents Play in the Lives and Marriages of Their Children?

In the third and seventh stories, fathers played a significant role in the outcome by encouraging their sons to invest in Torah study rather than their marital relationships. How did you react to that? What role do you believe parents should play in the life choices and priorities of their children? What role did your parents play in yours? What role do you play, or would you wish to play, in the lives of your children?

4. "A Righteous Man Knows the Life of His Beast"

In the penultimate story Rachel, the wife of R. Akiva, expresses her sense of purpose by likening herself to a beast of burden that serves its master without expectation of reward. Pirkei Avot 1:3 records this teaching of Antigonus of Sokho: "Do not be like servants who serve the master expecting to receive a reward, but rather like servants who serve the master without expectation of receiving a reward. Let reverence for Heaven guide your actions."

In our culture, service without recognition or reward is generally not viewed favorably; it is likely to be considered exploitation or abuse. Yet Rachel sees her service in a framework much larger than her own life. Her sacrifice serves God, Torah, and Israel.

Have you ever felt like a "beast of burden?" Do you make sacrifices that serve a larger purpose? If so, are recognition and reward necessary?

5. An Insidious Underbelly

An unavoidable, insidious underbelly to the stories in this passage is the contention that women are antithetical to Torah study: minimally, they are a distraction to men; at their worst, they are sirens separating men from Torah and thereby from God.

Many of the Sages viewed women as having four primary purposes: to enable men to fulfill the mitzvah of procreation, to raise children, to satisfy men's sexual urges, and to contribute to the economy of the family. In the Bavli, R. Eliezer b. Hyrcanus is quoted as saying, "One who teaches his daughter Torah teaches her obscenity" and "There is no wisdom in women other than the spinning wheel."[29]

Misogyny was not unique to the Talmud, of course; it pervaded the ancient world and sadly was not abandoned in antiquity. Does this chapter's passage toe the misogynistic line, or do you hear a more nuanced voice?

Summing Things Up

The Rabbis appreciated the significance of marriage and family life on both the individual and societal levels. While a strong and loving marital bond served both partners of the union, as well as the Jewish community and society as a whole, the values of Torah study and marriage sometimes clashed. This happened, for instance, when husbands would leave home for long periods to pursue Torah study. In such cases, women were deprived of their conjugal rights, and both husbands and wives made sacrifices and struggled to find balance. Through a series of seven stories, the Rabbis explore the challenges and pitfalls of balancing a love of Torah study with devotion to one's wife. Today, men and women also strive for balance between work and family, and between the pursuit of professional or religious goals and personal relationships. The Talmud does not present us with the ideal formula for success, but rather acknowledges the struggle and tension.

APPENDIX Theodicy, the Problem of God's Justice

Why would a good, loving, and compassionate God create a world in which evil flourishes and good people suffer? This perennial religious and theological conundrum underlies theodicy, the problem of God's justice and the vindication of God's goodness in the face of pervasive physical and moral evil.

A long and strong strain in many religious traditions teaches that a deity (or deities) possesses power and control over our life experiences. The ancient Greeks believed that human suffering was usually a sign of divine wrath in response to people's impiety.[1] In general, if one transgressed the law, failed to attend to a cultic obligation, or behaved immorally, the gods would respond by inflicting suffering. Righteousness, on the other hand, would be rewarded with good fortune. However, the gods were often capricious, competitive, and volatile, so human suffering was not *always* the result of condemnable behavior.

Fate also played a large role, and sometimes the only thing a person could control was his or her response to what life meted out. The late fifth-century BCE Athenian historian and general Thucydides wrote, "The sufferings that fate inflicts on us should be borne with patience, what enemies inflict with manly courage"—in other words, the measure of our character lies in how we play the hand we are dealt. But the Greek philosopher Epicurus, who lived a century after Thucydides, expressed the religious dilemma of theodicy (God's justice) as a trilemma, a way of presenting a serious issue as a choice between three unfavorable options; in a famous summary of Epicurus's trilemma, the eighteenth-century Scottish philosopher and skeptic David Hume writes:

If God is unable to prevent evil, then God is not omnipotent.
If God is not willing to prevent evil, then God is malevolent.
If God is both willing and able to prevent evil, then why does evil exist?[2]

The ancient Greeks were not alone in wrestling with suffering and its implications. For ancient Zoroastrians, the supreme god Ahura Mazda dealt out both reward and punishment, which was often set aside until the future world (after death) to lessen the human experience of suffering in this world. Thus here too there was not necessarily a direct and predictable correspondence between human behavior and its reward or punishment.

Much later, the sociologist and philosopher Max Weber (1860–1920) would observe that the gap between the real world of human experience and the ideal world as religion describes it grows at an accelerated pace within a climate of monotheism: "The more the development [of a religious tradition] tends toward the conception of a transcendental unitary god who is universal, the more there arises the problem of how the extraordinary power of such a god may be reconciled with the imperfection of the world that he has created and ruled over."[3] In other words, within a monotheistic understanding, one all-powerful or extremely powerful God *ought* to be able to institute justice and equity, even if God's creatures—humans beings—cannot or do not.

In the Torah, God who created the world is in charge and maintains control of it. Therefore, everything that happens—for good or ill—has a divine purpose. God rewards Israel's loyalty to the covenant and punishes violations of divine will. This idea permeates the Tanakh (Hebrew Scripture) as well. For example, we read in Deuteronomy 7: 9–10:

> Know, therefore, that only your God, Adonai, is God, the steadfast God who keeps the divine covenant faithfully to the thousandth generation of those who love [God] and keep the divine commandments, but who instantly requites with destruction those who reject [God]—never

slow with those who reject, but requiting them instantly. Therefore, observe faithfully the Instruction—the laws and rules—with which I charge you today.

Suffering, this thinking goes, is a result of our poor behavioral choices. Moreover, reward and punishment happen on a communal or national scale.

If, then, you obey the commandments that I enjoin upon you this day, loving your God Adonai and serving [God] with all your heart and all your being, I will grant the rain in your land in season, the early rain and the late. You shall gather in your new grain and wine and oil—I will also provide grass in the fields for your cattle—and thus you shall eat your fill. Take care not to be lured away to serve other gods and bow to them. For Adonai's anger will flare up against you, shutting up the skies so that there will be no rain and the ground will not yield its produce; and you will soon perish from the good land that Adonai is assigning to you. (Deuteronomy 11:13–17)

In this conception of suffering as punishment for sin, when Israel violates God's covenant as expressed through the mitzvot (commandments), God responds by visiting affliction on the Israelite nation. Numbers 13 and 14 convey that the Israelites are condemned to wander forty years in the wilderness of Sinai as punishment for their refusal to believe that God would stand by them when they entered *Eretz Yisrael* to claim their inheritance.

The classical prophets identify the corporate sins of Israel as the cause of national suffering. These sins are magnified in light of Israel's unique relationship with God and consequently God's lofty expectations concerning Israel's moral behavior. When the Assyrian Empire threatens the ten northern tribes in the eighth century BCE, the prophets Amos and Hosea understand their imminent destruction in precisely these terms. Amos speaks of moral failings:

Thus said Adonai:
For three transgressions of Israel,
For four, I will not revoke it:
Because they have sold for silver
Those whose cause was just,
And the needy for a pair of sandals.
[Ah,] you who trample the heads of the poor
Into the dust of the ground,
And make the humble walk a twisted course!
Father and son go to the same girl,
And thereby profane My holy name.
They recline by every altar
On garments taken in pledge,
And drink in the House of their God
Wine bought with fines they imposed. . . .

Hear this word, O people of Israel,
That Adonai has spoken concerning you,
Concerning the whole family that I brought up from the land of
    Egypt:
You alone have I singled out
Of all the families of the earth—
That is why I will call you to account
For all your iniquities. . . .

Assuredly, thus said Adonai my God:
An enemy, all about the land!
He shall strip you of your splendor,
And your fortresses shall be plundered. (Amos 2:6–8, 3:1–2,11)

Amos's younger contemporary, Hosea, preaches a message of imminent destruction. Sifting away other possible violations of God's law,

Hosea declares that idolatry is the root cause of the People of Israel's suffering, just as many centuries later the Rabbis will explain that the destruction of the Second Temple and the many tribulations it entailed (death, destruction, exile) resulted from the particular sin of *sinat chinam* (gratuitous hatred) within the Jewish community. Hosea's description of the coming punishment of the Northern Kingdom of Israel, whose capital is Samaria, is painfully graphic:

> Samaria must bear her guilt,
> For she has defied her God,
> They shall fall by the sword,
> Their infants shall be dashed to death,
> And their women with child ripped open. (Hosea 4:1)

The theology of divine reward and punishment affirms God's intense interest in human moral behavior and societal affairs. How people organize themselves and treat one another is a matter of divine, and hence cosmic, concern.

The prophet Ezekiel—who lived in the Southern Kingdom of Judah in the sixth century BCE, predicted the destruction of the First Temple (the Temple of Solomon), accompanied his people into exile in Babylonia, and promised God's restoration of Israel to her land—also introduced a significant change in perspective to the traditional theology: the personalization of reward and punishment. While Torah says that reward and punishment apply to the nation as a whole, Ezekiel, who wished to impress each individual with his or her responsibility for upholding God's high values, claims that divine recompense and retribution are meted out on an individual basis.

> The word of Adonai came to me: What do you mean by quoting this proverb upon the soil of Israel, "Parents eat sour grapes and their children's teeth are blunted?" As I live—declares Adonai—this proverb

shall no longer be current among you in Israel. Consider, all lives are Mine; the life of the parent and the life of the child are both Mine. Only the person who sins shall die." (Ezekiel 18:1–4)

Imploring the people to take full moral responsibility for what transpires in their society, Ezekiel rejected the notion that God punishes people for the sins of their parents and in its place introduced the notion that retribution is meted out on an individual, rather than communal, basis. This novel idea had significant implications for how people would come to think about their own suffering and that of others.

The question "Why do the innocent suffer?" is found throughout the Tanakh, with particular emphasis in the books of Deuteronomy, Esther, Daniel, Ecclesiastes, Job, and the Prophets. So fundamental to Torah is the notion of God's involvement in human suffering that the Rabbis included it in Jewish liturgy: Deuteronomy 11:13–21 (a portion of which is quoted earlier) comprises the middle section of the *Shema*, traditionally recited twice daily.

Yet the Rabbis of the Talmud recognized that the reality of life does not bear out the belief concerning reward and punishment on a granular level. How often do the righteous suffer and the evil prosper? They reasoned, therefore, that often reward and punishment happen not in *this* world, but in *olam ha-ba* (the world to come).[4] Yet this does not wholly solve the question of God's justice.

Scholar, theologian, and rabbi Louis Jacobs (1920–2006) summarizes the dilemma:

> The biblical authors and the Talmudic Rabbis, unlike the later Jewish philosophers, do not consider the general problem of evil in the universe, of why the benevolent Creator should have brought evil into being. The earlier writers seem to have accepted the existence of evil as a "given," seeing this, in so far as they gave any thought to it, as belonging, like questions on the true nature of God, to an area which

it is beyond the capacity of the human mind to grasp. Their difficulty was not with the problem of evil *per se* but rather with the apparently random way in which sufferings are visited on creatures.[5]

When we fast-forward to the nineteenth century, the early Reformers excised the second paragraph of the *Shema* from the siddur (prayer book) because they did not believe that God operates this way. Living in a post-Enlightenment world of science, they did not subscribe to the theological claim that God, like the Wizard of Oz, is managing the world from behind a curtain. Reconstructionist Judaism concurred; the Reconstructionist siddur provides an alternative passage for the second paragraph of *Shema*: Deuteronomy 28:1–6 and 30:15–19."[6]

Certainly, many people today do adhere to classical biblical theology, both in its pre-Ezekiel and post-Ezekiel formulations. But for many others it is a highly problematic theology that seems to "blame the victim" for suffering.

A second classical answer is that, on occasion, God metes out suffering to test our faithfulness. Each year, as part of the yearly cycle of Torah readings, and again on Rosh Hashanah, Jews read the story of Abraham's willing sacrifice of his son Isaac:

> Some time afterward, God put Abraham to the test. God said to him, "Abraham," and he answered, "Here I am." And God said, "Take your son, your favored one, Isaac, whom you love, and go to the land of Moriah, and offer him there as a burnt offering on one of the heights that I will point out to you." (Genesis 22:1–2)

The Torah makes clear that the ordeal Abraham is about to undergo, which will cause him inordinate suffering (whether or not God requires Abraham to actually carry out the sacrifice of Isaac), is a test administered by God.[7] This perspective offers worshipers the opportunity to view suffering as a trial, or challenge, in which constructive endurance is a measure of success.

This comports with the message of the book of Job, in which the protagonist, Job, endures sufferings of epic proportion. The narrative frame (chapters 1–2 and 42:7–17) in particular portrays a righteous and long-suffering man with limitless patience and faith. For this Job, suffering is a test of his faithfulness to God.[8] The angelic prosecuting attorney in God's heavenly court, Satan, has claimed that Job's faithfulness is purely a function of the riches and blessings God has bestowed on him. Take them away, Satan dares God, and Job's faithfulness will evaporate like a drop of water in the desert at high noon. God delegates to Satan the power to conduct precisely this experiment, and Job's suffering begins. Throughout the ordeal, despite his suffering, Job remains faithful. When his wife advises that he curse God and die, Job responds, *Should we accept only good from God and not accept evil?* (Job 1:10). In the end, Job is compensated for faithfully affirming God with restored fields, flocks, and herds, as well as ten new children. Job thus exemplifies the notion that human suffering can be a test of faithfulness administered by God, but also suggests that human suffering is often decoupled from divine reward and punishment and more a matter of divine caprice.

Many people find value in viewing their own suffering as a test of their faith in God, or perhaps of their ability to affirm God, life, goodness, and kindness, despite their suffering. In this way, they employ suffering in the service of righteousness.

A third classical understanding of suffering is that it is a necessary step on the path to a greater good. In other words, suffering can bring redemption in the long run. Joseph's brothers sell him into slavery to be rid of their bratty, favored younger sibling, the very sight of whom reminds them that they are not the preferred sons of Jacob. Had Jacob not shown such unremitting favoritism toward Joseph, the firstborn of his beloved departed wife, Rachel, Joseph's dreams that he would one day have power over the entire family might not have so rankled his brothers. But in the context of Jacob's powerful partiality the brothers sink to a despicable level, selling Joseph to a passing caravan of traders, who in turn sell him as a slave in Egypt.

Yet, many years later, when Joseph's brothers lie prostrate before Joseph offering themselves as slaves, Joseph, who has not forgotten a moment of the suffering he endured because of them, offers a surprising perspective:

> But Joseph said to them, "Have no fear! Am I a substitute for God? Besides, although you intended me harm, God intended it for good, so as to bring about the present result—the survival of many people. And so, fear not. I will sustain you and your children." Thus he reassured them, speaking kindly to them. (Genesis 50:19–21)

Speaking through Joseph, the author of this narrative is imparting that God imposes suffering as a necessary step in bringing redemption.

The Ten Plagues against Egypt provide another example. The Egyptians' suffering is not punishment for enslaving the Israelites, but a means to impress upon Pharaoh, his courtiers, and all the Egyptians the divine power of God, entirely above and beyond that of Pharaoh, whom the Egyptians erroneously worship as their god. The Egyptians' suffering is a by-product of this divine demonstration. As the Torah tells the tale, God choreographs Israel's spectacular redemption to make a statement about the nature of God in contrast with the idols and rulers that people might worship. The Ten Plagues—with all the suffering they inflict—enhance that spectacle by demonstrating God's incomparable power.

To summarize, the three classical views of how God operates in the world vis-à-vis suffering are (1) God rewards loyalty to the covenantal mitzvot and punishes violations; (2) God metes out suffering to test human faithfulness; and (3) human suffering is sometimes a necessary step on the road to redemption.

In the centuries after the Talmud was written, many Jewish thinkers would join the ongoing conversation about suffering, theodicy, and divine providence, offering other ideas for conceiving God, God's relationship with the physical universe, and the human experience of suffering.

GLOSSARY

aggadah (pl. *aggadot*): narrative, nonlegalistic exegetical commentaries on Torah that are a staple of Rabbinic literature in both Talmud and midrash; aggadic material consists generally of stories and parable

aliyah: lit. "going up"; the term is used in a number of ways, including moving to the Land of Israel or from within the Land of Israel to Jerusalem, as well as an individual "going up" to bless or read Torah in the synagogue

amah (pl. *amot*): "cubit"; a measure of length defined as the distance from the tip of the middle finger to the elbow, usually estimated as eighteen inches

Amidah: lit. "standing"; refers to the prayer also known as the *Shemoneh Esrei*, or "Eighteen Benedictions," which constitutes one of the pillars of statutory Jewish prayer; further referred to as the *Tefillah*, the *Amidah* is traditionally recited thrice daily; an additional *Amidah* is recited during the *Musaf* (or "additional") service on Shabbat and holy days

amora (pl. *amora'im*): one of the second stratum of Rabbis who lived and taught between 200 and 500 CE in Babylonia and the Land of Israel; the *amora'im* are the Sages who wrote the Gemara

amud (pl. *amudim*): one side of a talmudic folio (denoted "a" or "b")

av bet din: lit. "chief of the court," the second highest position in the Sanhedrin during the Second Jewish Commonwealth

baraita: lit. "outside"; refers to mishnaic-era Rabbinic teachings that are not included in the Mishnah or either Talmud—hence, are "outside" the canonical texts

bat kol: lit. "heavenly voice"; a literary device used in Torah to express God's viewpoint

Bavli/Babylonian Talmud: Talmud, lit. "teaching" or "learning," refers to the central text of Rabbinic Judaism that serves as the primary source for Jewish religious practice and ethics; the Babylonian Talmud is composed of two integrated texts: the Mishnah, a collection of first- and second-century oral traditions from *Eretz Yisrael* compiled by Rabbi Yehudah ha-Nasi at the end of the second century; and Gemara, an extended discussion and commentary on the Mishnah that features four centuries of complex discussions, debate, legal decisions, theological views, and Mishnah-inspired stories collected, organized, and redacted by the Sages in the Babylonian academies (primarily Sura, Pumbedita, and Machuza) between 200 and 600 CE; following the organization of the Mishnah substrate, the Talmud is divided into six *sedarim* (orders), which are, in turn, subdivided into *massekhtot* (tractates); this massive work, also known as the Bavli, and abbreviated BT, is typically published in twenty volumes, and in more recent editions with modern commentaries, many more volumes

bet midrash: lit. "study house" or academy

bikkurim: first fruits of the harvest, which were brought as a sacrificial gift to the Temple, in accordance with Exodus 23:16,19 and Deuteronomy 26:1–10

bikur cholim: lit. "visiting the sick"; helping take care of the sick is considered a mitzvah (religious obligation)

brit (pl. britot): lit. "covenant"

brit milah: "covenant of circumcision" performed on a boy's eighth day of life as prescribed in Genesis 17:9–14 and Leviticus 12:3

chag (pl. chagim): lit. "holy day"; the primary holy days are the three pilgrimage festivals: Sukkot, Pesach (Passover), and Shavuot; minor *chagim* include Tu B'Shevat, Purim, and Chanukah

chakham: lit. "wise"; a term applied to a Rabbi or Sage of the talmudic period who was learned in Torah

cheil: an area ten cubits wide that surrounded the courtyards of the Jerusalem Temple, demarcated by a fence called the *soreg*

chevruta: lit. "friendship" or "companionship"; refers to the traditional study partnership in the *bet midrash*, by which pairs of students studied, analyzed, discussed, and debated the Talmud

chilazon: a rare mollusk whose bodily fluid was used to produce the blue dye to make the blue thread attached to the fringes tied to the corners of a garment, as prescribed by Numbers 15:38

chuppah: wedding canopy under which the couple stands at their marriage ceremony

daf (pl. *dapim*): a folio of Talmud, consisting of the front and back of the folio (designated "a" and "b"); one *daf* comprises two *amudim* (single sides of a folio)

derekh eretz: lit. "the way of the earth"; kindness, courtesy, consideration

Eretz Yisrael: lit. "the Land of Israel"

exegesis: a critical explanation or interpretation of a text, usually a biblical text

galut: lit. "exile"

gaonic period: The period following the redaction of the Babylonian Talmud, from the seventh through the beginning of the eleventh century, named for the heads of the Rabbinic academies in Babylonia (the *Ge'onim*)

Gehenna/Gehinnom: purgatory; derived from the name of a valley outside Jerusalem (Valley of the Son of Hinnom) where, according to the Bible (2 Chronicles 28:3, 3:6; Jeremiah 7:31, 19:2–6), people sacrificed their children to the Canaanite god Molech

Gemara: the component of Talmud that comprises an extended discussion and commentary on the Mishnah, featuring complex discussions, debate, legal decisions, theological views, and Mishnah-inspired stories; there are two Gemaras, one composed in Babylonia (hence the "Babylonian Talmud") and one in the Land of Israel (the "Jerusalem Talmud")

gemilut chasadim: lit. "deeds of loving-kindness"; considered a mitzvah of paramount importance

gezerah shavah: lit. "similar law[s]"; a Rabbinic hermeneutical principle whereby a halakhic decision in one circumstance is inferred from a halakhic decision in a similar case; more specifically, when the same word or phrase appears in two scriptural passages, the halakhah applying to one is applied to the other because they share the same word or phrase

halakhah: lit. "the path" or "the way"; a term that has come to be used synonymously with "Jewish law," although its real meaning is the "path" or "way" decisions are made using sacred texts, classical hermeneutics, and reasoning; halakhah also refers to the corpus of Rabbinic legal texts

Hekhal: lit. "Sanctuary"; the Jerusalem Temple

kavanah: spiritual focus and intention in prayer; spontaneous prayer

kavod: honor, dignity, or glory

ketubah (pl. *ketubot*): a document that constituted a wife's legal lien on her husband's property, given to her at the time of marriage to ensure her economic viability should the marriage end through divorce or the husband's death; today *ketubot* have little economic force since civil laws in most locations protect women, but they tend to be more an expression of the couple's emotional and spiritual commitment to one another and, as illuminated documents, an art form

keva: fixed, statutory prayer

kibbud av va-em: lit. "honoring father and mother"; one of the Ten Commandments, found in Exodus 20:12 and Deuteronomy 5:16

Kodesh ha-Kodashim: lit. "Holy of Holies"; the inner sanctum of the Jerusalem Temple

kohen (pl. *kohanim*): lit. "priest"; those descended by family tradition from the line of Aaron, the first High Priest of Israel

k'vod ha-briot: human dignity

Ma'ariv: lit. "Evening"; the designation for the evening prayer service *machloket l'shem shamayim*: lit. "controversy for the sake of heaven"; debate and disagreement that generate insight and ideas and serve to promote Torah learning and practice

mamzer: a child conceived by a man and woman who were not halakhically permitted to marry one another at the time of conception; often translated "bastard," although the English term is not a perfect fit in meaning; the child's status is called *mamzerut*

massekhet (pl. *massekhtot*): lit. "tractate"; the organizational elements of talmudic literature, similar to chapters; there are sixty-three tractates in the Mishnah, organized in six "orders"

megillah (pl. *megillot*): lit. "scroll"; usually refers to the Five Scrolls: Song of Songs, Ruth, Lamentations, Ecclesiastes, and Esther, but during the Talmudic period referred to biblical books aside from Torah because they were written on scrolls

Mikdash: the "Holy" Temples in Jerusalem; the First Temple was built by King Solomon and destroyed by the Babylonians in 586 BCE, and the Second Temple, built after the Jews returned from exile in Babylonia, was destroyed by the Romans in 70 CE

mincha: lit. "present" or "meal offering"; refers to the daily afternoon sacrifice offered in the Temple in Jerusalem; today *Mincha* refers to the afternoon prayers, which replace the *mincha* offering

Mishkan: the "Tabernacle" in the wilderness

Mishnah: from the word meaning "to study" or "to review"; a collection of oral traditions of the *tanna'im* compiled by Rabbi Yehudah ha-Nasi (Judah the Prince, d. ~217 CE) at the end of the second century CE; it is divided into six *sedarim* (orders), with each order further divided into *massekhtot* (tractates); an individual oral teaching is also called a "mishnah," and the plural is *mishnayot*

Mishneh Torah: lit. "Repetition of the Torah"; law code written by Moses Maimonides between 1170 and 1180 in Egypt and subtitled *Sefer Yad ha-Chazakah* (Book of the strong hand)

mitzvah (pl. *mitzvot*): religious obligation or commandment *musaf*: lit. "additional," referring to additional sacrifices offered in the Temple in Jerusalem on Shabbat, holy days, and Rosh Chodesh (the new month); *Musaf* also refers to a prayer service consisting primarily of an additional *Amidah*, recited on Shabbat, holy days, and Rosh Chodesh in many synagogues, usually following *Shacharit*

musar: Jewish ethics; in the nineteenth century Rabbi Yisrael Lipkin Salanter originated the Musar Movement, an educational and cultural movement focusing on the refinement of individual character traits; it is enjoying a resurgence in popularity today

nasi: "president" of the Sanhedrin (the assembly of Rabbinic authorities in the Land of Israel), a position that, according to tradition, was reserved for direct descendants of Hillel

olam ha-ba: lit. "the world to come"; in traditional Jewish eschatology, history will end when the Messiah comes, heralding an age of peace and tranquility, resurrection of the dead, and the afterlife (world to come)

Oral Torah (*Torah she-b'al peh*): refers to the Babylonian Talmud; the Rabbis who composed the Talmud claimed that it was "Oral Torah" given to Moses on Mount Sinai along with the "Written Torah" (the Five Books of Moses), but transmitted orally through the generations until Rabbi Yehudah ha-Nasi commissioned its writing at the end of the second century CE

pasul: unfit or disqualified for use to fulfill a mitzvah

pe'ah: lit. "corner"; refers to the portion of the crop that must be left standing in the field for the poor to harvest for themselves as their due, in accordance with Leviticus 19:9 and 23:22; Pe'ah is also the name of a tractate of the Mishnah and the Talmud

Pentateuch: lit. "five books"; refers to the Five Books of Moses that the Written Torah comprises: Genesis, Exodus, Leviticus, Numbers, and Deuteronomy

Rabban: title of the *nasi* (president, patriarch) of the Sanhedrin (the assembly of Rabbinic authorities in the Land of Israel)

resh galuta: exilarch, lit. "head of the exile"; the Jewish leader representing the Jewish community to the government in Babylonia; the exilarchs traced their family line to King David

Rosh Chodesh: the "new moon" marking the beginning of the lunar month in the Jewish calendar

Sanhedrin: the "council" of Rabbinic judges that constituted the courts of justice in Israel from the late Second Temple period until 358 CE; the Great Sanhedrin consisted of seventy-one Rabbis convened in cases of national significance, such as declaration of war or the trial of a king; a Lesser Sanhedrin court of twenty-three heard criminal and civil cases

satan: "the adversary"; originally conceived as a position in the heavenly court approximately equivalent to the prosecuting attorney, filled by angels on a rotating basis; later, the position came to be conceived as the name of a particular angel, Satan, who was given the job of being the prosecuting attorney or adversary in the heavenly court

seder (pl. sedarim): lit. "order"; the broader organizing element of the Mishnah; orders were subdivided into tractates

sefer Torah (pl. *sifrei Torah*): scroll of Torah, written on parchment, for use in public Torah readings

Shacharit: the morning prayer service, so called because *shachar* means "dawn"

Shekhinah: God's indwelling Presence in the world, from the verb meaning "dwell" or "live"

shemitah: the biblical sabbatical year, every seventh year, during which the land lies fallow, debts are cancelled, and indentured servants are released (see Exodus 23:10–11, Leviticus 25:1–7,18–22, Deuteronomy 15:1–6)

Shemoneh Esrei (see *Amidah*): lit. "Eighteen Benedictions"; the central prayer of the evening, morning, and afternoon prayer services

shivah: the seven days of mourning following burial observed by a parent, spouse, sibling, or child of the deceased

siddur: the Jewish prayer book; from the word meaning "order," because there is a prescribed order to the prayers that are recited thrice daily

sinat chinam: baseless or gratuitous hatred

Stamma'im, stammaitic: the term *Stamma'im* refers to the unnamed redactors of the Talmud who followed the *amora'im*; stammaitic refers to the activity of these unnamed redactors and the stratum of Talmud they edited

sugya: literary unit of the Talmud

tagin: decorative "crowns" that some scribes add to certain letters of a Torah scroll

tahor/taharah: lit. "pure/ritual purity"; according to the Torah, a priest had to be in this state in order to offer sacrifices

talmidei chakhamim: lit. "students of the Sages"; full-time students of Torah in the academies of Babylonia and *Eretz Yisrael*

tame/tumah: lit. "impure/ritual impurity"; according to Leviticus, the primary source of ritual impurity is contact with the dead; others include being present in a building or under a roof where a dead body lies, contact with certain carrion (including many insects and all lizards), childbirth, a group of skin afflictions under the umbrella term *tzara'at*, and contact with certain body fluids; the rules concerning purification varied with the cause of *tumah*

tamid: lit. "continuous"; the daily sacrifice made in the Temple, morning and afternoon, also called the *olat tamid* (daily burnt offering), as set out in Exodus 29:38–42 and Numbers 28:1–8; Tamid is also the title of a Talmudic tractate that discusses the priests' activities and responsibilities from early morning through the offering of the *tamid*

Tanakh: Hebrew Scripture; "Tanakh" is an acronym for the three major sections that constitute the Hebrew Bible: T̲orah (Five Books of Moses), N̲evi'im (Prophets), and K̲etuvim (Writings)

tanna (pl. *tanna'im*): A Sage (pl. the Rabbinic Sages) of the first and second centuries CE, whose opinions are recorded in the Mishnah (the collection of oral traditions that serves as the substrate of the Talmud)

Tefillah: lit. "prayer"; refers both to prayer in general and to the central prayer of the formal prayer service, the *Amidah*, also called the *Shemoneh Esrei* (Eighteen Benedictions)

tefillin: phylacteries consisting of two small black lacquer boxes containing scriptural passages that are affixed to the head and arm with leather straps and worn during weekday morning prayer, a literal enactment of *Bind them as a sign on your hand and let them be as a frontlet between your eyes* (Deuteronomy 6:8)

tekhelet: Numbers 15:38 and Exodus 25:4 prescribe that a *p'til tekhelet* (thread of blue) be attached to the required fringes on the corners of a garment; also the term for the blue dye used to produce the threads for the fringes and in the High Priest's vestments; this dye was made from the bodily fluid of a rarely found (and consequently expensive) mollusk called a *chilazon*; the term has come to refer to the dye that produces the blue color

teshuvah: lit. "return"; repentance

tokhachah: rebuke or admonition; the term connotes a litany of curses that will befall Israel if they fail to keep God's law (see Leviticus chapter 26 and Deuteronomy 28:15–68)

Torah she-bi-khetav: the "Written Torah"; the Five Books of Moses (Genesis, Exodus, Leviticus, Numbers, and Deuteronomy)

Tosafot: medieval commentaries on the Talmud in the form of critical glosses (marginal annotation) composed in the eleventh and twelfth centuries by Rashi's students, sons-in-law, grandsons, and others in France and Germany

Tosefta: lit. "supplement"; a compilation of Jewish Oral Law from the period concurrent with the Mishnah (second century CE) that corresponds closely to the Mishnah but is not identical to it; Tosefta provides attributions for many laws that Mishnah reports anonymously and includes aggadic material and discussions not found in the Mishnah; tradition attributes the redaction of Tosefta to R. Chiyya and his student R. Oshayah; modern scholars disagree about its origins

tzedakah: righteousness or charity

tzitzit: ritual fringes attached to the four corners of a garment, as instructed in Numbers 15:37–41 and Deuteronomy 22:12; the tallit (prayer shawl) was produced to facilitate the observance of this mitzvah once clothing no longer had natural corners—by attaching tzitzit to the tallit's corners

world to come (see *olam haba*)

Written Torah (*Torah she-bi-khtav*): the Five Books of Moses: Genesis, Exodus, Leviticus, Numbers, and Deuteronomy

Yerushalmi/The Jerusalem Talmud: Like the Babylonian Talmud, the Jerusalem Talmud has two components: the Mishnah that was compiled at the end of the second century CE, and a discussion and commentary on the Mishnah written by the Sages in the Land of Israel (primarily in the academies in Tiberias, Tzippori, and Caesarea) from the end of the second century CE through the fifth century CE; the Yerushalmi, abbreviated JT, was completed earlier and is shorter than the Babylonian Talmud

yissurim shel ahavah: lit. "chastisements of love"; the belief that certain undeserved suffering is a gift from God through which the one who chooses to accept the *yissurim* atones in this world for sins committed and is thereby entitled to a larger reward in the world to come

yovel: jubilee year; occurring every fiftieth year, the jubilee year was biblically designated as a time when debts were annulled and land returned to its original owners (see Leviticus 25:8–17, 25–28)

NOTES

Introduction

1. The Hasidic teacher Reb Bunam told a similar story of a man named Yitzhak b. Yakil. The motif of this story is found in the folklore of many cultures; it conveys a universal message.
2. The tractate of Talmud known as Pirkei Avot (often translated Ethics of the Ancestors) tells us, "Shimon ha-Tzaddik was one of the last survivors of the Great Assembly. He used to say: The world is sustained by three things — by Torah [study], by worship, and by deeds of loving-kindness" (Pirkei Avot 1:2).
3. Shaye Cohen, *Maccabees to the Mishnah*, 219.
4. Stuart Cohen, *Three Crowns*, 3.
5. Holtz, *Rabbi Akiva*, 1.
6. Sukkot, celebrated in the autumn after the last crops are brought in, expresses thanksgiving at the end of the harvest. Passover, in early spring, marks the time of year when new lambs are born and the wheat is planted. Shavuot, in early summer, marks the early barley harvest.
7. Passover is associated with the Exodus from Egypt, the liberation of the Jews from servitude to Pharaoh, as told in the book of Exodus. Shavuot, seven weeks later, commemorates the giving of the Torah to Israel at Mount Sinai. Sukkot recalls the forty years the Israelites wandered through the wilderness after leaving Egypt before they entered *Eretz Yisrael*. Thus, the story of the people's redemption from Israel, covenant with God at Mount Sinai, and journey to reclaim and settle the land of their ancestors is told — indeed, relived — each year through the festivals.
8. Often translated "charity," tzedakah actually means "righteousness" and refers to a wide range of behaviors considered righteous, chief among them generosity toward those who have less than we do.

9. *Gemilut chasadim* means "deeds of loving-kindness." The distinction between tzedakah and *gemilut chasadim* is described beautifully in the Bavli: "Tzedakah can be achieved only with one's money, but *gemilut chasadim* can be accomplished with one's person [i.e., through an action] or one's money. Tzedakah can be given only to the poor; *gemilut chasadim* can be done for both the rich and the poor. Tzedakah can be given only to the living; *gemilut chasadim* can be done both for the living and for the dead" (BT Sukkot 49b).
10. *Derekh eretz*, literally, "the way of the land," means treating others with proper decency and courtesy, essential to a civilized and functional society.
11. Pirkei Avot 5:19.
12. They are often called "School/House of Hillel" and the "School/House of Shammai" or simply Bet Hillel and Bet Shammai.
13. BT Eruvin 13b.
14. Emerson, *Works*, 2:11.
15. This may be an urban legend, but at least it's entertaining.
16. *JPS Hebrew-English* TANAKH.
17. Stein, *Contemporary Torah*, 2006.

1. Finding Our Place

1. A group of Rabbinic scholars known as the Masoretes (from the Hebrew term *mesorah*, meaning "to pass down" and hence "tradition") between the seventh and tenth centuries CE copied, edited, and corrected the text of the Tanakh using extant manuscripts. They also added the diacritic markings (both vowels for vocalization and trope for chanting) that are in use today. Since the completion of their project, their version of the Torah text has been broadly accepted with few emendations.
2. BT Bava Metzia 59b.
3. Genesis Rabbah 1:14. Another version of this interpretation is found in the Babylonian Talmud, Tractate Chagigah 12a–b. Here R. Akiva recounts the following teaching as one he learned from his teacher Nachum Ish Gamzu. R. Akiva says that without the two occurrences of *et*, "Heaven" would be taken as God's name, rather than what God created. R. Ishmael then asks, "What need is there for the second iteration of *et* (wouldn't the first occurrence have sufficed)?"; R. Akiva responds that the second *et* tells us that

the heavens were created before the earth. Here, too, R. Akiva attributes significant meaning to a particle that has no translatable meaning.
4. *Pesikta de-Rav Kahana, Parah*, Buber ed. 39b.
5. BT Berakhot 61b.
6. Berlin, *Ha'amek Davar*, introduction to sec. 5.
7. Bruns, "Midrash and Allegory," 627–28.

2. Controlling Our Anger

1. Yoichi Chida and Andrew Steptoe, "The Association of Anger and Hostility with Future Coronary Heart Disease," *Journal of the American College of Cardiology* 53, no. 11 (2009): 936–46.
2. M. L. Staicu and M. Cutov, "Anger and Health Risk Behaviors," *Journal of Medicine and Life* 3, no. 4 (Nov. 15, 2010): 372–75. Also: R. S. Jorgensen et al., "Elevated Blood Pressure and Personality: A Meta-analytic Review." *Psychological Bulletin* 120 (September 1996): 293–320.
3. The notion that depression is anger turned inward was initially proposed by Sigmund Freud in "Mourning and Melancholia," in *The Standard Edition of the Complete Psychological Works of Sigmund Freud*, ed. and trans. James Strachey in collaboration with Anna Freud (London: Hogarth Press, 1914–16), 14:243–58 (accessible at http://www.english.upenn.edu/~cavitch/pdf-library/Freud_MourningAndMelancholia.pdf). R. L. Carhart-Harris et al., in "Mourning and Melancholia Revisited: Correspondences between Principles of Freudian Metapsychology and Empirical Findings in Neuropsychiatry," *Annals of General Psychiatry* (2008): 7–9, use evidence from neurophysiology to make the case for some of Freud's psychoanalytic theories.
4. Jennifer L. Steward et al., "Anger Style, Psychopathology, and Regional Brain Activity," *Emotion* 8, no. 5 (October 2008): 701–13.
5. These include the Virginia Tech shooting (2007), the assassination attempt on U.S. Rep. Gabrielle Giffords (2011), Sandy Hook Elementary School shooting (2012), and the Fort Hood shootings (2009 and 2014), among others.
6. Laura L. Hayes, "How to Stop Violence," *Slate*, April 9, 2014, http://www.slate.com/articles/health_and_science/medical_examiner/2014/04/anger_causes_violence_treat_it_rather_than_mental_illness_to_stop_mass_murder.html.

7. Eyder Peralta, "On the Streets of Baltimore, Trying to Understand the Anger," NPR.org, April 28, 2015, http://www.npr.org/sections/thetwo-way/2015/04/28/402739255/on-the-streets-of-baltimore-trying-to-understand-the-anger.
8. White, *Talking about God*, 2. Moses Maimonides (eleventh century) said that all human language is inherently limiting and hence inadequate to describe God. Were we to say, "God is good," we would of necessity be limiting God to our limited understanding of good. Therefore, the only statements we can accurately make about God are negative statements, such as "God is not evil and does no evil." Maimonides's philosophy, as articulated in *Guide for the Perplexed* 1:58, is termed *via negativa*. Of this approach, White says (p. 2): "Not even adopting the most rigorous *via negativa* can do more than testify to the dilemma that confronts us here: either it seeks to retain some content to its talk about God, in which case the basic problem remains, or it reduces language about God to talking about something-I-know-not-what about which nothing can be said."
9. While some have claimed that Akatriel-Yah is the name of an angelic figure, almost all agree that this is one of the names of God, as the additional appellation "Lord of Hosts" confirms. Yishmael's report is sometimes understood to be a vision of God seated on the heavenly throne, much like Ezekiel's vision of God's chariot (Ezekiel 1), but there is no reason not to accept Yishmael's report at face value: he believed he saw God seated on the Ark of the Covenant, God's earthly throne.
10. I have provided a literal translation because this understanding of the verse is what the Rabbis have in mind.
11. The New Jewish Publication Society translation in *JPS Hebrew-English* TANAKH.
12. Fox, *Five Books of Moses*.
13. Steinsaltz, *The Talmud*, 281.
14. "The enemies of Israel" is a euphemism for Israel. The very suggestion that God would destroy Israel was so anathema to the Rabbis that they employed a euphemism rather than state the idea outright.
15. Variant reading: heretic.

16. Both Temples in Jerusalem were situated so that the opening to the Holy of Holies, the inner sanctum that contained the Ark of the Covenant and where, according to tradition, God dwelled, was on the east side. One who faced God, therefore, faced west—back to the rising sun.
17. Barbara Summers and Brian Lanker, *I Dream a World: Portraits of Black Women Who Changed America* (New York: Stewart Tabori & Chang, 1989).
18. Maimonides, Mishneh Torah, *Hilkhot De'ot* 2:3.
19. Translation mine.
20. BT Eruvin 65b.
21. Rebbe Nachman of Breslov, *The Gentle Weapon*, 44.
22. Translation mine.

3. Understanding Our Suffering

1. This is not true for all human beings. Some individuals have a medical condition known as congenital insensitivity to pain (CIP), whereby one is completely insensitive to pain. This is exceptionally dangerous. People with CIP, particularly young children, can sustain a broken bone or severe burn without realizing it.
2. The world to come, or *olam ha-ba*, refers to a constellation of rabbinic ideas and beliefs related to the afterlife, ranging from a heavenly world enjoyed by a righteous person immediately after death to the eschatological messianic kingdom of God that will prevail after the "End of Days" and resurrection of all the righteous dead.
3. BT Sanhedrin 101a.
4. Ehrman, *God's Problem*, 1.
5. Who can forget the claim of religious conservatives Pat Robertson, Hal Lindsey, and Charles Colson that the devastation wrought by Hurricane Katrina in August 2005 was God's punishment for America's sins?
6. This verse concludes a long passage known as the *tokhachah* (rebuke), which describes the afflictions that will befall the nation of Israel if the people violate their covenant with God.
7. Understood here as the "way to eternal life."
8. BT Kiddushin 31b.

9. Yet another possibility is that the *baraita* intends to claim that one's time in Gehenna will be reduced. Gehenna (or *Gehinnom*) is purgatory, the place of punishment and spiritual purification where the Rabbis imagined one goes after death to atone for one's sins. They taught that one spends no more than a year in Gehenna and afterward the soul receives its reward in the world to come. A shortened stay in Gehenna means that the soul arrives in *olam ha-ba* sooner.

10. When Torah says that God *visits the iniquity of parents upon children, and children's children, upon the third and fourth generations*, does this mean that God causes children to suffer for their parents' sins? I would suggest that this is a poetic formulation intended to compare God's enormous inclination to forgive (to "the thousandth generation") to God's desire for revenge (to "the third and fourth generation"). On balance, God leans heavily toward forgiveness. Nonetheless, punishing a child for the sins of a parent is a morally troubling idea. When Jeremiah raises it in 32:18, he may be suggesting that Israel's enemies will, in time, suffer for the crimes they have committed against Israel, which explains why buying land in Anatot, near Jerusalem, is a good investment despite the imminent destruction of Jerusalem by Nebuchadnezzar, king of Babylonia: in the future God will punish Israel's enemies and restore the land to the Jewish people. Alternatively, Jeremiah may be repeating the refrain of Exodus 34:6–7 to assure the people that God is far more inclined to forgive them than to extend their punishment. Long before the Talmud was written, the prophet Ezekiel rejected the notion that God punishes children for their parents' sins, claiming unequivocally, *The person who sins alone shall die. A child shall not share the burden of a parent's guilt, nor shall a parent share the burden of a child's guilt; the righteousness of the righteous shall be accounted to that person alone, and the wickedness of the wicked shall be accounted to that person alone* (Ezekiel 18:20).

11. *Nega'im*, "plagues," is another term for *tzara'at*. Both terms refer to a category of eruptive skin diseases discussed in Leviticus 13. *Nega'im* and *tzara'at* are often incorrectly translated as "leprosy," a chronic bacterial infection known as Hansen's disease.

12. In *Eretz Yisrael*, a person afflicted by a *nega* was isolated outside the city in accordance with Leviticus 13:46. *Nega'im* were not considered chastisements of love due to the restrictive treatment required by Torah.
13. Tractate Nega'im (Blemishes) in the Order Tohorot (Purities) discusses the various forms of *tzara'at*, skin afflictions that affect skin, clothing, and houses, per Leviticus 12-15. Mishnah *Nega'im*, which has no Gemara to accompany it, describes the various manifestations of *tzara'at* and the rituals employed to purify a person or object afflicted with it.
14. BT Menachot 110b.
15. BT Berakhot 20a: R. Yochanan would go and sit at the gates of the bathhouse. He said, "When the daughters of Israel come out of the bathhouse, they will look at me and thereby have children as handsome as I am."
16. Ben-Shahar, *Pursuit of Perfect*, 193–94.
17. BT Berakhot 59a.
18. Recited in a message of healing and reconciliation at a service dedicated to HIV/AIDS sufferers in Johannesburg, South Africa, on December 6, 2000, Nelson Rolihlahla Mandela, 18 July 1918–5 December 2013, http://www.mandela.gov.za/mandela_speeches/2000/001206_healing.htm.
19. Nouwen, *Out of Solitude*, 34.
20. BT Nedarim 39b.

4. Approaching Prayer

1. Stern, *Gates of Prayer*, xi.
2. This is an Aristotelian conception of God.
3. Kaplan, *Meaning of God*, 76.
4. This verse from *Shir ha-Yichud* may well be more an expression of panentheism than pantheism. The distinction between the two is that according to the monism theory of pantheism, all is God (one could say that "God" is a label to the totality of the universe), whereas panentheism is the view that all is *in* God; that is, the entire universe is contained within God, but there is something of God that exists outside, or extends beyond, the universe. There is no consensus among panentheists concerning precisely how to characterize the aspect of God that exists outside the universe, but it is usually understood in abstract terms, such as existence itself. Many

biblical verses can be interpreted through a traditional, pantheistic, or panentheistic lens. For example, *The whole earth is filled with God's glory* (Isaiah 6:3) would be understood by a traditionalist to convey that God is manifest in every aspect of the universe. The pantheist would interpret the same verse to mean that the whole world is to be equated with God's glory, a way of saying God's essence. A panentheist would understand the verse to affirm that God encompasses all that we find in the universe; that is, God is in all things.

5. For example, see Rubenstein, *Creation and Composition*; *Culture of the Babylonian Talmud*, 5, 30–31; and *Stories of the Babylonian Talmud*, 21.
6. Rubenstein, *Culture of the Babylonian Talmud*, 2.
7. For example, BT Megillah 28a.
8. BT Shabbat 30b. The terms *akpid/yakpidu* and *kapdanut* have the same Hebrew root: *kof-peh-dalet*.
9. The unattributed material of the Talmud is called *stam* (anonymous). Rabbi David Weiss Halivni coined the term "stamma'im" to describe the anonymous redactors who shaped the *sugyot*.
10. Rubinstein, *Culture of the Babylonian Talmud*, 4–5.
11. Heschel, *Man's Quest for God*, 68.
12. Heschel, *Man's Quest for God*, 67.
13. M Berakhot 4:4, 28b.
14. BT Berakhot 29b.

5. Honoring Our Parents

1. Blidstein, *Honor Thy Father and Mother*, 4. Blidstein cites BT Kiddushin 31b, which recounts: "When R. Yosef heard his mother's footsteps, he would say, 'Let me rise before the *Shekhinah* ["Divine Presence"].'"
2. Op. cit., 5.
3. BT Kiddushin 31b.
4. BT Kiddushin 32a.
5. Leviticus 19:9 and 23:22. Related to *pe'ah* are several other forms of charity via agriculture, including: (1) the obligation to leave *leket* (gleanings), grain that falls from the reaper's hand or sickle (Leviticus 19:9 and 23:22); (2) *shikh'chah*

(forgotten sheaves) that are left or overlooked by harvesters (Deuteronomy 24:21); (3) *olelot* (clusters), immature clusters of grapes; and (4) *peret* (clusters of grapes that fall to the ground) (Leviticus 19:10 and Deuteronomy 24:21).

6. Exodus 23:19 and 34:26; Numbers 15:17–21 and 18:12–13; and especially Deuteronomy 26:1–11.
7. Another version of this story is found in the Bavli, Tractate Kiddushin 31a.
8. Torah describes the breastplate as made of gold, blue, purple, and crimson fine-twisted linen and encrusted with twelve precious and semiprecious stones on which the names of the twelve tribes are engraved. See Exodus 28:13–30 and 39:8–21; jasper is mentioned in Exodus 28:20.
9. In the Bavli version of this story, the Sages entered Dama ben Netina's shop with the intention of paying six hundred thousand gold *dinarim*.
10. There are several discrepant formulations of the Seven Noahide Laws, but none include honoring one's parents. BT Sanhedrin 56a enumerates one version, which requires the establishment of courts of law and outlaws blasphemy, idolatry, sexual immorality, murder, robbery, and eating a living animal's limb.
11. The mishnah asserts that one is rewarded for honoring one's parents in this world and also retains the full "principle" (credit toward reward) for the world to come. Dama's reward may well be the Rabbis' way of asserting that God is just and fair to all people, Jewish or not. Or perhaps they were divided concerning whether non-Jews are rewarded with *olam ha-ba*—in which case Dama could only have been compensated by heaven in this world.
12. According to Tosafot to BT Kiddushin 31b.
13. BT Kiddushin 31b.
14. BT Kiddushin 31a.
15. BT Kiddushin 31b.
16. *Sifra, Kedoshim* 1:5
17. My purpose here is *not* to suggest whether humans or nonhuman animals have greater worth; I am not weighing in on this question. In the value system of the Rabbis, human beings supersede nonhuman animals in moral worth and importance, and hence their comment is made in the context of this understanding. Many people today reject the notion that the life

of a human being supersedes that of a dog on philosophical and ethical grounds. As the eighteenth-century utilitarian Jeremy Bentham wrote in *The Principles of Morals and Legislation*, ch. 17, sec. 1: "The day may come when the rest of animal creation *may* acquire those rights which never could have been withholden from them but by the hand of tyranny. The French have already discovered that the blackness of the skin is no reason why a human being should be abandoned without redress to the caprice of a tormentor. It may one day come to be recognized that the number of legs, the villosity of the skin, or the termination of the *os sacrum* are reasons equally insufficient for abandoning a sensitive being to the same fate. What else is it that should trace the insuperable line? Is it the faculty of reason, or perhaps the faculty of discourse? But a full-grown horse or dog is beyond comparison a more rational, as well as a more conversable animal, than an infant of a day or a week or even a month old. But suppose they were otherwise, what would it avail? The question is not, Can they *reason*? nor Can they *talk*? but, Can they *suffer*?"
18. The most common examples in responsa literature concern a child's desire to move to Israel, learn Torah, or marry.
19. A Tolstoy version of the story can be found in Richard M. Gula, *The Good Life: Where Morality and Spirituality Converge* (Mahwah NJ: Paulist Press, 1999), 48–49. For the Grimm brothers' version, see Grimms' Fairy Tales: The Complete Fairy Tales of the Brothers Grimm, accessed November 29, 2016, https://www.grimmstories.com/en/grimm_fairy-tales/the_old_man_and_his_grandson. In classical publications of *Grimm's Fairy Tales*, published between 1812 and 1822, Tale #78 is one version of the story.
20. The Shulchan Arukh was published in Tzfat (Safed) in 1563.
21. *Yoreh De'ah* 240:18.
22. Maimonides, Mishneh Torah, *Hilkhot Mamrim*, ch. 6.
23. Dratch, "Honoring Abusive Parents," 110.
24. Engel, *Divorcing a Parent*, 101.

6. Affirming Our Sexuality

1. Numerous midrashim express the notion that forming good marital matches is such a difficult task that God finds it as challenging as parting the Reed

Sea. See Genesis Rabbah 68:4; Leviticus Rabbah 8:1 and 29:8; and Numbers Rabbah 3:6.

2. Specifically, in the sixth-to-seventh century CE midrashic compilation *Pesikta de-Rav Kahana* 22:2, the story is told of a couple who comes before R. Shimon bar Yochai for a divorce after ten years of marriage during which they were unable to produce a child. In the Rabbi's presence the man offers the woman any object in his home she considers precious. Although he should have written out a *get* (divorce decree), R. Shimon sends them home to enjoy one last night together, complete with good food and wine. After the husband falls asleep, the wife has *him* brought to her father's house, where he awakes in the middle of night and asks how he got there. She explains that she has done as he said and brought the most precious thing back to her father's house. The Rabbi prays on the couple's behalf and they conceive.

3. BT Ketubot 48a.
4. BT Ketubot 61–63.
5. BT Niddah 71a. Some Rabbis also believed that when the woman climaxes before the man there is a greater probability of conceiving a boy, which they considered highly desirable.
6. The Torah required people to separate a tenth portion of their produce, wine, oil, and cattle to give to the *kohanim* (priests) or the *levi'im* (Levites). This tenth was considered God's portion. The *kohanim* and *levi'im* used some of the tithes to purchase animals for sacrifice and others to support the poor, and they were permitted to keep a portion of the tithes for themselves. See, for example, Numbers 18 and Deuteronomy 14:22–29.
7. The Rabbis often identified cause and effect patterns of retributive justice in the complexities of life. For example, just as Jacob deceived his father, Isaac, his father-in-law, Laban, deceived him. Similarly, just as the Pharaoh of Egypt drowned Hebrew baby boys in the Nile River, so too were his chariots and horsemen drowned in the Reed Sea.
8. See Sarna, *JPS Torah Commentary: Exodus*, 26. In the enigmatic account of the night encampment (Exodus 4:24–26), Hebrew Bible scholar Michael D. Coogan explains that when Zipporah sensed that Moses's life was threatened by God because he was uncircumcised, she circumcised her infant son and "took the bloody piece of skin that she had deftly removed from her son's

penis . . . and touched Moses's 'feet'—his penis—with it, tricking the homicidal deity into thinking that Moses himself had just been circumcised" (*God and Sex*, 13). Other instances where "feet" is used as a euphemism for penis include Judges 3:24; 1 Samuel 24:3; 2 Samuel 11:8; and Isaiah 7:20. In Isaiah 6:2, the prophet describes the seraphim: *Each of them had six wings: with two he covered his face, with two he covered his legs [or: feet], and with two he would fly.* It has been suggested that the second set of wings covered the angelic creatures' genitals. The Targum Yonatan (Yonatan b. Uzziel), a first century BCE Aramaic translation of the Prophets, may have understood the verse this way; this is the cryptic translation, rendered in English: "Each had six wings. With two he would cover his face so that he would not see [God]. With two he would cover his genitals so he would not be seen. With two he would serve."

9. For some of the Rabbis, anal intercourse was considered *bi'ah lo k'darka* (unnatural sex) because it cannot lead to procreation, which they considered the primary purpose of sex. How then could the Talmud be permitting anal intercourse given that it might be seen as "spilling the seed" (prohibited by Genesis 38:9) or "unnatural"? One response is that there was disagreement among the Sages: some felt anal sex was permissible, and their view is codified in the Talmud. Concerning *bi'ah lo k'darka*, Tosafot to Yevamot 34 cites R. Yitzhak: "It is not considered like the act of Er and Onan unless it is his intention to destroy the seed and it is his habit to always do so. However, if it is occasional and the desire of his heart is to come upon his wife in an unnatural way, it is permitted." Maimonides writes: "A man's wife is permitted to him. Therefore, a man may do whatever he wishes with his wife. He may have intercourse with her at any time he wishes and kiss her on whatever limb of her body he wants. He may have natural or unnatural sex, as long as he does not bring forth seed in vain. However, it is a sign of piety not to show too much levity, but to sanctify himself at the time of intercourse . . . A man should not depart from the way of the world and its custom because its ultimate purpose is procreation" (*Mishneh Torah, Issurei Bi'ah* 21:9). Providing one's spouse pleasure is itself an obligation and therefore mitigates the concern about "bring[ing] forth seed in vain."

10. Pirkei Avot 2:11.

11. The Rabbis believed that the greater a Sage's intellectual prowess, the greater his sexual appetite.
12. In Jewish tradition a *mamzer* (bastard) is a child born of a relationship that was not licit at the time of conception and could not be made licit—most commonly an adulterous relationship.
13. BT Berakhot 62a.
14. Some fantasizing during sex is considered normal and natural behavior. Condemning it as wrong or sinful burdens people with guilt for an activity they cannot prevent. In a *New York Times* article, Dr. Daniel Goleman, psychologist and author of *Emotional Intelligence*, cites Dr. Mark Schwartz of the Masters and Johnson Institute: "If a man loses his arousal while making love with his wife, and uses a fantasy to get it back, then lets go of the fantasy to focus on the lovemaking again, it's irrelevant what the fantasy is about. It's a helpful bridge back to making love, and increases the couple's intimacy." Schwartz also noted that excessive fantasizing during sex can increase emotional distance between the partners and signal "what's missing in the sexual encounter" (Daniel Goleman, "Sexual Fantasies: What Are Their Hidden Meanings" *New York Times*, February 28, 1984).
15. BT Eruvin 100b.
16. Genesis 30:14–18 describes how Leah traded her sister, Rachel, mandrakes (presumed to be an aphrodisiac) for a night with Jacob that resulted in the conception of Issachar. Torah recounts: *When Jacob came home from the field in the evening, Leah went out to meet him and said, "You are to sleep with me, for I have hired you with my son's mandrakes." And he lay with her that night. God heeded Leah, and she conceived and bore [Jacob] a fifth son . . . She named him Issachar.* R. Shmuel b. Nachmani interprets Leah's actions as seducing Jacob.
17. Slapper and Kelly, *English Legal System*, 210.
18. Maimonides, Mishneh Torah, *Ishut* 15:17.

7. Balancing Family and Study

1. BT Berakhot 17a.
2. Pirkei Avot 2:2.
3. Neusner, *Evidence of the Mishna*; Neusner, *Judaism and Story*; Neusner, *Development of a Legend*; Neusner, *Rabbinic Traditions about the Pharisees*. As some

scholars have pointed out, Neusner focused on the structure of the story to extract its meaning, largely dismissing other salient literary features such as plot, language use, and narrative style. Nonetheless, his observation that talmudic stories served a didactic (and often theological) purpose, and were retold and reshaped to achieve that goal, is well accepted.

4. BT Ketubot 106a.
5. That Rav Pappa was a fifth-generation *amora* and Rav Ashi a sixth-generation *amora* inspires the conjecture that perhaps the story originally chronicled six amoraic generations and an arithmetic pattern of shrinking enrollment: 1,200; 1,000; 800; 600; 400; 200.
6. Rubenstein, *Culture of the Babylonian Talmud*, 18.
7. Goodblatt, *Rabbinic Instruction in Sasanian Babylonia*, 267.
8. Goodblatt, *Rabbinic Instruction in Sasanian Babylonia*, 7.
9. In chapter 6 of this volume, the story recounted in BT Berakhot 62a about Rav Kahana, who hid under the bed of his teacher, Rav, reflects this living arrangement. To gain such access, it is reasonable to suppose that Rav Kahana lived in Rav's house.
10. Ari L. Goldman, "Dalai Lama Meets Jews from 4 Major Branches," *New York Times*, September 26, 1989, http://www.nytimes.com/1989/09/26/nyregion/dalai-lama-meets-jews-from-4-major-branches.html.
11. Rubenstein, *Culture of the Babylonian Talmud*, 102.
12. The *JPS Hebrew-English TANAKH* (p. 158) translates *onah* as "conjugal rights" but footnotes as an alternative translation "ointments" (others say "oil"). Bible scholar Shalom M. Paul suggests the term may mean "oil" or "ointments," olive oil being a staple used for cooking, eating, medicine, unguents, and perfume in the ancient Near East; this would render the triad of Exodus 20:10 functionally equivalent to that found in other ancient documents (*Studies in the Book of the Covenant*, 59). Bible scholar Etan Levine points out that the documents in question concern divorced or incapacitated wives; the biblical case is a wife who is relegated to the status of co-wife. Levine quotes the late Bible scholar Nahum Sarna: "The Septuagint, Peshitta, and Targums [early Aramaic translations of Hebrew Scripture] all understood it to refer to the woman's conjugal rights. If correct, it would reflect a singular recognition in the laws of the ancient Near East that a wife is entitled to

sexual gratification" (Levine, "Biblical Women's Marital Rights," 94). Elsewhere, Levine points out that some scholars have claimed that *onah* derives from the root *ayin-vav-nun*, meaning "domicile"; hence *onatah* means "her abode." This view suggests that the husband is responsible for the triad of food, clothing, and shelter. Levine rejects this claim on three grounds: (1) no early biblical translations read *onah* as "habitation" (as Sarna noted above); (2) the Hebrew term for habitation as a third-person noun would be *m'onah* (her dwelling), not *onah*; (3) the woman under discussion in Exodus 21:10 is presumed to already be living with a man and hence "the very issue is her juridical right *not* to cohabit with him!" *Marital Relations in Ancient Judaism*, 212.

13. Gold, *God, Love, Sex, and Family*, 188.
14. A *kav* is a volume measure approximately equal to 1.2 liters or .28 gallon. Accordingly, nine *kabin* (pl. of *kav*) would equal 11 liters or 2.5 gallons.
15. M Sotah 3:4; 20a.
16. A parallel is found in the Middle Persian wisdom text of the Babylonian Sasanian period, the Book of *Joisht i Friyan*: "You think that wives have great joy from various sorts of clothes and the suitable station as mistress of the house, if she can call such a thing her own. Now it [is] not so. Wives [have] great joy being with their husbands" (Yaakov Elman in *Encyclopedia Judaica* [2008], s.v. "Talmud and Middle Persian culture").
17. Genesis 1:28, describing God's Creation of humanity, includes this phrase: *Be fertile and increase*. The same phrase is found in v. 22 in relation to animals that swim and fly. In v. 28 the phrase *Be fertile and increase* refers not only to human beings, but to the land animals also created on the sixth day. In context, the phrase is descriptive, applying not only to the human species, but also to birds, fish, and land animals. The Rabbis, however, chose to read *Be fertile and increase* as prescriptive, hence transforming procreation from a self-sustaining attribute of humanity (among other species) to an obligation God placed on Jews.
18. Travel throughout the ancient Near East during the Talmudic period (and earlier) is well attested. Getzel Cohen examines Talmudic sources, as well as Persian, Greek, and Roman sources from the fifth century BCE through the Talmudic period and archaeological evidence. Amoraic sources mention

Rabbis traveling both within Babylonia, and between Babylonia and *Eretz Yisrael*, for the purpose of study. Safety mandated that people travel in groups, or together with a caravan, along established routes. Amoraic literature describes trips by donkey, camel, wagon, and on foot. Cohen in "Travel between Palestine and Mesopotamia" writes that "the extant evidence suggests that the *average* rate for a caravan through the desert was 20 miles/day. The *actual* rate on any particular day would undoubtedly have varied somewhat, subject as it would have been to the terrain and other conditions, such as weather, security, the conditions of the animals and/or the travelers, etc." Cohen estimates that Jews traveling between Pumbedita (on the bank of the Euphrates near modern-day Fallujah, the site of the Rabbinic academy founded by R. Yehudah bar Yechezkel in the third century CE) and Jerusalem at a rate of 20 miles/day, allowing for rest on the Sabbath, would take approximately 35 days to cover the 600 miles. The distances between the Babylonian cities that boasted significant Jewish populations (Pumbedita, Nehardea, Machuza, Sura) were far less, but even a trip between Sura and Pumbedita (both located along the Euphrates, 109 miles apart as the crow flies) could take at least five days.

19. Numbers 30:3: "If a man makes a vow [*neder*] to Adonai or takes an oath imposing an obligation on himself, he shall not break his pledge; he must carry out all that has crossed his lips." In general, declaring a *neder* creates an obligation with respect to something that a person vows to refrain from enjoying, often as a sacrifice to God, or to a deed that person promises to do or refrain from doing. Hence, the person prohibits something to himself. The first vow uttered in the Torah was made by Jacob the night he fled from Esau (Genesis 28:20–22).
20. BT Nedarim 32a.
21. Lichtenstein, "Study," 932.
22. JT Ketubot 5:7; 30a–b expands this comment by saying that, with the wife's consent, the husband may absent himself from home for an unlimited period of time.
23. Catherin Hezser notes: "In comparison to ass drivers, camel drivers' marital duty is established by rabbis to (at least) once in thirty days (M. Ket. 5:6), due to the longer duration of their journeys" (*Jewish Travel in Antiquity*, 157)

and "Sailors' isolation from ordinary society due to their long absences from their families was also known to rabbis and taken into consideration in their recommendations for procreation: sailors are advised to have sexual intercourse with their wives at least once every six months, according to Bet Hillel's opinion transmitted in M. Ket. 5:6. The period of six months was probably seen as the maximum duration of a(n average) ship journey here" (*Jewish Travel in Antiquity*, 187).

24. While it might be assumed that resumption of sexual intimacy following a husband's long time away might be delayed by concerns regarding the wife's purity status and hence availability to him, M Niddah 2:4 expressed the opinion that "all women are under the presumption of being clean for their husbands. Those who come from a journey, their wives are for them under the presumption of being clean." This is to say that if the husband has been away for a long period, the couple is permitted to engage in sexual intercourse immediately without concern about menstruation or childbirth. Following this, the mishnah records opinions of Bet Shammai and Bet Hillel requiring the wife to check with a cloth — but the examination is conducted *after* the couple has had intercourse.

25. The earliest instances of the use of wedding imagery to connote the covenantal relationship between God and Israel are found in the books of the prophets Jeremiah and Ezekiel. For example, Jeremiah speaks of a time when God will enter into a new covenant with Israel which *will not be like the covenant I made with their ancestors, when I took them by the hand to lead them out of the land of Egypt, a covenant which they broke, though I espoused them* (Jeremiah 31:31; see also Ezekiel 31:8-14 and 59-60). Amoraic literature provides numerous examples: When Exodus 19:10 recounts God's command to Moses to instruct the people *kidash'tam* (sanctify yourself) in preparation for the revelation, the Rabbis connect the verb "sanctify" to the Hebrew term for marriage (*kiddushin*), which has the same root. Thus, Deuteronomy Rabbah 3:12 asks who is responsible for paying for writing the documents required for a marriage between a man and a woman and responds to its question by citing this verse from Exodus, making God's marriage to Israel the model: "Our Rabbis learned: Documents of betrothal and marriage [the ketubah] are written only with the consent of the two

parties and the bridegroom pays the fee. We learn this from God's betrothal to Israel at Mount Sinai, as it is written, *Adonai said to Moses, 'Go to the people and warn them: sanctify yourself today and tomorrow'* (Exodus 19:10). Who wrote this document? Moses. Whence do we know this? For it is said, *Moses wrote down this teaching* (Deuteronomy 31:9)." (See also Exodus Rabbah 46:1, which understands the Torah to be the ketubah God gives Israel.) From Midrash *Pirkei de-Rabbi Eliezer* 41: "The bridegroom wishes to lead the bride and to enter the bridal chamber. The hour has come for giving you the Torah, as it is said, *Moses led the people out of the camp toward God* (Exodus 19:17): the Holy Blessed One went forth to meet them like a bridegroom who goes forth to meet the bride, so the Holy One went forth to meet them and give them the Torah."

26. *Further, when two lie together they are warm; but how can he who is alone get warm? Also if one attacks, two can stand up to him. A threefold cord is not readily broken* (Ecclesiastes 4:12).

27. Rachel's name is not found in this passage of the Talmud. Here she is referred to as "the daughter of Ben Kalba Savua" (see also BT Nedarim 50a and JT Sotah 9:15; 24c). In the midrash *Avot de-Rabbi Natan*, which includes a version of the story in BT Ketubot, she is called Rachel. Historian Tal Ilan has postulated that her name comes from the tagline of the story in this passage in which she is metaphorically the ewe; the Hebrew for "ewe" is Rachel: "Only in Avot de-Rabbi Nathan version A (the later version of this midrash), is the name Rachel found. It seems to be based on a misreading of the text in BT Ketubot 63a, where we are informed that Rabbi Akiva's daughter had acted like her mother with regard to her husband—Simeon Ben Azzai—obviously allowing him to go away on his studies for a lengthy period. This statement is followed by a saying intended to describe the daughter's actions— [*r'cheila batar r'cheila*]—the sheep went after the sheep. The word [*r'cheila*] means sheep and the name [*Rachel*]—Rachel—is derived from the same root. Avot de-Rabbi Nathan interpreted the saying as naming the woman" (Hebrew words in article transliterated here) ("Rachel, Wife of Akiba," in *Jewish Women: A Comprehensive Historical Encyclopedia*, ed. Paula E. Hyman and Dalia Ofer (Jerusalem: Shalvi Publishing, 2006), accessed December 18, 2017, https://jwa.org/encyclopedia/article/rachel-wife-of-rabbi-akiva.

28. Eilberg-Schwartz, *Savage in Judaism*, 232–33.
29. The first quotation is from BT Sotah 20a and the second from BT Yoma 66b and also JT Sotah 3:4.

Appendix

1. R. Eliezer b. Hyrcanus, on his deathbed, says something strikingly similar in BT Sanhedrin 110a.
2. Hume, *Dialogues Concerning Natural Religion*, 186.
3. Weber, *Sociology of Religion*, 138–39. Also Weber, *Economy and Society*, 519, and other sources.
4. Later thinkers, including Moses Maimonides, affirm the Rabbis' formulation in one form or another, differing mostly in how they conceive *olam ha-ba*. The belief that God is in control had sticking power until the modern era.
5. Jacobs, *Jewish Religion*, 498.
6. The alternative biblical passage, according to the commentary by Rabbi Steven Sager, "begins by encouraging observance in the same language [as Deuteronomy 11:13–21], but concentrates on the positive ways in which observance of mitzvot focuses our attention on God's presence as perceived through productivity and the pursuit of abundant life" (*Kol Haneshamah*, 279).
7. It is both tempting and worthwhile to debate what kind of test this is and whether it is reasonable and constructive or cruel torture as well as what kind of God would put a person through this trauma—but those questions are outside the range of this discussion.
8. Inside the narrative frame, the substance of the book of Job consists of poetic dialogues (Job 3:1–42:6) that depict an entirely different Job: defiant, resentful, and certainly not submissive. This Job does not complacently accept his suffering as either a heavenly test or as a deserved punishment, despite his three friends' remonstrations that one who experiences such egregious suffering must surely have done something terrible to deserve it. Rather, he puts God on trial, demanding an answer to the eternal question, *Why do innocent people suffer?* It would appear that this Job provided such a radical challenge to prevailing theological views that a "safe" literary frame was placed around the story to "sanitize" it and make it appear

that Job is, in fact, the dutiful Job-of-the-narrative-frame who does not object to the suffering visited on him and who passes the test with distinction. While the Job-of-the-narrative-frame likely accepts God's response from out of the whirlwind that he is incapable of understanding God's reasons, the Job-of-the-poetic-dialogues seems not to find comfort in God's response. Rather, he recognizes that God holds all the cards and therefore argument is futile. Scholars presume that these passages were written by different authors.

BIBLIOGRAPHY

Alter, Robert, and Frank Kermode, eds. *The Literary Guide to the Bible*. Cambridge MA: Belknap Press, 1990.

Batnitzky, Leora. *How Judaism Became a Religion: An Introduction to Modern Jewish Thought*. Princeton: Princeton University Press, 2013.

Baumgarten, A. I. "The Akiban Opposition." *Hebrew Union College Annual* 50 (1979): 179–97.

Ben-Shahar, Tal. *The Pursuit of Perfect: How to Stop Chasing Perfection and Start Living a Richer, Happier Life*. Columbus OH: McGraw-Hill Education, 2009.

Berger, Peter L. *The Sacred Canopy: Elements of a Sociological Theory of Religion*. New York: Anchor Books, 1990.

Berlin, Adele, and Marc Zvi Brettler. *The Jewish Study Bible*. Oxford: Oxford University Press, 2004.

Berman, Joshua A. *Created Equal: How the Bible Broke with Ancient Political Thought*. Oxford: Oxford University Press, 2008.

Blidstein, Gerald. *Honor Thy Father and Mother: Filial Responsibility in Jewish Law and Ethics*. New York: Ktav, 1975.

Bokser, Baruch M. *The Origins of the Seder: The Passover Rite and Early Rabbinic Judaism*. Berkeley: University of California Press, 1984.

———. "Ritualizing the Seder." *Journal of the American Academy of Religion* 56 (1988): 443–71.

Bottéro, Jean. *Religion in Ancient Mesopotamia*. Translated by Teresa Lavender Fagan. Chicago: University of Chicago Press, 2004.

Boyarin, Daniel. *Carnal Israel: Reading Sex in Talmudic Culture*. Berkeley: University of California Press, 1993.

Brody, Heinrich, ed. *Selected Poems of Jehudah Halevi*. Philadelphia: Jewish Publication Society, 1924.

Bruns, Gerald L. "Midrash and Allegory: The Beginnings of Scriptural Interpretation." In Alter and Kermode, *Literary Guide*, 625–46.

Cahill, Thomas. *The Gifts of the Jews: How a Tribe of Desert Nomads Changed the Way Everyone Thinks and Feels*. New York: Anchor Books, 1999.

Cohen, Getzel. "Travel between Palestine and Mesopotamia." In Geller, *The Archaeology and Material Culture of the Babylonian Talmud*.

Cohen, Shaye J. D. *From the Maccabees to the Mishnah*. 3rd ed. Louisville KY: Westminster John Knox, 2014.

Cohen, Stuart A. *The Three Crowns: Structures of Communal Politics in Early Rabbinic Jewry*. Cambridge: Cambridge University Press, 1990.

Coogan, Michael D. *God and Sex: What the Bible Really Says*. New York: Twelve, 2011.

De Uzeda, Shmuel. *Midrash Shmuel: A Collection of Commentaries on Pirkei Avot*. Translated by Moshe Schapiro and David Rottenberg. Jerusalem: Haktav Institute, 1994.

Dratch, Mark. "Honoring Abusive Parents." *Hakirah* 12 (2011): 105–19.

Ehrman, Bart. *God's Problem: How the Bible Fails to Answer Our Most Important Question — Why We Suffer*. San Francisco: HarperOne, 2009.

Eilberg-Schwartz, Howard. *God's Phallus: And Other Problems for Men and Monotheism*. Boston: Beacon, 1994.

———. *The Savage in Judaism: An Anthropology of Israelite Religion and Ancient Judaism*. Bloomington: Indiana University Press, 1990.

Eliav, Yaron Z. "Bathhouses as Places of Social and Cultural Interaction." In *The Oxford Handbook of Jewish Daily Life in Roman Palestine*, edited by Catherine Hezser, 605–22. Oxford: Oxford University Press, 2010.

Emerson, Ralph Waldo. *Works of Ralph Waldo Emerson*. Vol. 2. Boston: Houghton, Osgood, 1880.

Engel, Beverly. *Divorcing a Parent: Free Yourself from the Past and Live the Life You've Always Wanted*. Brattleboro VT: Echo Point Books & Media, 2014.

Fine, Steven. "Review of Lapin, Rabbis as Romans: The Rabbinic Movement in Palestine, 100-400 CE." *Society of Biblical Literature*, 2013. Accessed April 24, 2017. https://www.academia.edu/3412357/Review_of_Lapin_--Rabbis_as_Romans_The_Rabbinic_Movement_in_Palestine_100_400_CE.

Fisch, Menachem. *Rational Rabbis: Science and Talmudic Culture*. Bloomington: University of Indiana Press, 1997.

Fitzmyer, Joseph. "The Languages of Palestine in the First Century A.D." *Catholic Biblical Quarterly* 32 (1970): 501–31.
Fox, Everett. *The Five Books of Moses: Genesis, Exodus, Leviticus, Numbers, and Deuteronomy.* New York: Schocken, 1983.
Friedman, Shamma. "La'aggadah hahistorit batalmud habavli." In *Saul Lieberman Memorial Volume,* edited by Shamma Friedman. New York: Jewish Theological Seminary, 1993.
Geertz, Clifford. *The Interpretation of Cultures.* New York: Basic Books, 1973.
Geller, Markham J., ed. *The Archaeology and Material Culture of the Babylonian Talmud.* Leiden: Brill, 2015.
Gillman, Neil. *The Death of Death: Resurrection and Immortality in Jewish Thought.* Woodstock VT: Jewish Lights, 2011.
———. *Doing Jewish Theology: God, Torah & Israel in Modern Judaism.* Woodstock VT: Jewish Lights, 2008.
———. "Problematics of Myth." *Sh'ma: A Journal of Jewish Ideas,* January 1, 2002. http://shma.com/2002/01/the-problematics-of-myth/.
Gino, Francesca and Michael I. Norton. "Why Rituals Work." *Scientific American* (May 14, 2013). https://www.scientificamerican.com/article/why-rituals-work/.
Gold, Michael. *God, Love, Sex, and Family: A Rabbi's Guide for Building Relationships That Last.* Lantham MD: Jason Aronson, 1998.
Goodblatt, David. *The Monarchic Principle: Studies in Jewish Self-Government in Antiquity.* Tübingen: Mohr Siebeck, 1994.
———. *Rabbinic Instruction in Sasanian Babylonia.* Leiden: Brill, 1975.
Goody, Jack. *The Logic of Writing and the Organization of Society.* Cambridge: Cambridge University Press, 1987.
Gordis, Daniel. *Saving Israel: How the Jewish People Can Win a War That May Never End.* Hoboken NJ: John Wiley, 2009.
Halbertal, Moshe. "Coexisting with the Enemy: Jews and Pagans in the Mishnah." In *Tolerance and Intolerance in Early Judaism and Christianity,* edited by G. N. Stanton and G. G. Stroumsa. Cambridge: Cambridge University Press, 1998.
Hartman, David. *A Living Covenant: The Innovative Spirit in Traditional Judaism.* Woodstock VT: Jewish Lights, 1998.
Heschel, Abraham J. *Man's Quest for God: Studies in Prayer and Symbolism.* New York: Scribner, 1954.
Hezser, Catherine. *Jewish Travel in Antiquity.* Tübingen: Mohr Siebeck, 2011.

———. *The Social Structure of the Rabbinic Movement in Roman Palestine*. Tübingen: Mohr Siebeck, 1997.

Hicks, Donna. *Dignity: Its Essential Role in Resolving Conflict*. New Haven: Yale University Press, 2013.

Holm, Jean, and John Bowker, eds. *Sacred Place*. New York: Continuum, 1994.

Holtz, Barry. *Rabbi Akiva: Sage of the Talmud*. New Haven: Yale University Press, 2017.

Hume, David. *Dialogues concerning Natural Religion*. Indianapolis: Hackett, 1998.

Jacobs, Louis. *The Jewish Religion: A Companion*. Oxford: Oxford University Press, 1995.

JPS Hebrew-English TANAKH. 2nd ed. Philadelphia: Jewish Publication Society, 1999.

Kaplan, Mordecai M. *The Meaning of God in Modern Jewish Religion*. Detroit MI: Wayne State University Press, 1995.

Katz, Michael, and Gershon Schwartz. *Swimming in the Sea of Talmud: Lessons for Everyday Living*. Philadelphia: Jewish Publication Society, 1997.

Kol Haneshamah: Shabbat Vehagim. 2nd ed. Wyncote PA: Reconstructionist Press, 1995.

Kraemer, David C. *Jewish Eating and Identity through the Ages*. Routledge Advances in Sociology. New York: Routledge, 2007.

Kunin, Seth Daniel. *Themes and Issues in Judaism*. New York: Cassell, 2000.

Langer, Susanne K. *Philosophy in a New Key: A Study in the Symbolism of Reason, Rite, and Art*. Cambridge: Harvard University Press, 1967.

Lapin, Hayim. *Rabbis as Romans: The Rabbinic Movement in Palestine, 100–400 CE*. New York: Oxford University Press, 2012.

Lempriere, J. *A Classical Dictionary*. London: Forgotten Books, 2017.

Levenson, Jon D. *Creation and the Persistence of Evil: The Jewish Drama of Divine Omnipotence*. Princeton: Princeton University Press, 1994.

Levine, Étan, "Biblical Women's Marital Rights." *Proceedings of the American Academy for Jewish Research* 63 (1997–2001).

———, ed. *Marital Relations in Ancient Judaism*. Wiesbaden: Harrassowitz Verlag, 2009.

Lichtenstein, Aharon. "Study." In *20th Century Jewish Religious Thought*, edited by Arthur A. Cohen and Paul Mendes-Flohr. Philadelphia PA: Jewish Publication Society, 2009.

Lightstone, Jack N. *Mishnah and the Social Formation of the Early Rabbinic Guild: A Socio-Rhetorical Approach*. Waterloo ON: Wilfrid Laurier University Press, 2002.

Mahfouz, Safi Mahmoud. "America's Melting Pot or the Salad Bowl: The Stage Immigrant's Dilemma." *Journal of Foreign Languages, Cultures & Civilizations* 1, no. 2 (December 2013): 1–17.

May, Rollo. *The Cry for Myth*. New York: Norton, 1991.

———. *Power and Innocence: A Search for the Sources of Violence*. New York: Norton, 1998.

Nachman of Breslov. *The Gentle Weapon: Prayers for Everyday and Not-So-Everyday Moments*, adapted from *Likutei Mohoran* 1:54 by Moshe Mykoff and S. C. Mizrahi. Woodstock VT: Jewish Lights, 1999.

Neusner, Jacob. *Development of a Legend: Studies on the Traditions concerning Yohanan ben Zakkai*. Leiden: Brill, 1970.

———. *Jeremiah in Talmud and Midrash: A Source Book*. Lanham MD: University Press of America, 2006.

———. *Judaism: The Evidence of the Mishnah*. Chicago: University of Chicago Press, 1981.

———. *Judaism and Story: The Evidence of The Fathers According to Rabbi Nathan*. Chicago IL: University of Chicago Press, 1992.

———. *The Mishnah: Religious Perspectives*. Leiden: Brill, 2002.

———. "The Mishnah Viewed Whole." In *The Mishnah in Contemporary Perspective: Part One*, edited by Alan J. Avery-Peck and Jacob Neusner. Boston: Brill, 2002.

———. *Rabbinic Traditions about the Pharisees before 70*. Eugene OR: Wipf & Stock, 2005.

Norenzayan, Ara. *Big Gods: How Religion Transformed Cooperation and Conflict*. Princeton: Princeton University Press, 2015.

Nouwen, Henri J. *Out of Solitude: Three Meditations on the Christian Life*. Notre Dame IN: Ave Maria Press, 2004.

Paul, Shalom M. *Studies in the Book of the Covenant in the Light of Cuneiform and Biblical Law*. Leiden: Brill, 1970.

Porath, Christine and Christine Pearson. "The Price of Incivility." *Harvard Business Review* (January–February 2013). https://hbr.org/2013/01/the-price-of-incivility.

Pritchard, James B., ed. *Ancient Near Eastern Tests Relating to the Old Testament.* 3rd ed. Princeton: Princeton University Press, 1969.

Raveh, Inbar. *Feminist Rereadings of Rabbinic Literature.* Translated by Kaeren Fish. Waltham: Brandeis University Press, 2014.

Rieser, Louis. *The Hillel Narratives: What the Tales of the First Rabbi Can Teach Us about Our Judaism.* Teaneck NJ: Ben Yehuda Press, 2009.

Rubenstein, Jeffrey L. *Creation and Composition.* Tübingen: Mohr Siebeck, 2005.

———. *The Culture of the Babylonian Talmud.* Baltimore: Johns Hopkins University Press, 2003.

———. *Rabbinic Stories.* New York: Paulist Press, 2002.

———. *Stories of the Babylonian Talmud.* Baltimore: Johns Hopkins University Press, 2010.

———. *Talmudic Stories: Narrative Art, Composition, and Culture.* Baltimore: Johns Hopkins University Press, 1999.

Sarna, Nahum M., ed. *JPS Torah Commentary: Exodus.* Philadelphia: Jewish Publication Society, 1991.

Satlow, Michael L. *How the Bible Became Holy.* New Haven: Yale University Press, 2014.

Schäfer, Peter, ed. *The Talmud Yerushalmi and Graeco-Roman Culture.* Vols. 1 and 3. Tübingen: Mohr Siebeck, 1998.

Scheinerman, Amy. "Giving Voice to the Unspeakable: Rabbinic Responses to Disaster." CCAR *Journal: The Reform Jewish Quarterly* (Fall 2015): 109–23.

Schwartz, Seth. "Gamliel in Aphrodite's Bath: Palestinian Judaism and Urban Culture in the Third and Fourth Centuries." In Schäfer, *The Talmud Yerushalmi and Graeco-Roman Culture,* 1:203–17.

———. *Imperialism and Jewish Society, 200 B.C.E. to 640 C.E.* Princeton: Princeton University Press, 2001.

Shavit, Ari. *My Promised Land: The Triumph and Tragedy of Israel.* New York: Spiegel & Grau, 2013.

Skibell, Joseph. *Six Memos from the Last Millennium: A Novelist Reads the Talmud.* Austin: University of Texas Press, 2013.

Slapper, Gary, and David Kelly. *The English Legal System.* 2nd ed. London: Routledge-Cavendish, 2003.

Slonimsky, Henry. *Essays.* Cincinnati: Hebrew Union College, 1967.

Stein, David E. S., ed. *The Contemporary Torah: A Gender-Sensitive Adaptation of the JPS Translation*. Philadelphia: Jewish Publication Society, 2006.

Stein, Siegfried. "The Influence of Symposia Literature on the Literary Form of the Pesah Haggadah." *Journal of Jewish Studies* 8 (1957): 33–44.

Steinsaltz, Adin. *The Essential Talmud*. New York: Basic Books, 1976.

———. *The Talmud: A Reference Guide*. Jerusalem: Koren, 2014.

Stern, Chaim, ed. *Gates of Prayer*. New York: Central Conference of American Rabbis, 1975.

Tigay, Jeffrey H. *JPS Torah Commentary: Deuteronomy*. Philadelphia: Jewish Publication Society, 1996.

Urbach, Ephraim E., ed. *Mei-olamam shel Chakhamim* (From the world of the sages). Jerusalem: Magnes, 1988.

Weber, Max. *Economy and Society*, vol. 1. Berkeley: University of California Press, 1978.

———. *The Sociology of Religion*. Translated by E. Fischoff. Boston: Beacon, 1993.

White, Roger M. *Talking about God: The Concept of Analogy and the Problem of Religious Language*. London: Routledge, 2010.

Wisse, Ruth R. *Jews and Power*. New York: Schocken, 2007.

Zborowski, Mark, and Elizabeth Herzog. *Life Is with People: The Culture of the Shtetl*. New York: Schocken, 1962.

Zohar, Noam. "Avodah Zarah and Its Annulment" (Heb.). *Sidra* 17 (2002): 63–77.